LONDON'S ARMED POLICE

UP CLOSE AND PERSONAL

This book is dedicated to

James Robert Wells QPM
1937-2018
An inspirational member and leader of the Force Firearms Unit
1968-1989

LONDON'S ARMED POLICE

POLICE

UP CLOSE AND PERSONAL

STEPHEN SMITH

PEN & SWORD
HISTORY

AN IMPRINT OF PEN & SWORD BOOKS LTD.
YORKSHIRE - PHILADELPHIA

First published in Great Britain in 2019
and reprinted in paperback format in 2021
by Pen and Sword History
An imprint of
Pen & Sword Books Ltd
Yorkshire - Philadelphia

ISBN 978 1 39900 496 1

Typeset by SJmagic DESIGN SERVICES, India.

Printed and bound in India by Replika Press Pvt. Ltd.

Pen & Sword Books Limited incorporates the imprints of
Archaeology, Atlas, Aviation, Battleground, Digital, Discovery, Family History, Fiction,
History, Local, Local History, Maritime, Military, Military Classics,
Politics, Select, Transport, True Crime, Air World, Claymore Press,
Frontline Publishing, Leo Cooper, Remember When, Seaforth Publishing,
The Praetorian Press, Wharncliffe Books, Wharncliffe Local History,
Wharncliffe Transport, Wharncliffe True Crime and White Owl.

For a complete list of Pen & Sword titles please contact
PEN & SWORD BOOKS LTD
47 Church Street, Barnsley, South Yorkshire, S70 2AS, England
E-mail: enquiries@pen-and-sword.co.uk
Website: www.pen-and-sword.co.uk
or
PEN & SWORD BOOKS
1950 Lawrence Rd, Havertown, PA 19083, USA
E-mail: uspen-and-sword@casematepublishers.com

Contents

CONTENTS

SCO19

XIX

SPECIALIST FIREARMS COMMAND

CTSFO firing his SIG MCX weapons system on the range at Leman Street. (*AH*)

Author's Note

Major General Orde Charles Wingate DSO, leader of the Chindits in the Second World War, said 'The boldest measures are the safest'. This has been true of many of the firearms operations I have been on in my career and continues to be the case with the new generation of armed officers of the Specialist Firearms Command SCO19 today.

Events in the firearms world are moving at an ever-increasing pace: terrorism, gang violence and gun and knife crime are the root causes, forcing us to call on more armed police to protect us. It is essential that these officers are well motivated, have the best available equipment and receive the most up-to-date training.

This book shows how our armed police have had to evolve in order to keep pace with criminals and terrorists. We cannot stand still or we run the risk of losing the streets – this cannot and will not happen.

I intend to bring the reader up to date with the most recent armed events in the capital. We will look at the fascinating developments in armed policing across the board, some of which are controversial. Some have never been mentioned in a public forum.

This book is written from the perspective of the firearms officer. I make no apology for that. There is enough 'police bashing' in the press from pressure groups and ill-informed people using social media. This is an attempt to balance the books. Please feel free to judge, but first read about the incidents, put yourself in the officers' shoes and identify the qualities they require to do a difficult, sometimes impossible, job.

This book continues from where my previous book *Stop! Armed Police!* (Robert Hale Ltd 2013) left off. There is a slight overlap, catching up with some earlier events that I was unable to cover in the first title.

I have included the names of violent criminals and terrorists (where known) and their antecedents. It is not my intention to add to their notoriety but to help the reader judge for themselves what type of person is capable of carrying out such atrocities and why.

I have referred to the Force Firearms Unit by the title it held at the time of the event I was writing about, for example D6, D11, PT17, SO19, CO19 and currently SCO19. (See Glossary for dates and meanings of these titles.)

All photographs have been credited where possible and I have made every effort to trace the copyright holders. Any errors relating to this are entirely mine. If you identify a photograph incorrectly credited please draw it to the publisher's attention and we shall take steps to correct this in future reprints.

Acknowledgements

No book is the sole work of one person, and this is no exception. I would like to show my appreciation of the following people who have afforded me help, encouragement, support and advice. Lee Horton and my daughter Phoebe Rose, along with those others close to me who afforded me space, and have shown patience and interest and acted as a sounding board when asked. My excellent editor, Kate Bohdanowicz, who has been both patient and understanding. Artist Heather Francombe for allowing me to use her work. Next my work colleagues past and present who are always enthusiastic about my writing projects. I hope this book lives up to your expectations. I would like to name the following people and organizations that have put themselves out to help with both their time and knowledge being free and generous with both. Steve Hartshorn (Assistant Firearms Lead for PFEW), Mark Williams (PFOA Chairman), Tony Long (ex SCO19), Paul Bickly (Curator Met Police Crime Museum), Chief Superintendent Andy Walker (SCO19), Superintendent Chris Nelson (SCO19), Bowen Pratt (SCO19), Dominique Andre and *Flashbang Magazine*. I would also like to thank each and every SCO19 officer both CTSFO and ARV, past and present, who took time to chat with me about the incidents within this book. I cannot put your names in this text but you know who you are! And last but by no means least, my publishers Pen & Sword who believed in this project.

PART 1

A LOOK BACK IN TIME

One of the three policemen murdered at the Massacre of Braybrook Street in 1966.

'Foxtrot One One' Fifty Years On

I recently had the privilege of being present at the fiftieth anniversary commemoration to honour the three murdered officers of the Massacre of Braybrook Street in Shepherd's Bush. It was a moving service, with wreath laying and speeches made at the scene of the atrocity. It was well attended and focused around the black marble memorial to the three fallen officers erected near the spot where they were murdered all those years ago.

I covered the horrific incident in detail in my last book but here is a brief account of events on that terrible day. It was 3.15pm on Friday, 12 August 1966, just twelve days after England's 4-2 victory over West Germany in the World Cup Final. Three career criminals, Harry Roberts, John Duddy and Jack Witney – who was driving his scruffy 1954 Ford Vanguard Estate motor vehicle – turned into Braybrook Street near Wormwood Scrubs Prison. The three had just left the Clay Pigeon pub in Harrow, after a liquid lunch, and were looking to steal a car. In a bag on the back seat were a set of false plates, some overalls and three firearms belonging to Roberts.

Unknown to the three, an unmarked Triumph 2000 police car had turned into the street behind them. Police Constable (PC) Fox accelerated and pulled alongside the Ford directing Witney to pull over.

The unmarked police vehicle, call sign Foxtrot One One, known in police circles as a Q-car, (see Glossary) was on a crime patrol from Shepherd's Bush Police Station. It was crewed by three officers – PC Geoffrey Fox, the driver and the oldest at 41, was posted from uniformed duties to drive the two detectives; Detective Sergeant (DS) Christopher Head, 30, and Temporary Detective Constable (DC) David Wombwell, the youngest of the three at 25.

What followed next was nothing short of cold-blooded murder. The Q-car had pulled across the front of the grey Vanguard Estate, stopping at an oblique angle across the road. TDC Wombwell exited and went across to speak to Witney about the absence of a tax disc. Finding that his insurance had also expired he returned to the police car to discuss the matter with his DS. Meanwhile, in the Vanguard, Roberts armed himself with one of the pistols.

Leaving PC Fox in the vehicle, the two detectives walked back over to the Vanguard. TDC Wombwell returned to Witney and took out his pocket book to make notes while DS Head went round to the passenger side. He asked Duddy, who was sitting in the back, to open the bag.

At this point Roberts leant across Witney and shot TDC Wombwell in the face through the open window. The bullet passed through his left eye killing him instantly. Realizing he was in imminent danger, DS Head ran back towards the police car but Roberts leapt out of the passenger door into the road and fired two more shots, one of which struck the DS in the middle of his back. He fell down into the roadway.

PC Fox tried to reverse the Q-car at Roberts but, having armed himself with a revolver from the bag, Duddy ran towards the police car managing to shoot a large hole in the windscreen. Fox ducked and slammed the car into drive hoping he could escape. Duddy, now level with the car, shot through the quarter light window hitting PC Fox in the temple killing him instantly.

The stricken police car, with the dead driver at the wheel, slowly moved forward, coming to a stop on top of the body of DS Head.

The murderers fled the scene in the Vanguard, but thanks to witnesses – some of them children – enough details were noted to track down the vehicle.

Witney was soon arrested and the vehicle recovered. Valuable evidence was retrieved inducing Witney to give up his associates. Duddy was arrested at Glasgow Airport, but Roberts, who was cut from a different cloth, used his military knowhow to evade capture for several days.

The Massacre of Braybrook Street, as it became known, hit the headlines. Its sheer brutality sparked public outrage and, as a national police manhunt began, the media and public watched on, determined to see justice for the three unarmed officers so senselessly killed in the line of duty. It also revealed flaws in the armed response of the Metropolitan (Met) Police and threw a spotlight on its lack of proper firearms training, equipment and policy.

Roberts was eventually tracked down and arrested. He and his accomplices narrowly avoided the death penalty as it had been abolished the year before in 1965.

Duddy died in Parkhurst Prison in 1981. Witney, who although present had not pulled the trigger, was released in 1991 and was brutally murdered by his flatmate in 1999 in an unconnected drug-induced hammer attack. Roberts was controversially released in 2014 and at the time of writing is still free.

Evening Standard, headline that shocked Londoners.

The fiftieth anniversary memorial service of this incident meant a lot to many officers from the firearms unit of the Met Police (which has had different names over the years such as D11, PT17, SO19, CO19 and SCO19) both serving and retired. This was why I, along with a group of officers, joined others in Braybrook Street to honour the fallen officers. Their deaths indirectly affected the course of my police career in firearms, as well as many others.

I was privileged to meet not only some of the relatives of the officers, but also some of the witnesses to the murders. One of them, who had been a child playing in the street, recounted that after giving evidence which helped convict the killers, Harry Roberts attempted to intimidate her in court and later made threats against her life.

The Massacre of Braybrook Street was the major driving force behind forming a dedicated training and operational firearms unit in the Met. The tragedy focused the media on the armed officers within the force and exposed the lack of training and lack of standardization of weapons, ammunition and equipment. It was obvious the Met needed to overhaul the way it carried out its business in relation to firearms. A modern firearms department that could keep pace with the fast-moving changes in violent crime was welcomed.

So, on 17 May 1967, less than a year after the massacre that shocked a nation, a small group of ex-Army police firearms instructors were gathered together to begin forming a training wing. The hope was to standardize training, select the most appropriate weapons and ammunition and develop viable tactics for dealing with firearms incidents.

A group of retired ex-SCO19 officers pay their respects at the Braybrook Street memorial on the fiftieth anniversary of the massacre. *(Stephen Smith)*

This new department within the police training unit began its life as D6. From twelve or so originals, the Met's firearms department has grown to over 500 officers. It has undergone many department name changes and, at the time of writing, it is Specialist Crime and Operations 19 (SCO19) and boasts of having some of the finest specialist trained firearms operators in the world.

The Massacre of Braybrook Street has now passed into history and is remembered for the right reasons – as a way to honour the three officers who lost their lives and as the catalyst for improving armed policing in the Met. It has special significance to those who work in the force firearms unit. I am a great believer that if we don't learn from the past, adapt and change, the past will come back and bite us.

Following this line of logic I have chosen to go back 110 years, to look at how the public behaved when confronted with armed criminals all that time ago and how the police service reacted to a spontaneous firearms incident, which developed in North London and spread over six miles, leaving four dead and fifteen wounded.

Death and Mayhem in Tottenham

The Tottenham Outrage – 23 January 1909

London illustrated Press impression of the tram hijack.

DEATH AND MAYHEM IN TOTTENHAM

Today the North London district of Tottenham in the London Borough of Haringey is a diverse and thriving area, but sadly it is no stranger to making the headlines and is frequently linked with riots, gang violence and shootings. In 1909, much of the built-up area we know today was covered with open space, wasteland, marshes and factories. The residential areas of Tottenham had gained the nickname of 'Little Russia' due to the influx of Russian immigrants following political unrest and pogroms against the Jews and other non-conformists. The British press named many of these religious and political refugees 'anarchists', meaning someone with revolutionary beliefs.

Very much like today, Britain welcomed political and religious exiles and was even then considered to be a very tolerant country.

The Anarchists

Paul Helfeld, 21, and Jacob Lepidus, 25, were both members of the Latvian Socialist Party, which was responsible for printing and smuggling revolutionary literature into Russia. They had been living in Paris until 1907 when Jacob's brother, Paul, was killed after the bomb he was carrying intended for the assassination of French President Armand Fallières exploded prematurely.

Helfeld and Lepidus were both Latvian Jews, (Latvia at that time being part of Russia), and had been actively involved in the 1905 revolution in Russia in which nearly 8,000 people were killed. Other than some reforms, its effects did not go far enough for many of the disillusioned revolutionaries who chose self-proclaimed exile.

The survivors of the gang fled first to Scotland and then moved south where they joined other Latvians melding into the political landscape of Tottenham. The men needed funding and so committed petty crime. Helfeld took a job at the Schnurmann rubber factory in Chestnut Road, Tottenham, where he was ideally positioned to case out the factory for theft or robbery.

The strange anomaly here was the fact that although Helfeld refused to give his name to his new employer, they still hired him. He was listed on their employment roster as 'Elephant' due to his enormous bulk.

The Robbery

Each week the factory paid out a total of £80 in wages to its workers, which is around £9,800 in today's money. This would go a long way to kickstarting the revolution back in Russia.

Helfeld found out that the wages were collected each week by the owner's chauffeur, Joseph Wilson, who drove to the bank in neighbouring Hackney with Albert Keyworth, a 17-year-old employee. The wages were made up of gold sovereigns, silver coin and loose coppers.

At 10.30am on 23 January 1909, the car returned to the factory gates. Keyworth jumped out with the bag of coins in his hand to open the gates. As he waited for the car to pull into the yard, Lepidus grabbed the boy and attempted to snatch the bag from him. Despite his youth,

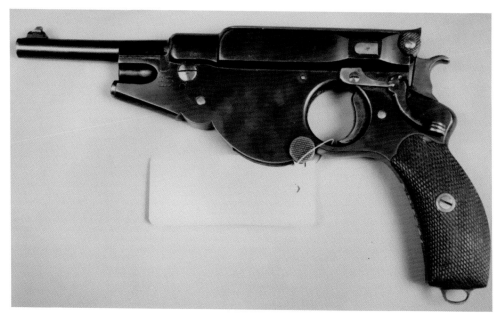

Above: A 6.5mm 1894 model Bergmann automatic pistol similar to the one used by Lepidus in the 1909 robbery.

Below: A .32 calibre Browning automatic pistol similar to the one used by Helfeld during the robbery.

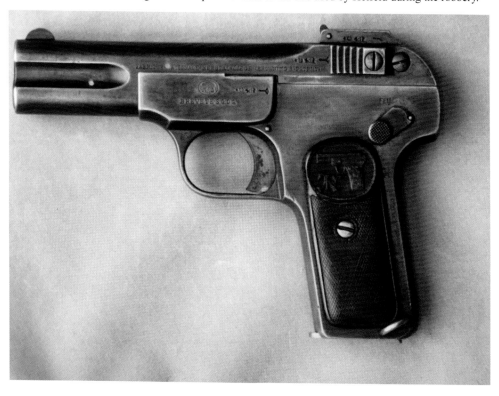

Keyworth was not going to hand over the wages without a fight. Wilson, the driver, saw what was happening and ran to the boy's assistance. As the three men wrestled on the pavement, Wilson was pushed and fell to the ground allowing Lepidus to pull the bag from the boy's hand.

Things now got serious as Helfeld, who for obvious reasons had hoped to maintain his distance from the crime, decided to join in. He drew his .32 calibre Browning pistol and fired several times at Wilson who was trying to get up and rescue the wages. The shots passed through his coat and loose clothing leaving him with only a scratch to his stomach.

The Chase

Two police constables, William Tyler and Albert Newman, were outside the nearby police station and, hearing the gunshots, gave chase down Chestnut Road. The officers, shouting most probably 'Stop thief!', attracted the attention of one George Smith who tackled Lepidus (the smaller of the two) to the ground. Helfeld now produced his pistol, a 6.5mm 1894 model Bergmann automatic. He fired four times at Smith – he hit his cloth cap twice leaving a nasty graze, one shot missed and the last hit him in the collarbone. The two men continued their escape.

Now we know the two police officers witnessed this shooting from further down the road but, undeterred and unarmed, they chose to continue their pursuit of the suspects.

The fracas and noise from gunshots had alerted the public and other police officers. Several off-duty policemen who lived in rooms above the police station (as was common practice for single men in those days) ran out of the building in various states of undress and joined in the pursuit. Some of the officers commandeered bicycles from passers-by. One of the officers managed to borrow a pistol from a member of the public and opened fire at the two fugitives from a distance, hitting neither of them and luckily no members of the public either.

The Motorcar

Wilson the driver had not been idle, starting up his boss's car and driving after the suspects. He slowed down to pick up PC Newman as PC Tyler ran beside the car managing to keep up. However, as the car began to make ground, the two fugitives turned and opened fire at their pursuers, first directing their shots at the approaching motorcar and then at the following crowd.

Wilson was hit in the neck, which caused a minor wound and PC Newman received a bullet wound to his cheek and ear. The car itself was disabled as a round had burst a water pipe, and steam and water spurted everywhere adding to the general confusion.

The growing posse following the car dived for cover under the fusillade of shots. All that is except for one 10-year-old boy, Ralph Joscelyne, who was struck in the chest by one of the rounds and fell to the ground mortally wounded. One of the crowd, possibly an off-duty officer on a borrowed bicycle, picked him up and carried him on the bike to hospital where sadly, following a long and bumpy ride, the lad was pronounced dead on arrival.

Tottenham Marshes

Having successfully delayed their pursuit, the two fugitives reloaded their pistols and moved off once more, this time in the direction of Tottenham Marshes. Tottenham Marshes, a semi-natural wetland that now forms part of the Lee Valley Park, covers an area of over 100 acres and was a good place for the two men to lose themselves. But their pursuers were having none of it. Tentatively at first and then with more determination than ever, they came out of cover and gave chase.

PC Tyler and the wounded PC Newman, showing some degree of local knowledge, took a short cut. It paid off and they confronted the robbers near a rubbish incinerator. PC Tyler advanced slowly towards the men who were now sandwiched between the two uniformed officers with the pursuing mob some distance behind. As Tyler got to within 10 metres he said, 'Come on give in, the game's up.' Helfeld, stationary and facing the officer, lifted his arm and with careful and deliberate aim shot him in the head.

Now adding 'cop killer' to the growing list of crimes, the two men calmly continued past the body of the dying officer. They crossed over the railway track and followed the west bank of the River Lee until they came to a small bridge, which they crossed over. Here they could hold off the crowd of pursuers who, far from being deterred by the killing of PC Tyler, were baying for the men's blood.

A standoff now occurred. No one could pass over the bridge as the pair was taking pot shots with their pistols at anyone who tried. However, the crowd was now joined by welcomed reinforcements – gentlemen who had been out shooting duck in the marshes. These men were armed with shotguns and began shooting across the bridge, returning fire and forcing them to give ground.

It was probable at this stage that Lepidus received wounds to his face and neck from shotgun pellets, as witnesses claimed they saw blood on his face.

Lee Navigation Canal

Outnumbered and possibly outgunned, Helfeld and Lepidus moved from the bridge and ran along the bank of the Lee Navigation Canal. The pursuing crowd grew again as a local football team joined in. Some canal workmen on the opposite bank kept pace with the two in the hope of cutting off their escape further up the canal at Stonebridge Lock. The two murderers opened up on the workmen, hitting several of them, wounding them and forcing them to abort their plan.

They crossed over the canal at Stonebridge Lock and then crossed another bridge, stopping on the parapet to catch their breath and once again hold up the crowd by shooting randomly at anyone daring to follow.

With a pistol he had borrowed from a bystander, PC William Nicod crept through some bushes and, when he was close enough to the two men, he pointed and pulled the trigger. The gun malfunctioned and he was spotted. It was an easy shot for them and both opened up on Nicod who was hit in the thigh and calf and was lucky to escape with his life.

Banbury Reservoir

Both men stayed together, running along the south side of the Banbury Reservoir. The lumbering bulk of Helfeld tried to keep pace with the smaller-framed Lepidus as both stopped occasionally to fire their pistols back at the pursuing crowd, which now numbered around twenty. They slowed to a walk while they reloaded their pistols from the plentiful supply of ammunition they had bought with them for such an eventuality.

They changed direction across some open ground and headed towards a haystack where they stopped to catch their breath and once again held the crowd at bay with gunfire.

The Number Nine Tram

The men could see Chingford Road in the distance. Maybe they thought it might just be possible to shake off their pursuers in a more built-up area; maybe hijack a tram and make good their escape. They ran across open ground towards the road.

They approached a stationary tram pointing their guns at the driver. The driver fled the cab and climbed the stairs where he hid between the seats. Most of the passengers also fled as the two gun-wielding men boarded the vehicle. They grabbed hold of the unfortunate conductor and threatened him with their guns, forcing him into the driver's cab.

Now the poor conductor had never driven a tram before, but it was surprising how quickly he learnt under pain of death and soon got it moving. Lepidus had squeezed into the cab with him and was pushing the muzzle of his Bergmann pistol against his head.

Helfeld took up position at the rear of the tram, firing his Browning automatic pistol from the platform at his pursuers who had not given up.

The crowd had now grown to around forty. More police had joined in, a few of whom had obtained firearms. One of these officers commandeered a horse and cart and was desperately encouraging the horse to get nearer the tram so he could try a shot at Helfeld who cut a fearsome figure on the platform of the tram brandishing his pistol. As the officer drew closer, his hopes were shattered when Helfeld shot his horse. The horse went down and the cart turned on its side, spilling the officer and the cart's contents out onto the road.

A police officer flagged down a number nine tram travelling in the opposite direction. Most of the pursuers jumped on board, the tram was put into reverse and soon started gaining on the two fugitives.

The Milk Cart

The conductor of the first tram, who was thinking on his feet, told Lepidus that just around the corner was a large police station where there were bound to be more police officers in wait. This was a lie, but it worked. Lepidus called to Helfeld and the two men jumped from the tram close to a stationary milk cart. Without waiting to make polite conversation with the milkman, they shot him and he fell from the cart, wounded. The two men climbed up onto the cart and whipped the horse into motion.

The cart moved off at a fast rate, changing direction towards Epping Forest, but a horse-drawn milk cart in 1909 was not known for its ability to go fast round corners and as the two attempted to steer it round a bend, it became unstable and turned over.

They picked themselves up and looked round for their next form of transport. It wasn't far away. A grocer's horse-drawn delivery cart was parked a short distance up the road and the grocer's boy, when threatened, willingly allowed them to take his cart.

Lepidus took the reins while Helfeld sat in the back with the intention of shooting at the pursuers who were now falling behind. One police officer commandeered a motorcar and, with an armed colleague, kept up the chase.

At this point Lepidus must have wondered why the grocer's cart was not going very fast. It turns out that he had not removed the handbrake and the poor horse was pulling the cart with only one wheel going round. The horse was soon worn out and would not move however many times he was whipped. Both men got out and continued on foot.

River Ching

Our two now very fatigued robbers were nearing the end of their endurance. They chose once again to go off the beaten track, running along the banks of the River Ching, but the path they had chosen was bordered by a 6 foot fence and the further the two men ran along it, the narrower it became.

They were desperate. They could not turn back so had no choice but to climb over the fence. The smaller and more nimble of the two, Lepidus, managed to get over easily while Helfeld, the now exhausted 'Elephant', failed. He had no energy left and was heard to shout to his partner in crime: 'Go. Save yourself.' Then, glancing back at the approaching police officers, he put his Browning pistol to his head and pulled the trigger. Although the .32 calibre bullet entered just above his right eye and exited his forehead, it failed to kill him and before he could finish the job he was overpowered by the constables and dragged away to hospital.

Oak Cottage

Lepidus, now alone and able to move quicker, ran on into Hale End, Walthamstow. He crossed some railway lines and headed towards a cottage in the distance. Hearing gunfire and police whistles, Mrs Rolstone left her three children inside the cottage and went outside to see what was going on.

Lepidus skirted around in the tree line before ducking through the open door and into the small, two-up, two-down cottage. He bolted the door. He had effectively lost his pursuers, but how long he could remain hidden in the cottage was yet to be seen.

Having returned to her front door to find it bolted, Mrs Rolstone looked through the window. She saw a strange man who was now inside with her children and, like any mother fearing for her children, screamed. This drew the attention of the police who were nearby searching the trees and bushes. Lepidus went up the stairs to the rear bedroom hoping he could still manage to escape capture.

DEATH AND MAYHEM IN TOTTENHAM

Seeing the children alone in the downstairs room, PC Dewhurst broke a window with his truncheon, called them over to him and helped them out of the cottage. His colleague, PC Eagle, found a ladder and, armed with a borrowed automatic pistol, climbed up it quietly and tentatively looked in through the upstairs window. He saw Lepidus with his back to him so he aimed the gun and pulled the trigger. But the trigger would not pull. He had failed to remove the safety catch.

PC Eagle quickly retraced his steps down the ladder. Meanwhile PC Cater and DC Dixon had entered the house. They noticed sooty handprints on the wall where Lepidus had tried to hide up the chimney. By following the prints, they knew he had gone upstairs and into one of the bedrooms. DC Dixon had obtained a shotgun and now reinforced by PC Eagle, who had finally worked out how to remove the safety catch, called PCs Eagle and Cater (who was also armed) together to form a plan. On a given signal all three of them began firing through the bedroom door before charging in still firing.

Lepidus was on the bed with a sheet over his head. Like his old friend a short time earlier, he put his gun to his temple and pulled the trigger.

The Tottenham Outrage, as it became known, originated as a wages snatch and ended following a 6-mile chase on foot, tram, milk cart and grocer's cart. The two robbers fired over 400 rounds during the two-hour chase, resulting in two dead and fifteen wounded by gunshot, three horses killed or injured, and the two would-be robbers coming to an untimely end. (Lepidus in Oak Cottage and Helfeld dying seventeen days later of meningitis following surgery to remove bone from his skull.)

The two murdered victims, 10-year-old Ralph Joscelyne and PC William Tyler, were buried on 29 January 1909 at Abney Park Cemetery. Crowds reported as numbering over 100,000 attended their joint funeral. Guns from the Royal Garrison Artillery fired a volley of shots at the end of the proceedings.

Money raised for PC Tyler's widow amounted to £1,055 – an enormous sum for that time – although she was only paid the monthly interest amounting to £15 per month.

The King's Police Medal was established to honour and recognize the bravery of the officers that day. It was presented to PCs Eagle and Cater, and DC Dixon. All three, along with PCs Nicod and Dewhurst, were promoted to the rank of sergeant without having to take an exam.

A plaque to PC Tyler was installed at Tottenham Police Station along with a monument built at his grave.

So how do we view the Tottenham Outrage today? Yes it is one of those interesting historic cases from over a century ago, but I wonder how it would be looked at and reported today?

Firstly, how would we have coped with a crime scene six-miles long? Imagine the work involved in taking several hundred witness statements and gathering the evidence strewn across such a vast area.

Today the title of 'active' or 'spree shooter' would have been applied but it would still have demanded the same determined response from police to hunt the suspects down and neutralize them. As far as tactics go, the police officers of 1909, mostly unarmed and later armed by various means, unwittingly fulfilled the tactics we teach today in dealing with armed and dangerous criminals: to 'identify, locate, contain and thereby neutralize.' Although it took them nearly six miles and two hours to contain the men, they never gave up and through sheer determination won the day, neutralizing them with their own hands.

PC William Tyler who was shot and killed as he bravely attempted to talk the robbers into giving up.

Today we have fast and effective armed response vehicles (ARVs), which would react quickly and be more than able to deal with a fast-moving shooting incident like that. Modern communications make it easier to coordinate and direct armed assets to a location. Today, we would discourage members of the public from joining in the pursuit of any suspect, armed or otherwise.

Back then some of the officers had issues with the weapons they obtained and the accuracy of their shooting and this was due to lack of experience and training. Certainly Lepidus and Helfeld were more confident and proficient with their weapons than most of the posse hunting them. They also had access to a large supply of magazines and ammunition for their guns. What fascinates me is the resourcefulness of those Edwardian bobbies to obtain firearms from members of the public and apparently from gun shops on the route of the chase, and to commandeer vehicles and carry on the chase. There were a large number of firearms in the public domain at this time, brought back from wars, handed down or bought privately. It is interesting how quickly and willingly these guns were produced on the day.

Having worked with similar resourceful officers during my service in the Metropolitan Police firearms command, I am under no illusion that the 1909 spirit survives in our British Police force and to a certain degree with the public we serve.

One final thing – not every person in the pursuit was noble, brave or honest. The £80 stolen by the robbers at the Schnurmann rubber factory in Chestnut Road, Tottenham was never recovered.

PART 2

TAKING ON THE GANGS

Detectives take over the scene following the shooting of Azelle Rodney in Edgware.

Operation Tayport

The Shooting of Azelle Rodney Edgware, 30 April 2005

In 2005, the Serious and Organised Crime Command known as SCD7 (Specialist Crime Directorate 7) had a department called the Projects Team, which was a sister department to the world-famous Flying Squad. The Projects Team, or SCD7 (2), had responsibility for proactive investigations into contract killings, serious crime groups, major drug importation, trafficking and distribution. They were active in combatting very serious criminality, and they certainly had the pedigree and experience to carry out this task.

The Projects Team often worked with other government and police agencies. They shared and pooled intelligence on major criminals, sometimes at an international level, so it was no surprise when, on 28 April 2005, they were passed intelligence from Her Majesty's Customs and Revenue.

This intelligence referred to two groups of individuals. One was a group of Colombian drug dealers who were in possession of a substantial amount of cocaine held at an unknown location in North London and the other was a North London gang of armed criminals who were intent on robbing them of their drugs.

Apparently this robbery, or 'drugs rip-off' in police slang, would take place that day as a meeting between the two groups had been planned in Edgware. The detective inspector (DI) given the unenviable task of being the 'silver commander' (officer in charge) hurried to gather enough of his detectives to cover the operation at such short notice.

He knew he couldn't do anything without the right armed back up, so he contacted the Force Firearms Unit, otherwise known as SO19. Although many SCD7 officers, particularly those on the Flying Squad – also known as SCD7(5) – were trained to carry firearms, the Projects Team were not, so it was thought prudent to use a team of specialist firearms officers (SFOs).

After the initial mad rush to get things moving, he received a welcome update that the meeting had been put off to the following day. He learned that the deal to buy the drugs was in its advanced stages and that the name of one of the gang members was Wesley Lovell, who lived in the north Finchley area of London. Apparently Lovell would be working with up to three other males, whose identities were as yet unknown.

It was also stated that Lovell and his accomplices had been responsible for several similar drugs rip-offs involving firearms. On one of these robberies they had apparently planned to shoot two Nigerian men in cold blood and rob them of their drugs. However, the robbery had been disrupted before it could be carried out when police arrested the two Nigerians with their drugs.

OPERATION TAYPORT

The DI now had some breathing space, but this latest information must have been of concern as it demonstrated how violent these individuals could be and that they represented a very serious threat to the safety of the public and everyone involved.

The SCD7(2) officers used the time to further explore the intelligence and look into Wesley Lovell who had many associates, including one who was wanted by police for attempted murder. His name was Azelle Rodney.

There was no intelligence that Rodney would be involved and the detectives on the squad kept an open mind – after all there were many other likely accomplices that could be called upon. They concentrated their efforts on finding Lovell to try and identify who he was running with.

Later that evening they got lucky, receiving a tip-off that the two groups would come together at an address in Edgware, controlled by the Colombians so that the prospective buyers could test a control sample of the drugs for its purity.

The bulk of the drugs were being held at another unknown location so it was unlikely any attempt to rob them would take place there.

Detectives moved to the Edgware area and were rewarded by seeing three possible subjects sitting in a VW Golf, parked outside Edgware Railway Station. This corroborated earlier intelligence as this vehicle had featured in reports connected to Lovell's address. The address the Colombians were using was still not known but was believed to be in the vicinity of Edgware General Hospital.

The operation was planned for the following day. Gold Commander Detective Superintendent Peter South, the senior officer overseeing SCD7 operations, was briefed and granted authority for it to take place. He also authorized the SFO team to use special tactics and specialist weapons and equipment.

This included any of the following:

- Shooting the tyres out with 'Hatton rounds' (shotgun rounds designed for disrupting tyres with minimum danger of ricochet).
- Round Irritant Personnel – or RIP rounds – containing granules of CS irritant that disperse on impact, also deployed from a shotgun (used against violent besieged criminals holed up in buildings).
- Distraction grenades to be used in a hostage rescue scenario (these are thrown into rooms when making an entry).
- High-velocity rifles and carbines. These are very important when subjects might be in a building or vehicle and critical shots may have to be fired through windows or into cars.

All these weapons and munitions would go with the teams in the covert armed response vehicles (CARVs) or 'gunships' as they were known on the teams.

As well as the crew of three SFOs, the gunships were loaded to the gunnels with kit, which included an extensive first aid backpack along with method of entry (MOE) equipment – indispensable if you needed to breach doors or windows in a stronghold – plus the weapons and equipment routinely carried by these officers on most of their firearms operations.

Operation Tayport began in earnest on the morning of Friday 29 April. These operation names are created at random by computer and actually Tayport had been running since 5 April and was a previous intelligence-gathering operation into Wesley Lovell. It was decided to continue using this as the operation name. At 7am the silver commander briefed the Specialist Surveillance Team (SCD11) and at 8am he briefed the SO19 SFO team (also known as Grey Team) with the latest information on the gang and their intention to rob the Colombians. They were reminded of their responsibilities and the legislation governing their use of force. They were advised that the subjects had access to firearms including automatic weapons and machine guns.

The SFO team were also told that if the location of the Colombians was identified they might be required to make an entry to secure drugs and evidence. After the briefing the various groups of officers went about their business, deploying to the vicinity of the known addresses and awaiting intelligence updates.

Around lunchtime further intelligence confirmed that Subject 2 (later identified, as Azelle Rodney) would be in possession of a machine gun. 'Silver' consulted with 'Gold' and they settled on the plan. Once they had Lovell's gang in a vehicle and information that weapons were in their possession, they would authorize stopping the vehicle en route, seize the firearms and thereby disrupt the planned robbery. They considered this to be the safest tactical option for all concerned.

Updates kept coming into the control vehicle and later that afternoon officers learned that Subject 1 (later identified as Frank Graham) and Subject 2 (Rodney) would both be armed.

As the day progressed, authorization was given to retain the SFO team on duty past their eight-hour shift, which was common practice on live operations. Later that evening an update stated that the robbery would not take place that day, but would happen the following day, 30 April. Operation Tayport was stood down once again.

At 7am Saturday, 30 April 2005 Grey Team booked out their weapons and attended a team briefing. On this occasion three officers from Black Team augmented their numbers. These extra SFOs would crew a fourth gunship as a contingency in case there was a need to stop two hostile vehicles. During this briefing, the officers were posted to their vehicles with the call signs Alpha, Bravo, Charlie and Delta. All tactics were discussed and any additional duties assigned.

One of Grey Team's officers, PC Tony Long, who had been posted to the Bravo car (which was second in the convoy) suggested that in the case of an 'enforced vehicle stop' he would remain in the front passenger seat to offer static firearms cover on the subject vehicle as the other officer deployed onto it. This was not unusual. Having a cover officer made good tactical sense. As the front-seat passenger in the Bravo vehicle, PC Long would be perfectly positioned to see into the subject vehicle and deal with any threat, thus protecting his colleagues as they deployed.

The officers prepared the four unmarked gunships. The control vehicle (call sign Control) made the convoy five and would sit at the rear of the covert police convoy. Control had an important role, and was usually a larger vehicle or people carrier driven by an SFO. The team leader (bronze commander) sat in the passenger seat with easy access to the radio communications. The silver commander and his bag carrier, who was usually a DS, would sit in the back of Control where all the important decisions would be made. This, in effect, was the brains of the convoy; the gunships were the limbs doing its bidding.

The SFO convoy travelled across to the main briefing at Albany Street Police Station. Silver again gave the briefing, which covered the same formula as the previous day including all the warnings regarding use of force. The intelligence had remained the same overnight and the favoured tactic of an armed interception was still chosen as the safest option. Shortly after 8.30am the SFO team, along with the control vehicle, deployed to Fulham Police Station where they were to remain while the surveillance teams monitored the gang.

The close proximity of Silver (ground commander) and Bronze (tactical firearms commander) had worked well in firearms operations through the years and had developed out of the necessity for quick, real-time decisions to be made and relayed immediately to the firearms officers who needed it. As in most police operations of this type, timing is critical – make a decision too early and the job is spoiled, too late and someone could be killed.

At 9.15am, intelligence came regarding Subject 1 (Graham), which said he was 'a bit mental and likes violence, and gets excited'. This information was useful to the officers who would later have to confront these individuals. It would help form part of their threat assessment, for instance make them take fewer chances and maybe be more dominant in dealing with them.

Surveillance found the three subjects in a café in Greyhound Road, Fulham. The three men left the café in two vehicles – a Mercedes and a Silver VW Golf hatchback (a vehicle hired by Rodney using a forged driving licence featuring his photograph). The identity of all associates, with the exception of Lovell, was still not known at this stage.

The team leader briefs the crew of one of the gunships in the yard of Fulham Police Station.

At 3.12pm the driver of the Mercedes went into a block of flats carrying a rucksack. Intelligence suggested that on leaving the flats the bag now concealed a firearm and that the robbery would take place later that evening.

It was a very warm day and the team did its best to stay cool while remaining in a high state of readiness. They were monitoring the radios and staying close to their gunships. The day dragged on.

Surveillance followed the Golf and its occupants to a barber's shop on High Street Harlesden closely followed by the SFO team, in case the lightly armed detectives were compromised. Silver had received intelligence that they were expecting the delivery of a final firearm and, after consultation with Bronze, it was decided that as soon as they could confirm the subjects were in possession of firearms, they would disrupt the robbery with an armed stop and arrest.

The barber's shop was known to be a criminal haunt which made it difficult for the surveillance team to operate close by. As a result, a covert aerial asset was deployed, which witnessed a red carrier bag being exchanged. Together with other intelligence this made Silver confident that the gang was now in possession of firearms, at least one of which was a submachine gun. He decided the Golf needed to be stopped at the earliest opportunity. He discussed this with Bronze and they decided they would be safer to do the intervention after the car had left the vicinity of the barber's shop.

At 6.30pm, surveillance officers stated that there were up to five black males around the car. One was identified as Wesley Lovell. Subject 2 (Rodney) was seen to put on a three-quarter-length coat. This seemed unusual, as it was a warm day. The team, concealed in a local car park, wondered if the coat could be hiding a weapon.

During the course of the operation, the subjects had been heard to discuss having access to 'two big macs and a little one'. This had been interpreted as criminal code for MAC-10 submachine guns. At the time there was a large number of MAC-10 submachine guns in circulation from a batch of deactivated weapons purchased originally for use in the film industry, then sold and illegally reactivated by a criminal armourer in Birmingham. These had been used in many gang-related shootings and murders.

The bronze commander visited each gunship in turn, updating them of this latest development, reminding them to be careful and advising them to deal with these dangerous subjects robustly.

After a while all three subjects got into the VW Golf, which pulled away and started to drive towards Edgware with surveillance in hot pursuit followed by the SFO gunships, who were still at 'state green', meaning the surveillance team still had precedence.

Satisfied that the subjects were armed and en route to carry out their robbery, after consultation with Bronze, Silver declared 'state amber'. This was the signal for the gunships to move through the surveillance vehicles and manoeuvre into a strike position. This was done seamlessly, leaving Alpha directly behind the Golf as it negotiated a roundabout turning from Mill Hill Broadway and right onto Hale Lane.

At 7.43pm 'state red' was declared over the radio. This was the final authority to complete the interception, and the decision about where it would be carried out now fell on the team's second-in-command, who was the front-seat passenger in the Alpha gunship. His decision would be time critical, but safety was paramount, taking into account parked cars, members of the public on the pavements or in the road, street furniture and oncoming traffic.

State amber in Hale Lane as the gunships move up for the enforced vehicle stop.

The unfolding situation was captured on film by one of the officers in the Delta gunship who recorded the manoeuvre on a digital camera. In 2005 it was thought beneficial to obtain video footage for training purposes. In this case, valuable footage of an enforced vehicle stop could be used to show senior officers the tactic they might be required to authorize at some point in their career. As there was only one subject vehicle, Delta's role was downgraded to one of support so there was no tactical disadvantage for one of its officers to film the manoeuvre.

Alpha accelerated past the Golf forcing its way in front. Bravo edged out and pulled alongside it, while Charlie closed with the rear of the Golf. This manoeuvre was designed to box the subject vehicle in, effectively containing it along with its occupants. Once stopped, the SFO team would deploy from the gunships, dominate the occupants, remove them from the vehicle and place them face down onto the pavement. This tactic had been used successfully on many occasions and although it has its own risks, it was by far the safest method to prevent a car load of armed criminals from making off across London.

The words 'Attack! Attack!' are clearly heard on the video. This was the signal for the Alpha, Bravo and Charlie gunships to perform an enforced vehicle stop, also known colloquially as a 'hard stop'. The Golf came to a halt just short of the roundabout at the end of Hale Lane close to the Railway Tavern pub, having been shunted by Charlie into the rear of Alpha. Simultaneously, Bravo came alongside to box it in and PC Long, manning its front passenger seat and convinced that the rear occupant of the Golf was about to fire a fully automatic weapon, engaged the subject, firing eight shots from his G36 carbine.

In the meantime, Delta was pushing past the group of now-stationary vehicles to cut off any potential runners, and the sharp cracks of PC Long's high-velocity rounds can be clearly

Moments before the shots are fired SFOs begin to deploy from their gunships.

heard on the recording, establishing that all of his shots had been fired in less than two seconds. To the layman this may sound excessive and ridiculously quick, but in a highly stressed close quarter confrontation, with a suspect who is believed to be armed with a weapon capable of firing 1,100 rounds a minute, it is an entirely reasonable response.

The officer had had the luxury of having 'eyes on' the vehicle for around ten seconds prior to firing, but his attention had been drawn to the rear-seat passenger whom he had seen looking around nervously as the team moved into position. The suspect's actions appeared to represent someone who was preparing for a fight. When, having looked around, he ducked down across the back seat, PC Long, who knew the dangers presented by a MAC-10 submachine gun, was convinced he was preparing to open fire on his vulnerable colleagues as they deployed from their vehicles.

Although he had not seen a weapon, when the subject reappeared suddenly, the officer felt he had no option but to open fire. In half a second a MAC-10 is capable of unleashing nine 9mm rounds so waiting to see a weapon was not an option. With the rear window only partially shattered, PC Long could not see the effect his rounds were having and continued to fire until the suspect slumped across the back seat and out of view.

Despite penetrating the vehicle's glass and bodywork, the subject, later identified as Azelle Rodney, had still been hit six times. His wounds extended to his face, neck, chest, right arm and two had penetrated the top of his head.

The silver VW Golf with its windows shot out, shown here shortly after the stop.

Unaware that PC Long had even fired, his colleagues had assaulted the vehicle. Some of its tyres were shot out using specialist Hatton rounds, fired from breaching shotguns, while others covered with their pistols and carbines.

While Rodney was ducking down in the back, seemingly making moves of resistance, Lovell and Graham in the front had both put their hands up in surrender and by doing so had survived the confrontation. Dragged from the vehicle and placed on the pavement, their wrists were secured with cable ties and they were searched thoroughly before being handed over to detectives from SCD7. Other officers had immediately pulled Rodney's limp body from the vehicle and begun the task of giving first aid. They attempted to resuscitate him for twenty minutes (the surveillance photographer from SCD11 captured their efforts on video) before the paramedics arrived and declared him dead at the scene.

Azelle Rodney, 24, was born in London and had apparently given up a promising sporting career after a hip injury. He quickly became a mid-level career criminal and at the time of the shooting was wanted by police for attempted murder following a double stabbing. His mother, Susan Alexander, was quoted in the press as saying that on the day of the shooting her son had only accepted a lift from the two men, whom he hardly knew, and was not a gangster. A daughter was born to his girlfriend a few days after the shooting.

While no MAC-10 submachine guns were found in the car, a colt .45 pistol was found on the seat next to Rodney's body among the debris from the window and his blood. Two further firearms, a 9mm K calibre Baikal Pistol and a .25 calibre key fob gun, plus ammunition, were found in a rucksack in the rear of the car.

Above: Azelle Rodney receives first aid from members of the SFO team.

Left: Clearly visible in the rear seat of the Golf is the barrel of the colt .45 pistol under a yellow plastic bag. You can also see the bag which contained two more firearms.

One of the gang lays face down by the car, securely cuffed and under arrest.

A search of Lovell's address found that it had been used to produce a large quantity of crack cocaine. Rodney's fingerprints and DNA were found extensively in the property and it seems appropriate to assume the gang were intending to replenish their raw materials in order to continue with production.

The SFO team left the scene to begin their long post-incident procedure. All the gunships were left in position along with any equipment used for first aid. These would all form part of the Independent Police Complaints Commission (IPCC) investigation. The shooting was the first to be investigated by the newly formed IPCC, which superseded its predecessor, the Police Complaints Authority.

The IPCC carried out a thorough investigation into the events of that day, which concluded in November 2005. Their findings were published and stated that E7 (the anonymity code granted to PC Long) had acted lawfully and in accordance with his training. The findings were passed to the Crown Prosecution Service (CPS) in order for them to carry out a legal review and in July 2006 they published their conclusion – there was insufficient evidence to convict any individual involved in Rodney's death. Assistant Commissioner John Yates issued a statement:

> 'The situation facing our officer that evening clearly left him with no option than to take the course of action he did. The officer's actions have been carefully examined by the IPCC during the course of a thorough investigation

and subsequently by the CPS and senior counsel. They have concluded that no criminal charges should be brought.... Without these officers standing between unarmed colleagues and the public and dealing with some of the most dangerous policing situations the threat to all Londoners from armed criminals would be very different indeed.'

In an internal memorandum, which contained this press statement, he added: 'These words sum up the high esteem in which you are all held and I remain proud to work with you.'

On 24 January 2006, following a short trial, Lovell and Graham changed their plea to guilty and were sentenced to seven years and six years' imprisonment respectively for drugs and firearms offences. They alleged that Rodney had played a major part in the manufacture and distribution of crack cocaine and in the planning of the drugs rip-off.

On 2 August 2007, an inquest was opened into the death of Azelle Rodney but the coroner, Andrew Walker, ruled that he could not proceed due to the large number of redacted statements. This was information withheld in order to prevent the source of the intelligence from being identified and to protect the covert techniques used to obtain evidence. These redactions were not made by the SFO team but by the Met Police legal department.

In May 2009, the British Government was forced by the European Court of Human Rights to apologize to Susan Alexander for the delay in holding a full investigation. On 30 March 2010, Justice Minister Lord Bach announced that there would be a public inquiry into Rodney's death.

This would be the first of its kind. The inquiry began on 6 October 2010 and was presided over by Sir Christopher Holland, a 73-year-old retired, former High Court judge.

In August 2011, in very similar circumstances to the death of Azelle Rodney, a young black man by the name of Mark Duggan would be shot dead by police in Tottenham, North London leading to riots across the country. The effect of this incident, if any, on the Rodney inquiry is a matter of conjecture but many now believe the incident may have impacted heavily on its eventual outcome.

It wasn't until 3 September 2012 that the witnesses' evidence was finally heard at the inquiry.

Officers who gave evidence began to feel uneasy at the direction in which it was being steered and the credence placed on the opinion of so-called professional witnesses and questionable reconstructions. Holland ruled that the public could now hear the redacted evidence previously kept secret, which begged the question, why then couldn't the evidence have been heard in front of a coroner and a jury in open court?

It was no secret that PC Long had been involved in two previous police shootings. The first being that of a hostage-taker at Northolt in 1985, where a man by the name of Errol Walker was stabbing a small child, having already murdered the child's mother. The second was at a meatpacking factory in Plumstead in 1987, when he had shot three armed robbers who had been aiming guns at a security guard (both incidents are covered in my previous book). This information was evidenced during the inquiry along with his discipline record.

The conclusion of the public inquiry was released in July 2013, two years from its commencement, and it was scathing. Holland said: 'The armed police officer that fired the fatal shots had no "lawful justification" for killing Azelle Rodney.' He added that the officer 'could not rationally be believed', and that in firing, the officer's use of force 'was disproportionate and therefore unreasonable and unlawful'.

The Met's high command, along with the officers of SO19, were stunned by the inquiry's conclusions and its implications for future firearms operations. Commissioner Sir Bernard Hogan-Howe, along with PC Long's legal team, immediately applied for a judicial review of the public inquiry claiming the chair's conclusions were 'irrational'. The judicial review found in favour of Holland and the case was referred back to the CPS to determine if a prosecution should now be brought.

PC Long now faced the jeopardy of a trial by jury for murder, but the effect it would have on future firearms operations and tactics could not be measured. There was an immediate drop in the unit's morale as officers were now confused as to what was expected of them when faced with dangerous armed subjects.

In this atmosphere of uncertainty, recruitment into the unit fell. Some firearms officers from various armed departments including SO19 (who all voluntarily carried firearms) handed in their authorization to carry them. Some said they did not wish to put their families through the same anguish that Tony Long and his loved ones had endured.

In July 2014, PC Tony Long was charged with the murder of Azelle Rodney and after thirty-three years of police service, suffered the indignity of being placed in cells at Westminster Magistrates' Court and the Old Bailey while his bail was settled. The charges were brought following claims that the public inquiry had uncovered new evidence. Long, who was now retired and who, up until this time, had been known publicly as E7, lost his anonymity and his face was splashed over the front pages of the newspapers. He now awaited his trial for murder at the Central Criminal Court and he and his family prepared for the worst with courage and dignity.

His trial began at No10 Court at the Old Bailey in June 2015. It would last just two weeks and before the jury was sent out, the judge asked them one simple question: 'Had the prosecution made us sure that, at the time he fired his first shot, the defendant did not genuinely believe (even if mistakenly) that he or others were about to be fired at, so that he needed to defend himself and or others by firing at Mr Rodney? If the answer is no, then you have reached a verdict of not guilty.'

The jury left the court and, after deliberating for just over twelve hours, on Friday, 3 July 2015 it acquitted him of murder by a majority verdict. Over ten years since he pulled the trigger Tony Long left the court a free man.

In a statement to the press he said: 'It has been very difficult facing trial for something that happened ten years ago when I had acted to protect the lives of others as part of my job and based on my experience and training. Police firearms officers do not go out intending to shoot people and, like me in this case, have to make split-second life or death decisions based on the information available at the time.'

Following his experiences Tony Long went on to write the book *Lethal Force: My Life as the Met's Most Controversial Marksman*, which explored his police career and the incidents in which he had been involved.

Meanwhile the case of Mark Duggan continued to cause controversy.

The Mark Duggan Shooting

Tottenham, 4 August 2011

Operation Trident, also known as SCD8, had been set up in 1998 to counter the huge rise in black-on-black shootings and gang violence that had been plaguing many inner London areas including Tottenham in North London.

With the help of the communities in which they worked and a network of good informants, they had been successful in arresting and recovering guns, weapons and drugs and frustrating the workings of many of the gangs who preyed on their own and neighbouring communities, many of whom were fed up with the anti-social behaviour of these gangs who seemed intent on peddling death, violence and drugs on their streets.

Mark Duggan in a gangster pose. (*Metropolitan Police*)

As early as March 2010, Trident had gathered information on the Tottenham Man Dem (TMD) gang, considered to be one of the most violent criminal street gangs in London, specializing in drug trafficking, armed robbery, kidnapping and contract killing. The gang traced its origins back to the Broadwater Farm Estate in Tottenham and was a major criminal presence on the estate before and after the riots there in 1985 during which PC Keith Blakelock was murdered. Trident gave this operation involving the TMD a randomly generated operational name of Dibri.

With the assistance of CO19's Tactical Support Team (TST), two vehicle stops were performed in Streatham, South London. One gang member and a female courier were arrested and a loaded Glock 17 pistol along with 150 rounds of 9mm ammunition were recovered. This was seen as a great success for Trident. The Glock pistol is a major status symbol within the gang culture and can be a devastating weapon in the right hands.

One example of this occurred in September 2012 when Dale Cregan, a Manchester drug dealer and gang member, ambushed and murdered two female police officers using a Glock 17 pistol, firing thirty-two rounds in thirty-one seconds. The barbarity of this attack resonated throughout the UK and was a snapshot of how these gangs viewed the value of life and how ready they were to use weapons on the vulnerable and the innocent. No one was safe and if you were caught in the wrong place at the wrong time, you too could be a victim. Consequently, there was always a great incentive to get these types of weapons off the streets and out of the hands of the gang members.

In August 2011, information came in that father-of-four Mark Duggan who, at the age of 29, was a prominent member of TMD, and possibly up to six other gang members were to be involved in a reprisal murder following the death of Duggan's cousin Kelvin Easton who was stabbed at a nightclub in March that year. Trident officers believed Duggan would at some point take possession of one of the firearms held for him by Kevin Hutchinson-Foster. The tactical advisors agreed that TMD was so dangerous that a firearms team would be required to offer support to surveillance and be ready to arrest Duggan, or any other gang member, when there was sufficient evidence to support a charge.

Trident continued receiving updates from informant-based intelligence and other sources, which included the Serious Organised Crime Agency. They hoped that by actively following these subjects, they could recover a firearm and prevent further violence and possibly a murder.

This operation was never going to be easy. To understand this, a good explanation of the type of people involved was given by one of the Trident officers later during the inquest:

'My experience of the criminals dealt with by Trident is that they often lead chaotic lives and are disorganized in their criminality. They often do not do things they have committed to, or at the times they say they will. Plans can be delayed for hours, days, and weeks or abandoned altogether. Equally, spontaneous violence or other criminality can occur without warning and with minimal provocation. This unpredictability poses real challenges in managing risk and planning proactive operations to disrupt criminality and arrest offenders.'

Operation Dibri would commence on Wednesday, 3 August 2011. The TST team CO19 supplied was made up from selected ARV officers. These officers were posted onto the third floor of the CO19 headquarters at Leman Street and would have offices close to the SFO teams.

Most TST officers saw this posting as a stepping stone to selection for the SFOs. In fact, owing to high demand for operations such as this, the TSTs were the busiest firearms teams in CO19 at the time. In 2010, records showed that the two TST teams were deployed 295 times and 272 times in 2011. TSTs also provided support to the SFO teams by carrying out long-term mobile armed support to surveillance (MASTS) operations, thus freeing up the SFO teams to concentrate on other equally serious crime operations, which were less protracted.

To help them in this, the TSTs received additional training, including MASTS training where they worked in the same configuration as their colleagues on the SFO teams, so they could work in plain clothes and in CARVs, or gunships. Their main armament was the Glock 17 pistol, and the MP5 carbine.

A week before the operation, and purely by chance, TST training featured input from an experienced SFO officer, who had been a principal officer – someone involved in a shooting incident – on operation Wondoola.

Operation Wondoola was a MASTS operation targeting one Terry Nicholas who had obtained a firearm for his own protection. Once in possession of this weapon, the SFO team had been given authority to arrest Terry. Terry was near the entrance to a car park in Acton at the rear of a restaurant, having just taken delivery of a firearm. As the officers deployed, Terry opened fire and they responded, killing him. The weapon he had taken delivery of was a 9mm CZ100 self-loading pistol, which was inside a sock.

The officer explained that this was common practice with some street gangs as the pistol was kept in a sock to prevent fingerprint and DNA evidence transferring onto it. The shooter fires it from the sock and the ejected cases are captured in the sock thus depriving investigators of further evidence. (For a full account of Operation Wondoola see my first book *Stop! Armed Police!*)

None of the officers on that training would believe that in a few short weeks they would be facing a man also armed with a gun in a sock.

As planned, Operation Dibri began on 3 August. Surveillance officers, backed up by the TSTs, followed various gang members trying to piece together any clues or signs that the gang was about to obtain firearms. Nothing was forthcoming and the operation was concluded at 3am following a loss of the main subjects. The officers stood down to their bases, dekitted and went home to get some well-earned rest before resuming the following day.

At 4pm the next day, the eleven TST officers returned to their base at Leman Street to begin another day's work. They drew weapons and ammunition and checked personal radio communications then went up to their office on the third floor for the tactical briefing given by the team leader (code name V59 given to maintain the officer's anonymity).

The briefing was almost identical to the previous day's but they were told that the focus this day would be on Duggan. Even at this stage it was just another ordinary day at work for the TST. Carrying out MASTS and trying to stay out of the way and not be seen by the local criminality was always a game of cat and mouse played for high stakes.

The officers were posted to four vehicles with the call signs Alpha, Bravo and Charlie with a control vehicle, call sign Control, bringing up the rear. Each of these would contain three officers – a driver, an operator/map-reader and a Hatton gunner sitting in the rear.

The briefing concluded with V59 giving the team the following firearms warnings as per the standing orders for conducting armed operations: 'Firearms may be discharged by AFOs [authorized firearms officers] only when absolutely necessary. An AFO, in discharging a firearm, must honestly believe that, given the immediacy and proximity of the threat, the immediate discharge of a firearm is absolutely necessary in the circumstances.' Every operator knew and understood these words. They were always read out verbatim.

The armed officers left the briefing and did their final equipment checks, preparing their kit for what could turn out to be a very long day tagged on behind a surveillance team. They moved down to the basement car park and kitted up the vehicles, testing that the Sepura radio sets worked, as bad communications on the day could cost lives.

At 5.15pm they were ready to leave. V59 signalled for them to form up outside and they set off in convoy, this time to meet with Trident officers at police premises known as Quicksilver Patrol Base in Wood Green. However, while making their way to this location things began to develop.

The tactical firearms commander (TFC) was the officer in overall command. He phoned V59 and gave what is known as a 'real-time briefing' based on 'fast time' intelligence that was coming in. There was no time for all the officers to attend another sit-down briefing so the team were updated over their covert personal radios as the wheels rolled.

The Trident officers had not been idle. While the TSTs had been kitting up and briefing they had been furiously trying to locate the subjects and find possible locations of where the firearms might be. Things were moving fast.

The TFC had received information that Duggan was in the vicinity of Tottenham and would be making his way across to the Broadwater Farm Estate. The TST moved across to support the surveillance in the hope that they would soon locate Duggan. This paid off, and at 5.55pm surveillance officers identified a gold Toyota people carrier and tried to confirm if Duggan was a passenger in the back.

The TST arrived in Tottenham and began to close in on the surveillance just as they confirmed Duggan was the rear-seat passenger of the people carrier, which was believed to be a minicab. Trident had also been given updated intelligence that Duggan was now in possession of a self-loading pistol with ammunition, and was on his way towards the Broadwater Farm Estate. (It was later pieced together that Duggan had briefly met with Hutchinson–Foster at his girlfriend's address in Leyton and taken delivery of a Bruni M92 handgun. The gun, placed inside a sock, was handed to Duggan in a River Island shoebox. Duggan then recommenced his journey.)

The TFC now had to make a decision. He could not afford to let a known gang member wander free in the knowledge he was in possession of a firearm. He had a duty of care to the public and now had sufficient evidence to justify an arrest.

The TST convoy quickly made up ground, moving into position within a street or two of the minicab. At 6pm, as the Toyota people carrier drove along Blackhorse Road, they were given state amber – permission for the armed interception and for CO19 to move through surveillance to final position ready for the strike.

The convoy turned left into Jarrow Road and as the vehicles jostled for position, state red – interception is imminent – was given. The deputy team leader in the Alpha gunship now had control over the timings and use of the appropriate tactics relating to a forced stop of suspects in vehicles, on foot or in premises. It was his sole decision as to when the strike would be called.

At 6.13pm, as they travelled along West Ferry Lane towards Tottenham Hale Station, the Alpha gunship decided it was the best location to call the strike. Alpha immediately passed the people carrier, swerving in and cutting across the front of the minicab, forcing it to stop. Bravo drew alongside the vehicle preventing it from pulling out, while Charlie stopped directly behind it, preventing it from reversing. The people carrier was effectively boxed in on three sides. The pavement was not an option, even if the driver had the intention of evading police.

View inside the Toyota people carrier. Duggan was sitting directly behind the driver and left via the sliding side door. (*Metropolitan Police*)

Nine officers in the three main gunships reverted to their default training roles. They had rehearsed this tactic and carried it out dozens of times both in training and operationally on the streets. It was designed to use speed and surprise along with physical and verbal domination in an effort to extract the suspect from the vehicle minimizing the risk to both the subject and the officers and to preserve evidence.

As the minicab, with its rear seat passenger, came to a halt, Charlie (a BMW Estate) stopped close to and directly behind it. V53 was the officer posted as the front-seat passenger and the map-reader and radio operator.

The armed officers, dressed in plain clothes and wearing blue Raid jackets with police markings and dark blue baseball caps with police markings on the front, deployed around the minicab. However, instead of sitting in the vehicle until instructed to get out, Duggan moved to the only available door, which was a sliding door on the passenger side of the vehicle. He flung open the door and jumped out onto the pavement to be met by challenges of 'Armed police! Show us your hands!' from the officers who had already deployed. Initially Duggan was facing an officer from Alpha. But as V53, who was behind him from Charlie, shouted 'Armed police!', Duggan turned to face him. We don't know what went through Duggan's mind but based on previous experience one can surmise that he intended one of two courses of action.

The first possibility is that Duggan, who had the pistol inside the sock, tucked into his belt, intended to fight his way out and would go for the gun. Even though he was outnumbered and outgunned, blood tests later identified that he had taken MDMA, a type of ecstasy and stimulant that speeds up breathing and heart rate and causes hallucinations. This may have caused him to act in an unexpected and extreme manner.

The second and far more likely scenario is that, as he was aware of the incriminating nature of being caught in possession of a loaded firearm and he knew he would be facing a long prison sentence, he may have decided to throw the weapon as far away as possible to get rid of the evidence. But to throw away the weapon, he would have to withdraw it from his waistband and, at some point during the act of throwing it, the barrel of the weapon would have pointed in the direction of V53. Either way V53, who was now pointing his MP5 carbine directly at Duggan and was fully expecting him to react to his shout of 'Armed police!', would have no idea of his intentions and could only assume Duggan's actions constituted a real and immediate threat to his life or that of his colleagues.

V53 remembers seeing Duggan move his clothing and go for what he honestly believed was a firearm. Later, at the inquest he said: 'I saw Duggan holding an object in his right hand, which I believed to be a gun, and his arm begin to move.' Even in this split second he properly identified that it was inside a sock and linked it back to the training from the previous week.

Photo of the Bruni Model 92 handgun supplied to Duggan by Hutchinson-Foster. (*Metropolitan Police*)

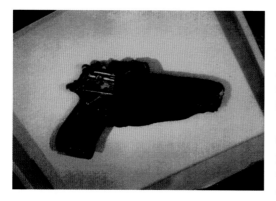

Same pistol shown in the sock in which it was concealed to prevent DNA evidence from Duggan getting on the firearm. (*Metropolitan Police*)

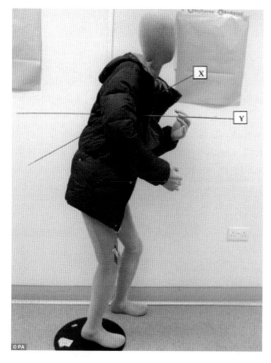

Mannequin shows Duggan's position when he was shot twice by police. (*Metropolitan Police*)

I have run many firearms training sessions in my career and I know that if you wait to see what an armed subject is going to do with a firearm, you may well be shot and killed. In fact, the accepted adage regarding this is 'action beats reaction'.

So V53, fearing for his life, fired two shots from his carbine. His first round passed through the right side of Duggan's chest causing a 'flinch reaction'. He quickly reassessed and, now that the gun was pointing in his direction, feared his life was still in immediate danger and fired again. This second shot hit Duggan's right arm, overpenetrating and passing through the edge of his jacket before hitting one of V53's teammates who was approaching from Alpha. Luckily, the 9mm round embedded itself in his covert radio causing no injury, but Duggan, now mortally wounded, collapsed to the ground.

All CO19 firearms officers are trained to a high standard of ballistic first aid. They spend hours each month refreshing these skills. Particular officers are sent away for advanced training with medical personnel, including trauma specialists, so as soon as the danger from an armed subject has passed these officers will go to extreme lengths to offer first aid to any injured party whether a suspect or a police officer. This case was no exception and the TST officers, including V53, attempted to stabilize Duggan until paramedics arrived. Sadly their efforts were in vain. His wounds were too severe and he was pronounced dead at the scene at 6.41pm.

The course of events from that point on has been the cause of much anger and hostility from certain quarters. V53 admitted he saw the firearm as Duggan drew it and brought it up towards him and he reacted by opening fire. We have no reason to doubt the officer's account.

In fact, the first account V53 gave at the scene was recorded at 6.50pm, just nine minutes after Duggan was pronounced dead. In an effort to be open and transparent he stated: 'I got out of the Charlie car, subject got out of the rear nearside of the taxi holding a gun-shaped item in a sock in his hand. Began to raise it up in my direction. I fired several shots.'

It's interesting that in the officer's account, at no time does he mention Duggan fired at police and we can confirm that he never did. The fact that the weapon was found 4 metres (14 feet) from Duggan, on the other side of a fence on grass near some bushes, has laid it open to allegations that the weapon was planted by police. I would respond by saying, why plant a weapon that far away? Surely it would have been placed closer to Duggan's body. I refer you again to my earlier explanation.

We will never stop conspiracy theories – the media thrive on them as they sell papers – but they also sow confusion, blurring the truth and feeding the anger. In this case they were to have terrible far-reaching consequences. The gun, being found some distance away from the subject, fuelled allegations of corrupt behaviour, which was latched onto by the media. However, one of the more troubling factors was that the IPCC made an incorrect statement to the press stating that: 'Duggan was shot dead during a shootout with police where an officer had been hit', thus implying Duggan had shot the officer. This did not fit in with the account of the recovered firearm being found some distance from the body. It smelled like a cover-up and the Police Federation and the officers asked that this be quickly put right.

Another glaring problem was that police had failed to notify Duggan's family that he had been fatally shot during this incident and they would learn about his death from other sources.

Image used during the inquest showing the position of the Bravo and Charlie gunships and the Toyota minicab. (*Metropolitan Police*)

Image used during the inquest showing the grass area where the handgun was found. (*Metropolitan Police*)

The family were understandably angry. They were unable to begin the grieving process because they were not kept in the loop. They needed to hear the truth and the sooner the better.

Things were beginning to get out of control due to a mixture of ineffective local command, and an independent body (the IPCC) failing to correct a glaring mistake. There was an ominous atmosphere brewing in the local community. News reporters, smelling a big story, were flocking to the scene. They knew something big was about to happen.

On Saturday, 6 August over 300 demonstrators gathered outside Tottenham Police Station demanding answers and chanting 'Justice for Mark Duggan and his family'. Empathy for the family hit an all-time high when Duggan's sister was filmed being physically restrained by officers as she marched with others to Tottenham Police Station. The video went viral. Any effort the police made to placate the situation was now met with hostility. The pot was boiling and about to boil over. That evening the first missiles were thrown in Tottenham and two patrol cars were set alight.

Riot officers and mounted police were deployed to disperse the crowds but came under renewed attacks with more missiles being thrown, including fireworks aimed at the mounted officers. The violence continued throughout the night; petrol bombs began to appear in great numbers and were being used against the police, vehicles and property. Things were escalating out of control.

On Sunday, 7 August the London Fire Brigade reported that it had dealt with forty-nine fires in the Tottenham area and there had been over 250 emergency calls from the public. A police incident room was set up to investigate the riots and given the name Operation Withen. The Duggan family made a statement that they did not condone the rioting.

Aftermath of the rioting and arson attacks that caused so much damage and misery.

On Monday, 8 August the rioting spread to Croydon, Clapham, Hackney, Lewisham, Peckham, Newham, East Ham, Enfield, Woolwich, Ealing and Colliers Wood. The first fatal victims of the rioting died that day: Trevor Ellis, 26, was found shot in his car in Brixton and Richard Bowes, 68, was found dying from injuries received attempting to put out a fire. Further bloodshed was inevitable as the unrest spread northwards to Birmingham, Liverpool, Nottingham as well as Bristol.

On Tuesday, 9 August the IPCC released a statement claiming there was no evidence that Duggan had fired at police (the officers involved had never claimed he had) and that the gun found near the scene had not been fired during the incident. This statement did nothing to halt the violence.

On Wednesday, 10 August three more people were killed in the disorder, this time in Winson Green, Birmingham. Haroon Jahan, 21, Shazad Ali, 31, and Abdul Musavir, also 31, died when a car was driven at them as they attempted to protect their property from rioters.

In the following days, the rioting and disorder began to subside. London had suffered the worst rioting of recent times. Lasting over five days, it affected twenty-two of the thirty-two London boroughs, with thousands of people, many of them known criminals, actively involved. The rioting in London resulted in five deaths and damage valued at over £200 million, with hundreds losing homes and businesses. The Metropolitan Police Service (MPS) had received police reinforcements from forces as far away as Scotland. The disorder had been so severe that MPs were recalled to parliament. Over 1,400 rioters were arrested with the majority receiving prison sentences for offences including arson. The MPS remained on high alert throughout the summer and autumn of 2011.

Former Deputy Assistant Commissioner Brain Paddick criticized the Met's handing of the riots, saying, 'They should have responded properly to the initial disturbances in Tottenham.' The IPCC admitted it might have misled journalists into believing Mr Duggan fired at officers before he was killed. A friend of the Duggan family and local gang mediator, Ken Hinds, said he had warned police of the prospect of rioting on 6 August. The Duggan family told reporters they had no faith in the IPCC investigation.

We can only imagine what the officer who shot Duggan was going through. Although he had clearly acted within his training, and the law, he now found himself at the centre of not only a high-profile investigation, but also the focus of a trial by media who referred to him as 'the officer who started the riots.' This was grossly unfair. He was only doing his job and acted exactly as most of us would have done faced with the same circumstances. No one could have foreseen that while attempting to arrest a subject believed to be armed and dangerous, he would personally be blamed for causing the worst rioting, arson and looting that this country has ever seen.

Were the riots orchestrated? Certainly, fellow gang members and 'activists' encouraged the initial disorder. It was then a case of others jumping on the bandwagon. It has always struck me that whenever police are blamed, rightly or wrongly, for overstepping the mark, the ensuing public outcry would often end in riots and looting with many of the rioters walking off with flatscreen TVs and other electrical goods. Often it was just an excuse for theft on a grand scale.

Critics of the police were quick to step up, adding weight to the feeling that the police, particularly the firearms department CO19, had acted inappropriately. Statements that Duggan was unarmed at the time he was shot were circulated. As usual, those acting on V53's behalf were unable to respond to these allegations as they were bound by legal requirements to remain quiet until the court cases.

Kevin Hutchinson-Foster, the gang member who had supplied Duggan with the firearm, was arrested on 24 October 2011. He had given Duggan the firearm just fifteen minutes before he had been shot.

It transpired that Hutchinson-Foster had 'pistol whipped' a rival gang member at the Lagoon Salon in Dalston just days before supplying that same Bruni handgun to Duggan. That firearm was found to have traces of Hutchinson-Foster's DNA along with that of the person he had pistol-whipped on 29 July. Hutchinson-Foster was sentenced to twelve years' imprisonment for these offences, and for supplying a loaded firearm to Duggan on 4 August 2011.

On 9 January 2013, Judge Keith Cutler CBE was appointed to conduct the inquest into the death of Mark Duggan. The inquest began in September 2013 and officer V53 told the jury that, when he confronted Duggan, he had an 'honest held belief he was going to shoot me.' He added, 'It was complete rubbish to say that Duggan was not armed when he was shot.' The officers were accused in the press of planting the handgun found 7 metres from Duggan's body.

V59, the sergeant in charge of the TST team said, 'It was highly offensive to claim that police had planted the gun at the scene.'

On 8 January 2014, 888 days after the incident and four months since the beginning of the inquest, the jury returned a verdict of lawful killing. Following the verdict, the IPCC admitted it had given false information to journalists in the wake of the shooting. Scotland Yard also apologized for not telling the Duggan family about his death straight away.

In March 2015, following a three-and-a-half-year investigation into the shooting, the IPCC published its 500-page report. It stated that the most plausible explanation for the location of the gun was that Duggan 'was in the process of throwing it to his right as he was shot.' It added that there was 'no evidence that sufficiently undermines the accounts provided by V53' and there was 'no credible evidence to uphold complaints by Duggan's family that police had relocated the firearm in the sock, or that officer V53 did not fire live shots in the belief Duggan was pointing a firearm at him or that he did not use lawful force.'

In conclusion, the report found no wrongdoing or misconduct by any of the armed officers involved. It did, however, recommend changes regarding officers conferring prior to making notes as well as some other procedural changes.

This incident had impacted on the lives of everyone involved, including the family of Mark Duggan, the families of the five people who lost their lives in the riots and every person who suffered injury or lost property or businesses following the disorder. Added to that list, and always forgotten, are V53 and his family who suffered long spells of uncertainty, stress, mental strain and all the other emotions that go along with being scrutinized by the media and investigated by police and independent agencies. The effect a shooting has on an officer's family can never be underestimated.

The delays between investigations and court dates also have a debilitating effect. In this case the officer was required to give evidence at two separate court cases, followed by a lengthy inquest, and all under the glare of the media. This officer's career was put on hold for many years while the investigation ran its course; each twist and turn threatening to make him a scapegoat for what had happened on that day in 2011. Consider this and it might make you ask if we pay the people who put their lives on the line for us enough.

Gangs in London

I was always told that to be a good copper you need to know how the criminals you deal with operate. Well, during my time in the firearms unit between 1991 and 2013, we were dealing with organized criminal gangs and not so organized criminal gangs and both had their own problems. However, over the years I got to see how violent and evil they all were. Whatever way you look at it, they are bad for the community, the country and the young people who seem so ready to join them. What follows is how I viewed them from the perspective of an armed police officer. Many of the criminals in these groups respected nothing but the firearms we were carrying when we arrested them.

Gangs, or crime syndicates, have been present in one form or another in London probably since Roman times. More recently, immigrant groups settling in the East End after fleeing persecution formed gangs for their own protection in a strange country and also to pool their skills and capitalize from criminal opportunities that presented themselves in a bustling big city.

Today it is no different. However, the violence used impacts more on the public than it did in the 1950s when it was generally tit-for-tat gang-related power struggles. It has also spread, and instead of being contained in a few central areas, it is now across the capital. Due to the willingness of the criminals to use lethal weapons such as guns and knives, local unarmed officers policing that community appear unable to deal with it effectively without the assistance of SCO19. ARVs are frequently attached to borough police stations for long periods of time to carry out proactive policing and to take on any armed elements. Not an ideal situation, but necessary.

The word 'gang' instils a sense of dread in most people. It is usually prefixed with another word, for example armed gang, drugs gang, motorcycle gang or kidnap gang. It implies criminality of some sort and that the group has a combined sense of purpose. In my experience, most individual criminals who feed off vulnerable victims are cowards, bullies, chancers or opportunists. When confronted with the force of law or bold civilians they will mostly back off, capitulate or divert to an easier victim. However, when part of a gang they are far more formidable and difficult to stop.

It is important that we understand how much of the crime in London is committed by these organized gangs, many of which specialize in intimidation, violence, blackmail, extortion, kidnap, gun running, vehicle hijacking, theft, robbery, burglary, drug dealing, drug trafficking, people trafficking, prostitution, fraud, murder and contract killings. Some will pick one speciality but in the main they will flip between most of the above if the opportunity arises.

Many of the accounts in this book relate to gangs and organized crime in one way or another. These phenomena exist among us and have, by far, the biggest impact on residents who live and work close by to where they operate. Many members of these groups come from the communities in which they live. These communities grieve when one of their young men becomes a victim of violence, or is arrested and incarcerated because of crimes committed while doing the gang's bidding. Members of the community are frequently the victims. These gangs prey on the weak and elderly or those who travel into the community to work. They commit knifepoint robberies, handbag snatches, assaults and random and gang-related stabbings and shootings. They declare their territorial kingdoms with borders based on sometimes nothing more than a postcode, a block of flats or a street name.

There was a time, in living memory, when these local street gangs were all known to the police and could be contained and dealt with by local unarmed bobbies on the beat, but not anymore. These violent groups, who model themselves on gangs from New York, give themselves names such as Peckham Boys, Tottenham Man Dem, London Fields Boys, MDP (Murder Dem Pussies), Ghetto Boys and have no respect for the police in any way shape or form.

They stake out territories, often daring neighbouring gangs to trespass onto their 'turf' on pain of death. These petty turf wars, which have been in the news recently, are responsible for the horrific rise in stabbings and shootings of young people. The number of gang-related murders in London by May 2018 had reached a staggering sixty-four, overtaking gang capital New York for the first time. By the end of December 2018, we had seen seventy-nine murders in London, which could be attributed to gang-related crime. These included sixty-three fatal stabbings and sixteen fatal shootings. Fifty of the victims were 25 or under.

These statistics were even used by US President Donald Trump at a gun convention to claim that by not arming our citizens, the UK was more dangerous than the US with its liberal gun laws. The only truth in that comment is that knife crime in London is as bad, if not worse, than UK gun crime. Both guns and knives are lethal in the hands of criminals and terrorists alike, but the availability of bladed weapons is almost impossible to control.

Some aggravating factors include population growth and migration of other groups into these areas, some of whom have come from violent places and are no strangers to using violence. They are often more than willing to take on those already-established groups in an effort to carve out their own territory. This causes a tinderbox effect that erupts in the form of turf wars, tit-for-tat stabbings and drive-by-shootings with civilians occasionally becoming victims in the crossfire. A growing number of victims are not affiliated to any gang and are not killed during so-called gang wars. Some are just innocent victims who are stabbed during the course of a robbery, sometimes even after handing over property or valuables. Others are in the wrong place at the wrong time: victims of random violence for no other reason than the perpetrator wants to prove they're a loyal member, a soldier, who is ready and willing to commit murder for the gang.

To understand why these gangs are so appealing to the young men and women they attract, we must ask if society is partly to blame. Have we created an underclass whose only recourse is to form its own subculture outside the law? We place great stock on success and wealth, as do these criminal gangs. They also want to become rich and use crime (much of it through the supply and distribution of drugs) to achieve it. The members of these groups advertise their wealth openly, with nice cars, jewellery, designer clothes and watches, all seen as badges of their success. This is what makes them role models for other young vulnerable members of these communities. If we wish to stop this process, we must provide better accessible role models for these disillusioned young men and women.

Many of the inner city criminal gangs have complex social structures based around violence, drugs and sex. The gang is like a club and, as in many clubs, its members have to prove their loyalty. This may involve the prospective member sustaining a beating from his peers, or performing an illegal task from robbery to murder. Gang members often record these crimes on mobile phones so other members can see how their prospect performed. The fact they have committed a terrible crime means they can be trusted not to go to the authorities. The more violent the initiation, the more kudos and standing within the gang.

Many victims of knife and gun violence are young black males, although not all are affiliated to gangs. Chief Superintendent Nicholas Davies told the Middle East-based broadcaster Al Jazeera in February 2018: 'The gangs don't necessarily follow racial groups. Some can be very multicultural, but as a rule we're finding the biggest threat to a young black male is indeed a young black male.' While it is mostly young black males who are recruited into these inner London postcode gangs, a growing number of females are being drawn into the web. These girls are generally recruited between 12 and 14 and are used to carry or store drugs or firearms in their homes for other gang members. They know police are less inclined to search females on the street. These young girls are victims of the gangs themselves and are often forced or placed under immense pressure to provide sex for gang members. Some are raped as part of their initiation.

The gangs have historically followed violent music, such as heavy rap, or more recently drill music, which glorifies their violent lifestyle. The accompanying video will often show gang members holding knives, baseball bats or occasionally guns and wearing masks or scarves to cover their faces. By using music videos to promote gang culture, it becomes even more desirable to young men and women who mostly live in deprived areas. It gives them a sense of belonging, a pseudo family with added excitement and status among their peers. It is a hard pattern to break.

The street gang culture often shields itself behind the community in which it lives. Police find it difficult to operate within the community as people may be in fear of – or have an overriding loyalty to – a gang member who is related to them.

Where police take direct action that ends in a confrontation or a shooting, such as in the Duggan case, the community can react with the threat of – or actual – public disorder. When I worked on the SFO teams and the ARVs, it made me angry that these gangs could ruin so many young lives by killing and maiming, but then have the support of some in their community.

You only have to look back to March 2011, when three members of the so-called Tottenham Gas Gang entered a grocery shop in Stockwell and discharged a pistol at rival gang members, hitting two of them along with 5-year-old Thusha Kamaleswaran. Just minutes after she had been dancing in the aisle of her father's shop, she was hit in the chest and left permanently disabled and owing her life to the heroic efforts of the NHS.

There were no demonstrations or riots on her behalf and no apology from the gang for shooting an innocent child. In fact one of the gang members, when later convicted of the shooting, made a derogatory comment about her race, implying that she was insignificant. He showed no remorse for ruining this innocent child's life. Meanwhile, local detectives and police staff raised over £180,000 for her treatment.

The police do their best fighting with one hand tied behind their back but maybe changes in the law are needed. Outlawing some gangs and perhaps making membership or association with them a criminal offence. Certainly educating the public in how they can help is required. We also need to identify vulnerable people, often the brothers and sisters of gang members, and make them aware of what these gangs are really doing and how they wreck lives.

We need better legislation to cut off the sources of income that helps these gangs thrive. Maybe we need to engage social media in a more positive way to reverse the cool image of drugs and guns, and the violent music lyrics that seem to indoctrinate these youngsters. On the other hand, would that just succeed in driving it more underground?

Either way, we need to equip and openly support our police, some of whom are bending under the strain of attending stabbings and shootings literally on a daily basis. I know of one young ARV officer who knelt at the side of a victim of a gang fight with his fingers inside the youth's neck trying to stop an arterial bleed, only to see the young man die in his arms. He was horribly affected by this incident, which was one of several similar he had attended within days of each other.

Because these violent gangs have been allowed to grow and develop while we argue over the rights and wrongs of using armed police to arrest them – with the occasional consequence of a police-related shooting – the criminals feel safer and more entrenched in the knowledge that we are tying ourselves up in knots. We need the armed officers of SCO19 more than ever.

On a good note, on 14 July 2018, tens of thousands of young people from every ethnic background took to the streets of North London in a march against knife and gun crime. Chanting 'No more violence! No more bloodshed!', they marched through areas blighted by the murder of young people.

How Armed Police Reach Out to the Community

Part of winning the battle against armed gangs and violent street crime is undoubtedly early intervention. Those who regularly deal with youth offenders understand the value of educating young people, helping them appreciate the consequences of bad decisions and diverting them from the gang culture, which is prevalent in many London boroughs. The message is simple: crime and violence are not glamorous. Every young person we can save from this fate has the potential to be a valuable member of our society, contributing at every level, which includes leading a normal family life and not being a drain on society.

I was recently invited to visit SCO19's headquarters at Leman Street, East London and I had the pleasure of meeting members of a specially selected engagement team who proactively take the message out to communities on behalf of SCO19. These are serving firearms officers, chosen because they understand the issues surrounding youth violence, including the gang, gun and knife cultures. They have empathy with the communities they visit and the ability to deliver hard-hitting presentations that give a clear message about the reality of violence and its consequences. These officers seek to empower young people, encouraging them to have a positive impact on their peers and make a difference to society.

These presentations are carried out under the banner of Operation Makepeace which was set up in 2008 by CO19 with the intention of reducing incidents of young people carrying knives and guns.

In 2017, SCO19's engagement programme connected with over 10,000 young Londoners, all of whom were encouraged to participate fully in the presentations, enabling discussion along with relevant question and answer sessions. The talks take place in secondary schools, pupil referral units, youth forums and community groups. The team also work alongside other organizations in the delivery of Operation Makepeace, including The Prince's Trust, The NSPCC, Red Cross, London Fire Brigade, through their own multi-agency events called Impact Factor, and an organization called Prison, Me? No Way, which includes priceless inputs from ex-offenders and the prison service.

As well as working with young people, the team also reach out to local community groups to discuss their operational work, dispel myths and promote the professionalism and restraint displayed by the officers, which is evidenced by the very low number of occasions they discharge their weapons each year. Interestingly, in 2017 there were more reassurances sought over Taser deployments than there were about officers with firearms.

Officers from the engagement team talk with pupils at a secondary school.

SCO19 have also called upon the engagement team to work with the media and Independent Office for Police Conduct (IOPC – which has replaced the IPCC) in an effort to promote awareness of our role along with its unique challenges, thus helping them understand the wider picture during police firearms investigations.

The engagement team continue to be an important and valued asset.

PART 3

THE SPECIALISTS

CTSFOs in grey kit deploy from an armoured Jankel support vehicle. (*AH*)

Counter Terrorist Specialist Firearms Officers

Due to the number of terrorist attacks in the UK in the first two decades of this century, along with the countless foiled attacks discovered and disrupted by the security services, it became necessary to standardize the training and equipment of our counter-terrorist armed police assets. The 2012 London Olympic Games provided the perfect jumping board to make this happen.

Part of the plan was to create large specialist firearms teams that could be lifted and shifted (by Chinook helicopters if necessary, or by vehicle convoy) to any Olympic site,

The hard-earned shoulder patch of London's CTSFO teams. (*Stephen Smith*)

Above: Current CTSFO officers alongside a jump-off van with a small selection of kit laid out in the foreground. This includes ballistic shields, an assortment of weapons and door-opening MOE kit. (*Stephen Smith*)

Below: Weaponry used by CTSFOs. Top left: Heckler & Koch G3 .762 with collapsible stock and eyes-on-tech sight. Middle left: Benelli semi-automatic breaching shotgun. Left bottom: SIG MCX .556 rifle full spec. Top right: SIG 716, .762 sniper rifle. Right middle: full length Benelli semi-automatic shotgun. Right bottom: Heckler & Koch 9mm MP5K (personal defence weapon) with side-folding stock. Bottom: Glocks 17, 19 and 26, Taser X-26. (*Stephen Smith*)

Above left: A CTSFO face-on showing body armour, ballistic plates, extra magazines for his SIG MCX, respirator, press-to-talk button for radio comms, flame-retardant, two-piece grey op clothing and ballistic helmet with ear defenders linked to radio comms. (*Stephen Smith*)

Above right: Rear of CTSFO showing, radio comms, first aid pouch, respirator, multi-tool, rear ballistic plate. (*Stephen Smith*)

or anywhere else in the UK where a terrorist attack had occurred, was occurring or was believed to be imminent. It would involve SFO teams from various UK police forces working closely together.

While the Met's SFO teams were already trained in most of the skill sets needed to be a counter terrorism specialist firearms officer (CTSFO), many of their counterparts in other UK firearms commands were not. The differences were largely confined to skills such as maritime operations, aircraft intervention and deploying from helicopters onto buildings using 'fast rope', along with some other specialist skills.

Therefore, in the run up to the London Olympics, a massive inter-force training programme was set in place. The SFO teams from Thames Valley Police, West Yorkshire Police, West Midlands Police, Greater Manchester Police and Strathclyde Police (now Police Scotland) joined the Met and underwent standardization training to enhance interoperability.

Combined Response Firearms Team training in Essex for the 2012 London Olympic Games. Officers from many UK forces trained together; here they are deploying on fast ropes from a Chinook helicopter. (*Stephen Smith*)

Above and below: (CTSFOs carrying out counter-terrorist training on the London underground. (*Dominique Andre*)

Above: Officer begins fast-rope descent from police EC 145 helicopter. (*AH*)

Below: CTSFOs provide cover while colleagues fast rope. (*Dominique Andre*)

These new combined teams were given the working title of Combined Response Firearms Teams (CRFT). They were known as this throughout the 2012 Games but then, instead of reverting back to the title of SFO, the officers who underwent the enhanced training were given the new title of CTSFO.

In April 2016, a nationwide CTSFO recruitment programme was launched with the objective of doubling the number of these highly trained officers. The regional CTSFO hubs increased with the additions of South Wales and a tri-force of English police forces to create a south-west CTSFO hub. The benefits to the smaller forces around the country were immense as they could now tap into this resource when needed. Many of these subsequently amalgamated different specialist assets with other forces, including surveillance teams, traffic and dogs, both to save money on training and equipment and to make better use of the resources available.

The skills required to attain the title CTSFO are listed below. This is not a definitive list as it changes and evolves as the role expands. However it is clear looking at this list that these are highly trained and motivated individuals.

The CTSFO Role Profile

All applicants should be experienced firearms officers who must be trained to a minimum of ARV standard. To become a CTSFO, officers must undergo additional selection and training and prove that they meet the following standards and have the following skills:

- High level of physical fitness – enough to achieve a 10.5 bleep test – and meet hearing and eyesight standards, which are tested annually
- Expert in firearms tactics
- Expert marksman with pistols, carbine and shotguns
- Proficient in less-lethal means such as Taser and baton launcher
- Ballistic trauma medic
- Trained in handheld distraction devices
- Trained in method of entry (MOE) and conversant with all types of mechanical entry equipment deployed by SCO19
- Dynamic search, both entry for evidential recovery and intervention for hostage rescue (used to be known as close quarter combat)
- Trained in siege management and resolution
- Mobile armed support to surveillance (MASTS)
- Aircraft intervention for resolving hostage situations on board aircraft
- Counter-terrorist tactics for resolving incidents involving terrorist subjects including use of critical shot
- Trained in chemical, biological, radiological and nuclear (also known as CBRN)
- Fast-rope trained to deploy from helicopters or urban access rigs
- Helicopter transit deployments via hover deplaning
- Small team intervention tactics. Working in small covert cells in support of other tactics or as a stand-alone option. Officers must also be National Surveillance trained

- Waterborne tactics for working from rigid-hulled inflatable boats (RHIB)
- Close target reconnaissance

MPS CTSFO are also trained in the following:

- Counter-ambush tactics for enhanced armed protection for dignitary and at-risk persons
- Smoke-filled environment tactics. Provision of dynamic and deliberate search wearing fire fighting breathing apparatus
- Abseiling for high-rise access
- Waterborne advanced boarding tactics for climbing ships underway in support of hostage rescue and counter-terrorist interdiction

Many more specialized skill sets and courses are available to CTSFO personnel once qualified. but they are not a requirement. These include becoming a nationally qualified rifle officer (sniper), explosive method of entry (EMOE), advanced motorcycle riding, armoured vehicle driving and anti-hijack driving. If you're a qualified firearms instructor there are many other options and you could, potentially, instruct on all of the above and even the CTSFO course itself. Needless to say, each officer must be in the peak of physical fitness to do this role and, of course, avoid injuries.

Two team members move into position around the side of a warehouse, both armed with the SIG MCX. (*AH*)

An ARV officer can progress to become CTSFO but it takes dedication and determination and is not always conducive to a good family and work-life balance.

It is both physically and mentally draining and at times extremely stressful. Officers must be aware that as a result of their actions they may be investigated and even prosecuted. This is not a job for the faint hearted, but, in my opinion, it can be one of the most engaging and challenging jobs that exists in modern-day law enforcement.

Ambush and Rapid Deployment

Another technique used frequently by SCO19, mostly by CTSFO and TST and occasionally by ARV, is rapid deployment, usually from the back of a covert 'jump-off' van or sometimes from premises nearby to where a robbery or other armed crime is due to occur.

The vehicle can be driven in and left in situ, or in the case of premises, the officers wearing plain clothes will infiltrate it, carrying their light-order kit and weapons, sometimes with their kit disguised as tools or a delivery of some description. The officers will then kit-up inside, check radio communications with their control and play the waiting game for the armed crime to shape up. They will always focus on speed and surprise to achieve rapid domination of the subjects.

Here are a series of training photos showing officers inside and deploying from a jump-off van or car.

CTSFOs in training deploy from a high-performance covert gunship in training wearing a hybrid of plain clothes and overt armour. The combination provides flexibility in how they deploy and adapt as the operational environment changes. (*Dominique Andre*)

Above: Two officers move forward using the small MCX Rattler to cover their advance onto the armed subject. (*Dominique Andre*)

Left: Officer in hybrid kit with MCX carbine held at low port. (*Dominique Andre*)

Above: CTSFOs in plain clothes with Aegis plate armour and Cora ballistic helmet inside their reactive jump-off van. (*Dominique Andre*)

Below: Having deployed, the team is now covering the armed suspect after a successful intervention. (*Dominique Andre*)

Hostage Rescue

Believe it or not, this is still one of the major roles of specialist firearms commands and it is carried out far more than you would imagine. Over the years there have been many incidents where SCO19 have effected a dynamic rescue of persons held against their will, whether it be for ransom or in a domestic or terrorist environment. While the domestic hostage situation is far more common, there have been several spates of armed criminal gangs forcing persons, who have been smuggled into the country illegally, to work for them in a form of modern-day slavery. These have resulted in the firearms department performing hostage rescue operations to free them and arrest the organizers and their enforcers.

Officers train regularly in dynamic entry and will use many of the tactics already mentioned, such as mechanical method of entry, EMOE, breaching shotguns, deployment of gas into premises, use of distraction stun grenades and the use of specialist vehicles. Here are photos of CTSFO using some of these methods.

CTSFO team ready to carry out a dynamic entry. Second officer shows a prepped stun grenade to the number one. (*Dominique Andre*)

Above left: An MOE breacher fires his breaching shotgun into the hinges to disrupt them and effect an entry through the door. (*AH*)

Above right: A shot gunner delivers CS irritant through a window as the door is being breached in order to render those inside submissive. (*AH*)

Below: Post-entry hostage rescue photo showing suspects secured with cable ties and the premises secured.

Aircraft Intervention

With two London airports falling within the jurisdiction of the Metropolitan Police district, SCO19 have the capability to carry out some form of aircraft intervention at short notice should the need arise. Fortunately, it is not a regular occurrence.

The last plane hijacking in the UK took place in February 2000 when an Afghanistan Ariana Airlines passenger jet containing 164 passengers and fourteen crew was taken over by men armed with grenades and handguns, who forced it to land at Stansted Airport. SO19 were called in to assist Essex Police and took on a major role during the siege, which lasted four days and ended peaceably with the surrender of the hijackers and the release of all passengers (many of the crew had escaped before the end).

Although SO19 were trained in aircraft intervention, in 2000 it would have been highly unlikely that they would have been able to mount a full-blown successful intervention on anything other than one of the smaller airlines. However since then, as a result of funding and additional

SCO19 carry out valuable aircraft intervention training at an airfield in the south east of England. (*Stephen Smith*)

training and equipment in the form of specialist vehicles, I believe SCO19 would today be capable of mounting an emergency intervention if required, prior to the arrival of Special Forces.

It is not my intention to give away specialist tactics in this book. I can however point out that, if required, entry to the aircraft will be made with the intention of neutralizing all hostiles on board and rescuing the passengers and crew with minimum casualties.

This is one of the most dangerous operations any armed unit, military or not, can be called upon to carry out and it would be undertaken only as a last resort. Most aircraft interventions rarely end without some loss of life on both sides but thankfully they are so rare that to illustrate such an incident we have to go back to December 1994. This was when an Air France flight was hijacked from Algiers by four members of the Groupe Islamique Armé who were planning to crash into the Eiffel Tower in central Paris.

Following the murder of three of the passengers, the elite tactical unit of the French Gendarme (Groupe D'Intervention de la Gendarmerie Nationale) stormed the plane in Marseilles, killing all the hijackers and freeing all remaining passengers. This operation was very daring and a great success, and set an example of what was needed should this event occur closer to home.

In preparation for this happening, today's CTSFOs undergo vigorous training using all the specialist vehicles and equipment available to them. As well as a high level of fitness, a certain agility is needed when effecting entry into a commercial aircraft under an 'emergency assault'. However, given time, during a 'deliberate assault', police or military units can plan and utilize all their assets to give the assaulters and the passengers the best chance of survival.

CTSFO units also share ideas and information with Special Forces and specialist police units around Europe using the ATLAS Network (see page 177), a mutual specialist police forum for sharing best practice with other European police units, which was established after 9/11.

CTSFOs use available cover to move into position ready to storm the aircraft. (*Dominique Andre*)

Left: CTSFOs prepare to make an entry from one of their ladder vehicles while an officer maintains cover on the cockpit. (*Dominique Andre*)

Below: CTSFOs make a dynamic entry into the aircraft covering all arcs of fire. (*Dominique Andre*)

Having made an entry, two officers cover and clear the galley and aisles and begin hunting down and neutralizing any hostiles. (*Dominique Andre*)

CTSFO Training Programme

Like most skills, practice makes perfect and so officers need regular training. Thankfully, the Metropolitan Police Service Specialist Training Centre at Gravesend has most of the resources needed to maintain and practise these skills.

In the last five years there has been increased investment in the equipment and training these officers receive. There has also been better understanding and acceptance from the public as to what their specialist armed police are capable of. In the spirit of transparency, SCO19 have begun to open up to the public and showcase exactly what they do in order to keep the country safe. Many of the tactics used by specialist police and anti-terrorist units around the world are on the internet and here is a series of photographs taken of CTSFO officers during training. It gives an idea of what they do to ensure they're always prepared.

CTSFOs in grey kit move up in 'stick' order using cover officers behind a short ballistic shield. Note the officers behind are carrying MOE equipment. This would be the standard for most 'dig out' arrest operations. (*Dominique Andre*)

Above: CTSFOs, using a ladder vehicle, deploy onto a balcony to set up on a front door protected by a door grill. Once the balcony has been secured, the MOE officers will set up on the door ready for breaching. (*Dominique Andre*)

Below: MOE officers set up on the iron door grill using a 'Hooli' bar and an enforcer ram to defeat the grill and access the door behind. (*Dominique Andre*)

Above: Other options for mechanical MOE: this officer has set up a Libervit HR5 hydraulic ram on the front door, which is carried on a backpack. (*Dominique Andre*)

Below: A CTSFO in a training scenario covers a tube train carriage with his SIG MCX. Officers will always look for the best cover available. (*Dominique Andre*)

Above: Officers carry out a search of a tube carriage covering as many points of danger as possible. (*Dominique Andre*)

Below: Officers make use of cover on the tracks of the London Underground searching for a suspect who has fled into the tunnel. It would be imperative that the power is turned off before using this tactic. (*Dominique Andre*)

A CTSFO uses night vision goggles to penetrate the darkness on the London Underground system. He has a suppressed SIG MCX weapons system. (*Dominique Andre*)

Team Sniper

CTSFO officers can apply to be a team rifleman or sniper, although some are already qualified as such before they start work on the CTSFO teams, and bring that skill with them. While their main role will be as an assaulter, if the operation requires a rifleman, their skills will be put to use. Here is a series of photos showing officers on rifle support duties.

Right: CTSFO sniper using his Accuracy International rifle with the City of London in the background. (*Dominique Andre*)

Below: Pair of snipers on a counter-sniper/surveillance operation with the SIG 716G2 suppressed rifle, chambered for 7.62 x 51mm. (*Dominique Andre*)

Left: Sniper prepares to move into position with his AI 7.62 rifle at the ready. (*Dominique Andre*)

Below: A rifle officer uses the SIG 716 rifle system on the range in 2018. (*AH*)

Maritime Operations

Working on the River Thames

Ever since Roman times, the River Thames has been a rich source of income both legally and illegally. The river has seen its fair share of criminality, from smuggling and theft in the dockyards and wharfs, to piracy. The police have had a responsibility for maintaining the rule of law in this section of waterway since before the formation of the Met in 1829. In fact one of the oldest police forces was the Thames River Police, who formed in 1798. It amalgamated

A Thames Division special ops rigid hull inflatable boat (RHIB) prepares to receive CTSFOs as they abseil down the side of a large 'ship underway'. (*AH*)

with the Met in 1839 becoming Thames Division, with its headquarters at Wapping Police Station in East London.

Thames Division has undergone many changes in its long history but one of its biggest transformations was following the terrible disaster on the river when *Bowbelle* (a Thames dredger) collided with *Marchioness* (a pleasure steamer and ex-Dunkirk veteran) on 20 August 1989. The collision occurred close to Cannon Street Railway Bridge, with the terrible loss of fifty-one lives. The tragedy resulted in more stringent river safety protocols, which included Thames Division taking a bigger role in river safety and rescue. This required the need for faster launches and the purchase of rigid-hulled inflatable boats (RHIB), which were more efficient and thus capable of getting to the scene of a river disaster quickly. This required sending officers on courses to become RHIB coxswains, capable of handling the craft in any weather condition.

Although a relationship with the force firearms unit had existed probably since the mid-1980s, it was placed on a more permanent and structured footing in 1991. For Thames Division it was like taking a step back in time – but without the cutlasses – as once again it would be able to practise armed boarding of moving vessels.

The criteria for SO19 was as follows: to respond to a spontaneous firearms incident upon a vessel on the Thames or other waterway; to assist other agencies to board a vessel, when moving or when moored, where there is a perceived firearms threat; to use a waterborne environment as

Two Met RHIBs cut across the water in front of wind turbines in the Thames Estuary. (*AH*)

means of approach when mounting an operation against a riverside property or moored vessel and, lastly, to provide waterborne insertion and extraction of covert firearms support teams.

Thames Division was happy to put forward its RHIBs and RHIB coxswains for SO19's specialist training. The units joined forces to become the Thames Special Operations Unit (Thames SOU). In training, the most challenging aspect was the boarding of ships underway along the Thames and out in the estuary. On occasion, the Thames SOU would be taken away on other operations and training exercises further afield within British waters, although this is no longer the case. The Met now confines itself solely to working on waterways within the Metropolitan Police district.

At first the SOU and SO19 trialled small rigid inflatable boats (RIB) craft in combination with Thames police launches but these proved inadequate. Later, two powerful, large RHIBs were purchased, each capable of delivering twelve fully equipped assaulters onto a target, whether it be a waterside premises, moving pleasure craft or ship. Each SFO (later reclassified as CTSFO) would undergo familiarization training with the boats and equipment to qualify them as an advanced boarder, and use specialist techniques to board the vessel.

Any officer working on the river would wear a fire-retardant immersion suit, enabling them to keep warm in the water and have a degree of buoyancy. SO19 also purchased a number of stainless steel shotguns to minimize any rusting of the mechanism when used in saltwater

Two CTSFOs abseil down to the RHIB from a ship underway. The usual method was to jump from the stern. *(AH)*

CTSFOs train to do the long climb up the narrow caving ladder to get to the deck of a large freighter in the Thames Estuary. (*AH*)

conditions. These weapons were ideal for using on a RHIB as rifles or carbines required a more stable platform to shoot from.

These maritime skills required a high degree of fitness owing to the amount of physical effort needed to pull the officer, along with all their weapons and equipment, up 15 metres of narrow caving ladder while being dragged along the side of a big cargo ship in a high wind. And that's before they've fought their way to the ship's bridge to take control of the vessel.

It's dangerous work. The huge swell of open water makes the RIB craft rise and fall, sometimes in excess of 5 metres. Some injuries are to be expected with this type of training but thankfully they're kept to a minimum with only a few broken bones and burst eardrums.

In training, the quickest way of leaving a vessel of any size is to jump off into the water. To practise this, they would stand on the stern rail of the vessel, cross their arms over their weapon, tuck their chin in and step off into mid-air, hitting the water maybe 30 feet below before waiting patiently to be picked up by the RHIB and the smiling crew from Thames SOU.

In recent times the River Thames has featured in many firearms operations, notably Operation Emerge in November 1992. SFOs from the Met, working for UK Customs and Excise and the Regional Crime Squad, assaulted and secured *Fox Trot Five*, which was an ocean-going barge registered in Panama. The operation netted cocaine valued at £160 million.

Above: The sleek hull of a Thames Special Ops RHIB with SCO19 CTSFOs returns from boarding a cargo boat in the Thames Estuary. (*AH*)

Below: A CTSFO in training begins an abseil from the upper deck of a large container ship. (*AH*)

LONDON'S ARMED POLICE UP CLOSE AND PERSONAL

In November 2000, SO19 worked closely with the Thames SOU, who were covering the Millennium Dome raid. The Dome, now the O2 Arena, was targeted by a gang dubbed by the press as the 'River Rats', who were planning to rob the De Beers diamond exhibition and had a powerboat on standby in which to make their getaway. The plot was foiled with all arrested and anyway, the diamonds had been swapped with fakes.

More recently, armed police carried out some high profile maritime anti-terrorist patrols and exercises to act as a deterrent to anyone hoping to use the River Thames for terrorist attacks.

Both units continue to improve their efficiency on the water, looking at new boats, equipment and tactics. In the near future we will see advanced boarders using powered rope ascenders and being delivered onto ships underway, by means of fast roping from helicopters. The ever-changing landscape of crime and criminal endeavours means armed policing can never sleep.

PART 4

TACTICAL SUPPORT AND EQUIPMENT

An ARV officer firing his SIG MCX on the range at Leman Street. (*AH*)

Support Vehicles

The Jankel Guardian and Nissan Warrior

Like all counter-terrorist police, special weapons and tactics (SWAT) type units anywhere in the world, SCO19 have use of specialist vehicles. These are required to carry out the range of tasks presented to them on a daily basis and they also need to be updated when better and more versatile vehicles are developed and become available.

Back in1979, D11 – as it was then – had use of armoured Land Rovers. These were used extensively at the Libyan hostage incident in 1984, and made appearances at several other notable firearms operations including the Hungerford massacre in 1987 and the Stansted hijacking in 2000.

The need for armoured vehicles was hammered home following a siege in Leicester in 1975, when two police officers were shot, one fatally, in front of a building occupied by an armed suspect following a domestic incident. Two further people were also killed, including the suspect's wife and an ambulance driver.

Neither the police sergeant who died nor his wounded female colleague could be recovered for fear of there being further casualties. The siege ended when a fire in the house forced the gunman to jump from an upstairs window into the arms of police.

The Met realized they had no contingency for casualty retrieval, so they developed a heavy steel-plated movable shield system. This was superseded by the armoured Land Rover, which remained in service until being replaced by the Jankel armoured vehicle around 2003.

CTSFO team pose for a photo in grey op kit with weapons and equipment in front of the Jankel Guardian and the Nissan Warrior support vehicles. (*IJ*)

Above: The Armoured Defender Land Rover, used by D11-SO19 from 1979 until 2003 when it was replaced by the Jankel.

Below: Armoured police Jankel Guardian, based on the Ford F-450 4X4 truck, converted for police use by the Surrey-based company which supplies them. Used by SO19, CO19 and SCO19 since 2003. (*Stephen Smith*)

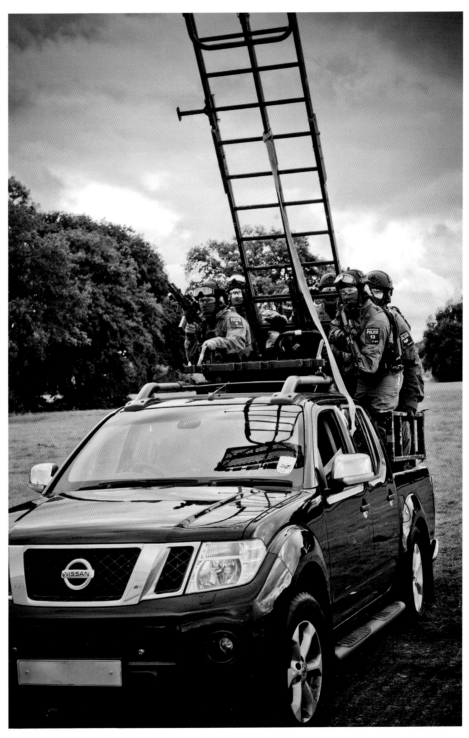

Ford and Nissan 4X4 pick-up trucks have been used by CO19 and SCO19 since 2003. Here this Nissan is equipped as a ladder vehicle to provide access to an aircraft. (*Stephen Smith*)

The author, centre, receives instruction on assembling the assault ramp for delivering assaulters onto an elevated entry point, August 2004. (*Stephen Smith*)

Based on the Ford 4X4 F-450 and converted by the Surrey-based company Jankel Armouring Ltd, the Jankel Guardian has been used extensively in the last two decades. It is a versatile firearms support vehicle, which can be used, among other things, for containment, casualty retrieval, hostage rescue, overt observation post and sniper position, hostage negotiation and anti-terrorist operations. It weighs just under 7 tons and is powered by a 6-litre, 325bhp turbo diesel engine.

Another well-used favourite of the firearms department is the Nissan Warrior. This versatile vehicle has a multitude of uses, which includes providing delivery options from first to third-floor balconies or windows. It can be fitted with ladders or ramps or used in a simple pick-up truck configuration to place alongside a bus or coach in order to make an assault or provide firearms cover.

Both the Jankel and the Warrior are coming towards the end of their lives with SCO19 who are looking at replacements for both. You can rest assured the next generation of support and specialist vehicles will be even more adaptable and innovative than these old favourites.

Specialist Rifle Team

White Team 2007-2013

In 2007, CO19 were looking at ways to improve their ability to tackle the ever-changing face of armed crime and terrorism. A dedicated rifle and sniper team had been considered for some years, but this would be no ordinary team of rifle-trained officers. The intention was to train selected officers in the art of covert reconnaissance and the ability to establish both rural and urban observation points (OP). They would also be trained in using ropes at height – ideal for working on exposed elevated rooftop locations including high-rise blocks – and firing from helicopters, which were versatile and mobile gun platforms. They would also research weaponry and equipment that would be useful in the run-up to the 2012 London Olympic Games.

An SFO sergeant and a rifle officer were assigned to carry out a feasibility study of how it would work. They came up with the idea of drawing personnel from both SFO and ARV, so as not to deplete the already understrength SFO teams. They would have to be rifle-trained officers with operational experience, as their main role would be to provide rifle support to ARV and SFO during pre-planned or spontaneous firearms operations, whether terrorist or domestic crime. They would also have to trial new weapons and equipment.

Applications were invited, the best of which would form a dedicated rifle team based on the third floor with the SFO teams. They would be used either as a complete team (as in the case of a state visit or major sporting event) or in smaller groups of no less than two to provide cover for SFO team deployments. They would have a responsibility to provide twenty-four-hour rifle cover for call outs should a siege develop anywhere in the capital.

In May 2007, following the selection of suitable candidates, a specialist rifle team (SRT) was formed called White Team. They were given a budget to research and purchase weaponry, along with the responsibility for planning training and operational rotas that could accommodate their roles.

They hit the ground running, offering support to SFO teams on numerous operations, both spontaneous and pre-planned. Shortly after going live, in September 2007 they were involved in Operation Hurlock at Chandler's Ford in Hampshire where two officers in a robbery OP, both attached to the SRT, shot and killed two armed robbers who were threatening a security guard on a cash-in-transit delivery to an HSBC bank.

However, they were victims of their own success. Although the inquest found the shooting of the two armed robbers to be lawful and it drastically reduced the number of cash-in-transit

White Team sniper in a rural hide with SIG 553. 5.56mm with 10-inch barrel and Elcan sight. (*Tony Long*)

robberies in London and the Home Counties, the practice of placing rifle officers in active robbery OPs was halted for many months. (See *Stop! Armed Police!*)

Later that year, White Team trialled and took delivery of the 5.56 mm, 10-inch barrelled SIG Sauer 553 with Brügger and Thomet suppressors, along with Elcan Specter sights. These were purchased with the intention of providing the team with a small, folding, but accurate close-range (100 metres max) sniper weapon that could be concealed in a sports bag or under a coat or jacket and smuggled into an urban OP. Due to the built-up, high-rise nature of the London skyline, the sniper team worked mainly at ranges within 100 metres.

However, after prolonged use, the suppressors on the SIGs developed problems so in 2010, following negotiations with the suppliers, they were exchanged for the 14-inch barrelled SIG 516.

Above: An officer holds the SIG 516 in its early configuration. (*Stephen Smith*)

Below: A White Team sniper uses a helicopter platform to line up on the cockpit during an aircraft assault training exercise. (*Tony Long*)

The workload increased, and due to the demands placed on these officers, it became apparent that it would be beneficial if all White Team officers were trained to SFO standard. If they didn't pass the course, they were returned to normal duties within the firearms unit. Although harsh on those who could not make the step up, it was necessary to fit in with the new CTSFO work, which was looking towards the 2012 London Olympics.

Two White Team snipers settle down in a mobile hide in the back of a covert van. (*Tony Long*)

White Team planned and carried out invaluable reconnaissance on the Olympic sites in order to provide unbroken sniper cover over all the main stadium areas where observation platforms were built. Many used rope skills to allow rifle officers to be securely roped off, thus being safer in high winds. These OPs would give a bird's-eye view of the proceedings.

Ironically, White Team would not be used in this role during the Games – it was handed over to other rifle officers brought in solely for the occasion. White Team were split among the new CTSFO teams, allowing them to be lifted and dropped (by helicopter if necessary) anywhere in the country to support local police units should the need arise.

White Team's work in preparation for the Games gave those on the ground a feeling of protection throughout the event. Sadly, in 2013 White Team were disbanded due to financial cutbacks, along with the fact the new CTSFO role and training took some of the special skills back to the teams.

In 2012, the 10-inch barrelled version of the SIG 516 was adopted by the SFO teams where it proved successful until 2015 when it was superseded by the SIG MCX weapons system.

Conflict Management Dogs

In the early 1970s, shortly after D11 was given its full operational remit, the department identified the benefits of using police dogs to assist in certain tasks. It looked to the dog section for help with duties such as tracking armed criminals across open country, locating weapons and arms caches in rural areas and containing armed besieged criminals in buildings, with a view to giving chase to any subjects who broke out and attempted to run for it. The Metropolitan Police Dog Section was only too happy to oblige.

The dog section provided German Shepherd dogs and police dog handlers to assist the firearms teams when called upon to do so. The early dog handlers picked for this role were sent on basic firearms courses, the rationale being that if they were in close proximity to armed criminals they would need to be able to defend themselves. This practice of arming dog handlers ceased in the 1980s when it was considered unreasonable to expect them to concentrate on controlling a police dog and a firearm at the same time.

By the mid-1980s, handlers went on tough selection courses with their dogs and were trained to work closely with the level one firearms teams, (predecessors to the CTSFO teams). The German Shepherd dog was considered the ideal breed for this role. Picked for its temperament, it had two main attributes: one was its ability to remain calm and not bark or whine, which would risk compromising the operation, and it was also excellent at searching for persons hiding within a structure.

These dogs proved to be invaluable. They were able to search in confined spaces, such as lofts and basements, and areas where fully equipped armed officers would have trouble accessing. The dogs would indicate when they found a suspect, either with a single bark or a wag of the tail. They are a great asset to the firearms unit and over the years have been responsible for locating hundreds of armed suspects who may well have gone on to shoot or harm the firearms officers had they not been there.

In the early 1990s when the term 'Trojan' was adopted for armed ARV units on patrol in London, the specially trained police dogs were known as Trojan dogs. Trojan dog handlers are proud of their affiliation with SCO19. They share a great working relationship with the operators on both the ARV's and firearms teams.

As a breed, the German Shepherd has cornered the market in general police work. These dogs are called upon to assist in most firearms operations and, when not utilized, are held in reserve to cover contingencies.

I have acted as the armed criminal role player on many training exercises and had the terrifying experience of a police dog breathing down my neck and taking me down to the ground by my arm as I attempted to outrun him. Thankfully I was wearing a bite pad. I have also experienced an accidental bite from a German Shepherd on a live firearms operation, which required stitches. I would rather have them on my side than have them coming after me.

The German Shepherd is truly exceptional. However due to the changing tactics used by terrorists and violent criminals, along with the success of these types of dogs in the military, the department needed to look for the perfect addition. They did not have to look far. The Belgian Malinois, already used by the Army for its ability to locate improvised explosive devices, was the obvious choice for the kind of work SCO19 had in mind. Intelligent and hardy, these dogs have a knack for seizing a suspect and locking on to them.

In May 2017, money was found to run a pilot scheme within SCO19. The department purchased two Belgian Malinois. These dogs are slightly smaller than German Shepherds and slightly more versatile and SCO19 needed them because they were more aggressive. This

Trojan dog and handler abseil down the tower at the Firearms Training Centre in Gravesend. Believe it or not, many of the dogs enjoyed the training. (*Pete Cox*)

breed is famed for its aggressive nature; even the puppies cannot be trained with other breeds of police dogs. However, if trained correctly, this aggression can be harnessed and used in the correct circumstances.

These dogs have been tried and tested in battlefield conditions by US Special Forces and were later adopted by the British Special Forces for use in Afghanistan. The breed was made famous by the Malinois called Cairo, who was attached to US SEAL Team Six and was present on the mission to kill Osama bin Laden.

In May 2018, there was press interest in the canine newcomers with claims that the Met's firearms unit had trained two so-called 'attack dogs' to hunt down terrorists in the event of a marauding attack. This was not far from the truth. They were given the name conflict management dogs (CMDs) and trained specifically to stop terrorists.

One of the benefits of using such a dog against terrorists is that it can attack, hold and detain a subject who may have otherwise been shot by armed police, thus giving them a less-lethal option when Taser would not be considered owing to the possible sympathetic detonation of a body-borne device.

The downside of training and running a programme of this type is that it comes with a big price tag. The dogs have to be housed at the SCO19 base in specially built pens with

Above: A conflict management dog waits for the release to go after a suspect in training. Cameras can be attached to its harness. In this photo it has a muzzle to protect the role player. (*AH*)

Left: This dog clearly enjoys its work and training. These dogs have been used successfully on many operations without incident and are a fantastic addition to SCO19. (*AH*)

Dog on an operation with its handler. The dogs are part of the CTSFO team and live in the building in which the officers work. (*AH*)

their own runs. They need adapted vehicles to transport them to jobs and their handlers are required to undergo extensive training and be on twenty-four-hour call out to respond to terrorist operations.

These two dedicated intervention Belgian Malinois dogs are the first of their kind in the UK and the Met is hoping to expand the programme. Ultimately, each of the CTSFO teams will have its own dogs, allowing them to work independently of other teams on a protracted operation with multiple addresses or subjects.

With new tools come new rules and they dictate that the CMDs cannot be deployed without the authority of a superintendent, who will have to ascertain the risk posed by the subject compared with the risk posed by deploying the dogs. Their use must be reasonable, necessary and proportionate.

These CMDs have been successfully deployed many times. The dogs are trained to bite the extremities and release on special commands known only to the handler and a few of the firearms team.

On some occasions the German Shepherd and the Belgian Malinois may be used on the same operation as they fulfil different and unique roles, which give added tactical flexibility. Consequently, it's important their handlers fully understand the attributes of each breed.

I find it refreshing that in this atmosphere of accountability and litigation we are still prepared to push the boundaries and try new things. This is essential if we wish to contain this current wave of terrorist attacks and have effective methods that we can develop going forward.

I have seen these dogs at the SCO19 base. Although they are not treated as pets, I can assure anyone who may think this type of police dog training is cruel, that they are well looked after and live in state-of-the-art, centrally heated accommodation and are treated with respect from the specialist operators who realize the true value of their canine teammates.

Drones

One of the most innovative modern-day developments is the drone. I became aware of drones when they were used by Britain and the US on the battlefield in Iraq, Afghanistan and Syria. However their use in theatres of war has led to a rapid development in this type of vehicle.

They are now frequently used in civilian life. Hobbyists use them for aerial photography and drone racing, where they pilot them around a course against the clock. They are used in the oil industry for surveying vast areas of uninhabitable terrain, for traffic management and road safety, by film and documentary-makers, giving them infinite creative choices. They have even been used on humanitarian missions in cases of earthquake, volcanic eruptions and other international disasters, where aerial observations can be used to find the safest pathways to rescue and get aid to those injured and displaced. They are also being used effectively in understanding the importance of climate change.

Our police service is also developing and using them in its fight against crime in general, and more importantly against armed and violent criminals and terrorists.

A commercially available SkyRanger drone used daily by SCO19 to provide video and still images at firearms incidents. (*Stephen Smith*)

But is the drone, or unmanned aerial vehicle (UAV) as it was first known, a new innovation or old technology reinvented? I was surprised to learn that the concept of UAVs has been around since the end of the First World War. In fact the first pilotless vehicles were used by the US Army in January 1918, launched by catapult and flown using radio control. Although the war ended before their impact could make a difference, they continued to be developed. Britain developed its own radio-controlled aircraft, which was mainly used as an aerial target system.

The term drone began to creep in around 1935 and originated from the name given to the first mass-produced target UAV – the De Havilland DH82B Queen Bee – bee hence drone.

Reconnaissance drones were first used on a large scale during the Vietnam War. They were adapted for use as combat decoys, for launching missiles against fixed targets and for leaflet drops. They even fitted speakers to them for propaganda announcements.

Following the Vietnam War, other countries saw the benefits of this technology and they became more sophisticated with improved endurance (some now recharge in flight using solar power), higher altitude, better load-carrying capabilities and, with the advent of GPS, more accurate targeting of locations and routes. Modern drones are used for delivering supplies, military reconnaissance, surveillance and, since 9/11, for delivering a military airstrike capability against enemy assets.

Drones are now being used to assist London's armed police. Since 2017, SCO19 have been looking at ways to provide better support to its officers and its 'command and control' at the scenes of armed incidents. The use of a drone, in particular during an armed siege, may prevent sending officers into a potential area of danger. The drone can be sent in first to check if it's safe. This technology comes into its own when dealing with terrorist safe houses or bomb factories. Previously, an officer would have to go forward for a 'close quarter reconnaissance' with the possibility of a compromise and spoiling months of good work. However, a drone can be sent, gathering all the information needed to plan a raid or intervention and with minimal risk.

SCO19 use a variety of drones. Some are based on commercial models, which can be purchased online or from high street outlets, while others are sourced from specialist suppliers, which I am not permitted to name. They are fitted with a variety of high-resolution, all-weather cameras with the capability of zooming in on the smallest detail. The advantages of using drones fitted with cameras is the potential for landing them on high buildings and using them as OPs to give a 'live real-time feed' to a firearms control room, which is known as 'land, leave and look'. They have the added ability of evidence-gathering, identifying suspects using facial recognition and helping with decision-making regarding the best time to send in armed officers to arrest suspects.

In this climate of cutbacks and budget reforms it is pleasing to know that the use of drones delivers great value for money. In the past, the unit would have had to employ a police helicopter to fulfil many of these functions and the cost of the helicopter is between ten to fifteen times more than the drone. Drones are also quieter than helicopters, which would frequently drown out police communications, or its downdraft would interfere with evidence.

The police helicopter could also be easy to spot when hovering over an incident. On more than one occasion it has drawn fire from armed criminals and has also been shot at while aerial evidence-gathering at riots. All these tasks can now be covered using drones, whose pilots and observers are safely on the ground watching from a live feed.

Recently, police drones were used to provide aerial spotting of potential threats at Windsor during the wedding of Prince Harry and Meghan Markle. The drones hover unobserved over

DRONES

The SkyRanger, shown here fitted with an under slung, remote-controlled surveillance camera. (*Stephen Smith*)

crowds, sending vital information to the control, which is using the live feed and can spot any potential attackers moving into position or terrorists preparing for an attack.

A few years ago, it would have been ridiculous to think that we would be talking so openly and in such a matter-of-fact way about the police use of drones. But I'm sure that in the not-too-distant future, we shall see their use expanding in ways we never thought possible. Who knows? Maybe they'll replace the need for police patrols. Maybe drone technology will be able to identify criminals and crimes being committed and assign officers in more efficient ways, such as gathering evidence and vectoring officers to intercept offenders while maintaining an aerial observation platform that few would be able to outrun.

The potential for SCO19 drones is vast. I don't know what the implications or legal standing would be around using them as a weapons platform, even for less-lethal delivery. I would be surprised if that was ever the case, but who knows what the demands of policing armed criminals and terrorists may be in the future?

With regards to the increased use of domestic drones, the government is introducing new laws in 2019 to control their use. This will include a 400-feet height restriction, along with a one kilometre no-fly zone around airports. All owners of drones weighing over 250 grams will have to register with the Civil Aviation Authority. Of course, like most restrictions they will only apply to those who use them *legally*.

Interestingly, in August 2018, an alleged attack against the President of Venezuela Nicolás Maduro occurred using two low-tech commercial DJI M600 drones, each carrying a kilogram of the military-grade explosive C-4. The drones exploded away from their intended target in the capital city Caracas, causing damage but no casualties. This is a worrying development in their use and one we should watch carefully, as the technology and the weight of the potential payload increases for commercial and hobbyist drones.

In December 2018, drone sightings caused chaos at Gatwick Airport causing thousands of flights to be cancelled. This was a wake-up call to the authorities who quickly initiated long-overdue countermeasures to be put in place. We can expect to see many developments in this field on all sides.

New Rifle for SC&O19

2015

Following the success of the SIG 516 systems, weapon improvements were sought and the new multi-calibre SIG MCX was selected as its replacement. This was initially for the CTSFO teams but after the Paris attacks in November 2016, it was extended as personal issue to all ARV officers within SCO19 and SO18 (Aviation Security Operational Command Unit, which was part of Specialist Operations).

The key benefit of the MCX system was the fact it came with varying barrel lengths and could convert from .556 to 300 Blackout (7.62 x 35mm, similar to the AK47 round) which allowed a smaller suppressed weapon system to support the evolving tactics the armed officers needed to adopt. The 300 Blackout round offers more terminal energy when compared to the 556 and is an ideal calibre for law enforcement.

In 2015, following familiarization training, the SIG 516s were handed over to the ARV crews as personal issue weapons to standardize the SCO19 weapon fleet, but this was just a stopgap until they could purchase more MCX weapons systems.

Finally, all ARV officers were equipped with the SIG MCX weapons systems making it the standard personal issue carbine for all SCO19 officers. These new weapons were put to the test

The versatile SIG MCX weapons system, which has become the standard primary weapon of SCO19 officers. This one is configured for CTSFO use and is fitted with the Surefire M600 torch, Aimpoint micro T2 sight with 3 X magnifier and PTL4 IR for use with night vision goggles. (*Stephen Smith*)

Close up of the SIG MCX carbine showing the etching placed on each weapon to celebrate the 50th anniversary of the Force Firearms Unit in 2016. (*Stephen Smith*)

during the terrorist attacks at London Bridge and Borough Market where ARV officers used them to engage the terrorists (more about that later).

The G36 carbines from the ARVs were shared across all the other armed departments in the Met to increase high velocity firepower, which is important when taking on terrorists in vehicles. The magazine wells were standardized to receive NATO magazines to increase nationwide AFO interoperability. The famous, and highly dependable, Heckler & Koch 9mm MP5 carbines still remain in service within the MPS but are likely to be phased out in the coming years.

Improved Taser

2018

The word Taser is an acronym of 'Thomas A. Swift's Electric Rifle', which is inspired by the *Tom Swift* series of novels from 1911. It is the brand chosen by the Met to supply its stun gun devices for a less-lethal resolution during confrontations and has been used by all UK police forces since January 2003, when the first M26 model (2003-2006) went into service. After a few teething problems, mainly around safe working practices and aftercare of persons stunned, it has continued to be a lifesaver. The M26 Taser was replaced in 2006 by the X26, which continued in use until the introduction of the X2 in mid-2018.

There are hundreds of documented cases where Taser has been used to bring a violent situation to a safe conclusion. One that attracted great interest was the terror attack at Leytonstone Underground Station (which is covered later), when Muhiddin Mire, a self-radicalized Islamic fundamentalist, stabbed two people before being stunned by police armed with an X26 Taser. As in most cases, its use allowed officers to safely arrest Mire without incurring further injury.

When the M26 Taser was first used in 2003, it attracted a lot of press attention. Each activation was given as many column inches as a shooting incident, but this has subsided, with only a few incidents being considered newsworthy or serious enough to warrant such treatment.

SO19, as it was known then, was the first UK police unit to trial Taser, and it has since been carried on every firearms operation and has been built into the 'less-lethal' planning phase of every firearms operation. It has been used hundreds of times by both CTSFO and ARV officers and continues to be an integral piece of firearms equipment.

During the Taser working party meetings, which meet to discuss its use and development, it was established that most problems had occurred with the X-26, following a failure of one or more of the barbs (darts) attaching to a subject and thus necessitating a reload. As this was time critical, it was not a good recipe for a successful second deployment. In response, Taser produced a new model, the X2, which had the addition of a second cartridge, making it a multiple-shot weapon. This would allow the firer to have a second attempt at disabling a subject without having to take their eye off the subject to reload. Each cartridge had its own dual-laser red dot sighting system, which meant the firer could tell where each barb would hit, (the X26 had only one red dot denoting the top barb). The range was also extended to 7.6 metres (the X26 was 7 metres) and it could penetrate thicker clothing, making it the ideal choice for SCO19.

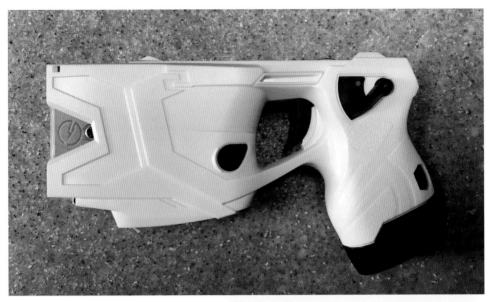

Above and right: The X-2 Taser, which replaced the X-26 model in January 2018. This new model has two cartridges and a slightly longer range. (*Stephen Smith*)

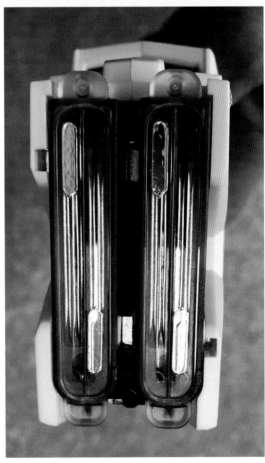

An officer in training aims the X-2 at a target, placing the lasers/barbs either side of the belt line for maximum effect. (*Stephen Smith*)

The Taser has to be used responsibly. The advice given to police in training is that it may cause cardiac arrhythmia in persons of very small stature and children. There is also a risk of injury if it is used on someone who may fall from a height, as has happened in the USA, leading to some fatalities.

However, I hope this valuable piece of police equipment continues to save the lives of the public and its officers. In the advertising blurb for its new model, Taser boasts that the X-2 is like going from a revolver to an automatic and the single shot is a thing of the past. The proof of the pudding will be in the eating.

Body Worn Video

Seeing is Believing – How Evidence-Gathering Has Evolved 2015

Since 2014, body worn video (BWV) has become a common sight on our police officers. The Met alone has purchased 22,000 of these BWV cameras, but its adoption by the police was no easy journey. Many officers considered their job was hard enough without having to record every interaction with the public.

Some reacted with suspicion, believing it was 'big brother' monitoring their every move and trying to catch them out. The department was split. The CTSFOs were worried about issues such as an officer's anonymity, as well as revealing tactics, methodology and operational techniques when the film was shown in open court. There was also the fear that certain confrontations filmed from obscure angles could mislead a jury at an inquest and bring about a perverse verdict. With these factors in mind, CTSFOs thought there was more to lose than

The AXON Body 2 body worn video (BWV) camera as used by SCO19 officers. (*Stephen Smith*)

there was to gain. However, this was not the case with many ARV officers, whose interaction with some members of the public often left them wishing it had been captured on film. On the whole, they were keen to embrace the new technology.

Certain public bodies overseeing our police (IPCC and more recently the IOPC) had pushed for officers, especially armed officers, to carry personal camera equipment to aid investigations and allow them to prove or disprove allegations made against the police. Change was certainly needed; it was fast becoming an age of transparency and the public had lost faith and trust in their police.

Years ago a police officer's word was their bond and considered to be the undisputed truth. This trust was slowly eroded following some major police corruption investigations across the country. These include Operation Countryman in 1978 to 1982, which was a massive investigation into police corruption in London and resulted in the prosecution of eight officers; the 1989 release of the 'Guildford four', who were wrongly convicted for the Guildford pub bombings in 1974 and the 1999 Macpherson report into the Stephen Lawrence killing, which claimed the police force was 'institutionally racist', adding to the perception in some communities that armed police were targeting young black males.

Video evidence has long been used during surveillance operations and has been invaluable in convicting many major criminals. It was always compelling evidence when a jury was shown the offender actually committing the crime they were accused of. Seeing is believing.

Traffic police cars have used dashboard cameras for decades to convict drivers, but there was still a long way to go in persuading specialist police departments, or even local borough officers, to adopt BWV as a matter of course.

One incident that fuelled the debate in favour of BWV occurred in 2005 after the shooting of Azelle Rodney, during which one of the specialist firearms officers filmed the 'non-compliant vehicle stop' from one of the gunships at the rear of the convoy.

This video evidence was used by the IPCC during its investigation and, with its help, it came to the conclusion that 'all the officers had acted within the law.' That same video footage was later used in the public inquiry to back up claims that the officer did not have enough time to assess the threat and react as he did. It was, therefore, alleged that his actions were premeditated, and he was charged with murder. Then again, that same video evidence was used by counsel for the defence to prove the officer did in fact have time to assess the threat, thus backing up his testimony. He was acquitted of murder.

Even with video evidence available to an investigation, it is not always cut and dry. Film footage can be open to conjecture. Video shot at different camera angles can give different viewpoints and result in different opinions.

It should always be viewed 'in the round', which means taking into account all the facts and evidence. It is, after all, only one aspect of a multi-faceted gathering of the facts.

The idea of BWV was bounced around and pondered over for many years in police circles at every level, but one of the pivotal incidents which finally galvanized all parties to make it happen was the shooting of Mark Duggan in 2011.

This incident and its aftermath resulted in rioting across the country, ultimately costing more lives and millions of pounds worth of damage. Would BWV have proved the officer's actions were correct and thus alleviated the public outrage?

It was only a matter of time before technology and political will would prevail and officers would become walking evidence-gatherers. But the police and the public had different ideas of what they wanted from this technology.

The police investigators and the IOPC wanted it to help investigate wrongdoing. But once the IOPC had the footage, it would become evidence, and as such would not normally be released for viewing by the public until after any legal proceedings had taken place and maybe not even then.

However, the public felt the need to view and judge for themselves whether the police's account was truthful. In this age, when everything is on social media the moment it happens, people not only expect to make their own minds up, they want to view it immediately.

You only have to look at other countries where BWV is used, such as the United States. They are very quick to release police video, normally at a press conference following an incident that may have potential for an escalation of violence on the streets.

Finally, after much deliberation, all parties agreed to a commencement date of January 2014. Certain London boroughs would trial BWV and it soon became an essential piece of police equipment and a valuable tool in the ever-changing fight against crime. However, it was not until 2015 that SC&O19 received a variant of this device for trial with its armed officers.

Small numbers of BWV cameras were given to ARV officers on the proactive tasking team and it soon proved its worth. In August 2015, it featured in two IPCC investigations – the non-fatal shooting of Nathaniel Brophy and the fatal shooting of James Fox.

As well as developing the physical and practical aspects of using BWV, a post-incident procedure (PIP) was developed in conjunction with the Directorate of Professional Standards to safeguard the handover of the unit and the downloading and onward handling of the footage to protect its integrity.

Attitudes slowly changed as BWV answered a lot of questions about how the police operated. As officers had more positive experiences, the more accepted it became. One of the main advantages was the noticeable decline in complaints against police. After a complainant was shown footage of their interaction with police, accusations were usually dropped, thus avoiding the long and damaging internal investigation process, which cost many police hours and wasted time.

The BWV also provided valuable evidence, not only in most cases by justifying the officer's actions, but saving time in court as many defendants changed their plea after being shown video footage of their crime. Yes, there were occasions when an officer's BWV recorded their own speech or actions that went beyond what was expected of a pillar of society and this often lead to disciplinary action or even dismissal or prosecution. However, in the main, the evidence provided has been positive and the police have regained some of the trust and confidence required to do the job.

A spate of incidents proved BWV had a place within the firearms world. Both ARVs and the CTSFOs now carry BWV when deploying on all overt firearms operations (where possible).

Following operational problems with the mounting systems that came with the cameras, new ones were designed. They had to be versatile and have the ability to be moved between body armour and be placed on ballistic helmets and even cloth 'plot-hats'. This negated the problems first encountered during the James Fox shooting, when the camera worked loose

An ARV officer with BWV fitted to his ballistic helmet. The camera is small and discreet and can be mounted on the officer's shoulder or on the visor of the police baseball cap. (*Stephen Smith*)

after the officer shouldered his G36. It was not possible for it to be mounted in the conventional place at the front of the body armour due to the amount of equipment already fixed to the body armour.

Research is ongoing into evidence obtained from BWV in an attempt to establish how we view and interpret the information, and understand how a human brain reacts under stress. Should allowances be made for officers who make mistakes?

There is now a greater and legally accepted understanding that events captured on BWV may not reflect 100 per cent of the evidence submitted by those involved. The brain does not record the same way a CCTV camera does. It's not limited to auditory and visual exclusion, peripheral vision capture and lighting levels.

There has been much work done on this subject and this is reflected in a 2008 research paper produced by the British Psychological Society called *Guidelines on Memory and the Law*. It explains that officers cannot be expected to recall second-by-second detail of what took place, especially during a traumatic event. The BWV shows a one-dimensional view – the officers providing their dimension – which helps to complete the overall picture, so it should always be used in conjunction with the officer's account. It can also be used after the event to learn from and give feedback, which is invaluable for training to improve safety, skills and avoid making mistakes.

PART 5

OPERATIONAL DEVELOPMENTS

CTSFO officers 'form up' at the side of the building while the door is breached by an explosive charge. (*AH*)

Jean Charles de Menezes: The Effect on Police Tactics

Following the Stockwell Investigation, implemented in the wake of the tragic 2005 shooting of Jean Charles de Menezes, who was wrongly believed to be the failed suicide bomber Osman Hussain, it was identified that the SFO officers who had entered the tube train carriage had gone into that space cold, meaning they'd never had 'eyes on' the subject. There had never been the opportunity for a proper handover from surveillance to firearms, and officers worked off a description given over the radio.

In the aftermath, the question was asked: had the officers been partly integrated with the surveillance team, would they have seen the subject earlier, making it easier to identify him

A three-handed 'small team' of CTSFOs put in a strike on a cash-in–transit robber at the SCO19 training site at Gravesend. With this tactic, they can integrate with surveillance and get on top of the action at the right moment, having had 'eyes on' the suspect. (*Neil Francombe*)

within a crowded tube carriage? This is pure speculation but it may have led to an opportunity to intervene prior to him getting onto the tube and thus, possibly, avoiding the necessity to shoot him. This procedure has merit in other situations whether the officers be arresting armed criminals or terrorists.

It was apparent that there needed to be a more versatile working relationship with the surveillance teams and this would involve training both parties to work better together. The CTSFO officers would need to change some of their working practices and learn how they could blend in with their colleagues, who were highly trained in the covert art of surveillance.

They named this new course the Small Teams Intervention Course (STIC), on the basis that instead of working as a CTSFO team of between seven and twelve officers, and deploying from static jump-off vans or mobile gunships, they were trained in tactics that allowed for independent work in groups of two to four officers. This allowed them to integrate with the surveillance team and even share vehicles, meaning they could get 'eyes on' the subject, thus avoiding any confusion.

These officers could now be trusted to work in close proximity with the surveillance teams who had previously not allowed them to get near to their subjects for fear of compromising the job. They would be in a better position to deploy and deal with the subject and, when required, be able to make an arrest. They would generally wear plain clothes but could, at the very last moment before deploying, throw on plate carriers (lightweight covers which carry the ceramic ballistic plates worn as armour) along with other protective equipment and signage which identified them as police.

This tactic proved invaluable during the 2012 London Olympic Games where small teams of highly trained and equipped officers could move among the crowds with impunity, being directed to potential suspects by rifle observation points high up in the stadia.

Small team training has since been written into the CTSFO course and remains an integral tactic during the planning phase of any armed operation.

Covert Motorcycles

CO19 Terrorist Response 2006

Following the terror attacks on the Twin Towers in New York in September 2001 (which I'll refer to as 9/11), and the subsequent invasions of Afghanistan later that year and of Iraq in 2003, we saw a huge growth in the use of suicide bombers, on foot and in vehicles, causing mass slaughter in towns and cities. Terrorist attacks in the UK were now a very real threat and one of the big fears for the security services was that of vehicle-borne devices being driven into one of our cities in lorries, vans or cars.

To prepare for this, several new tactics were introduced around this time. One of these was Operation Kratos, which involved taking critical shots to stop suicide bombers. However, one of the main issues to consider was that once a vehicle had been identified as a potential bomb carrier and was en route to its target, how do you get your armed assets into contact before it reaches its critical point? Also, with London's traffic sometimes reaching gridlock, how do you get up close to the vehicle to neutralize the threat?

The solution was not difficult to find. For some time, officers within the firearms unit had been pushing to use covert police motorcycles on crime operations. During the Dome robbery in 2000, motorcycles had been requested as a contingency for moving armed officers quickly across public open spaces. In preparation for their use, selected officers had been sent to Hendon Driving school for a 'crash course' (bad choice of words) in riding covert motorcycles with a pillion passenger. It was set up so fast it surprised even the officers sent on the course. It involved riding up and down concrete steps and around obstacles, then deploying quickly off the bike to arrest suspects, in this case unarmed colleagues. The bike riders and pillions became extremely proficient in this tactic and wondered why it was not part of the normal operational firearms tactics of SO19.

The weapons chosen to complement this tactic were the MP5 carbines with collapsible stock. These were carried in backpacks, with pistols in bum bags around the waist. In the run up to the Dome robbery the bikes, along with riders and pillions, were held at locations near to the Dome itself. Alas, they were not deployed on that occasion and it was to be years before this tactic was considered again.

In late 2004 a small group of officers was chosen to be trained using suitable covert motorcycles. There were to be no short cuts. Selected officers, mostly SFOs who had private experience of riding motorcycles, were required to attend and pass a three-week course at Hendon, which authorized them to ride unmarked police bikes.

Following the 7 July terror attacks on the London transport system in 2005, the programme took a jolt forward and suddenly these selected officers found themselves on standby for further attacks. They were present during the manhunt operations to catch the failed suicide bombers responsible for four attempted bombings, again on the London transport system, on 21 July of that year. During this deployment, the officers were frustrated following problems with radio communications on the bikes, resulting in them being of no practical use.

CO19 (as it was then) solved the radio issues and expanded its motorcycle programme, sending further officers for training. This was kept under wraps and away from the public gaze, but the concept was very similar to that prepared for the Dome robbery. The motorcycle was the delivery system to get armed officers onto a terrorist target quickly, whether they were on foot or in a vehicle. The pillion would then neutralize the threat with the level of force appropriate for the circumstances.

CO19 finally took delivery of a fleet of specially chosen hybrid on-and-off-road covert motorcycles in late 2006.

The CTSFOs still train using the bikes on a regular basis. Qualified riders take them onto the ranges at Gravesend where they practise armed deployments from the bikes, and engaging hostile targets using the bike as a platform to shoot from.

Every officer trained in these tactics realizes that shooting from a motorcycle is dangerous and a last resort when used against potential terrorists. Even when used against armed criminals, it is not without its inherent dangers. It would only be used in extreme circumstances as it is generally safer to deploy from the bike on foot to engage the threat

The use of motorcycles is now built into SCO19 tactics, and in 2017, in the spirit of transparency, Police Commissioner Sir Bernard Hogan-Howe showed the CTSFOs and their motorcycles to members of the press for photo opportunities.

The tactics around motorcycles is still evolving and new equipment is always being assessed to make it work. This includes new bikes, in-helmet radio communications, weapons carriage systems and more suitable body armour.

Early SFO training on motorcycles around 2008. They were still developing their tactics. (*Stephen Smith*)

Above: Two pairs of CTSFOs prepare to 'move up' in a training scenario using their BMW motorcycles to get through the traffic and deploy. (*Dominique Andre*)

Left: CTSFOs in training engage from the pillion of a covert police motorcycle using a SIG MCX carbine. (*Dominique Andre*)

Explosive Method of Entry

2006

Our security services, including the police and the military, will use the best and most efficient tactics to achieve the purpose of arresting and neutralizing those who would do us harm. This includes the method of using explosives to effect an entry into a stronghold, whether it is a crack house in a squat or a bomb-making factory in suburbia.

In medieval times, armies laying siege to castles or fortified defensive positions used barrels of gunpowder to breach the gates and walls, thus allowing a direct assault hopefully with the element of surprise to guarantee a swift victory with minimal losses. Nothing much has changed, except the type of explosives and the tactics used to set them in place and detonate them. We have all seen explosive method of entry (EMOE) used in films and dramas on TV. We've even seen clips of our soldiers fighting in Afghanistan using charges to breach gaps in the walls of enclosures and compounds.

The equipment used has come a long way since the fifteenth century. The explosives and charges can now 'surgically' cut an opening in a door, window or wall to minimize the danger to people nearby and limit the collateral damage to the building or the environment.

When the 2005 terrorist attacks took place in London, followed by one of the country's biggest manhunts to track down members of the terrorist cell still at large, CO19 officers were not trained in EMOE and they had to look towards the military for help. This military liaison worked well and was successfully put to use on several occasions, although at the time it was reserved for terrorist-related operations. Eventually, protocols were set in place to allow CO19 to be trained in EMOE.

It is not my intention to give away any tactics or operational methods as the techniques and construction are secret and could be of use to an enemy. However, it would be foolish to suppose that the generic tactics used by SWAT and the security services throughout the world would be much different to those used by SCO19 today.

CTSFO teams have had access to EMOE since 2006. Its use has been identified as critical where the need for a rapid or quick entry into premises is required to save life or preserve important evidence and it is used only in extreme cases.

Selected SCO19 officers are trained in these skills and undergo stringent testing and exams. These skills, used by police in the civilian environment, undergo scrutiny by government bodies and certain licensing criteria are required in the use and storage of the explosives and detonators.

Above: The team waits around the corner for the door to be breached. (*AH*)

Below: Officers use the body of the armoured police Jankel to shield from the blast and debris following a breach to an upstairs door. (*AH*)

One of the early exponents of this tactic was an experienced SFO team sergeant, Kurt Bechtel. Kurt managed and arranged the training courses that would become the gold standard within the police. After qualifying in EMOE, he went on to help set up and run the national training programme.

Above: The team set a charge against a window in training at the Firearms Training Centre, Gravesend. (*AH*)

Below: EMOE officers set a frame charge on a wall while another offers cover with his MCX. (*Dominique Andre*)

Kurt Bechtel who helped develop EMOE within SCO19. Sadly, he passed away in 2016 having contracted mesothelioma, probably from asbestos disturbed while training in old buildings.

Many redundant buildings were identified for use in training – mostly old hospitals, which were built in the1890s and were no longer viable. Kurt and the other EMOE training staff taught their SFO students how to set charges and blow holes in doors and walls. This was built into the SFO training programme and continues to this day, with all officers required to familiarize themselves with the tactics involved in the use of EMOE.

Sadly in 2016 Kurt succumbed to mesothelioma, possibly contracted by inhaling asbestos disturbed by explosions during training. Kurt was a major player in developing EMOE within SCO19 and is sorely missed.

Fighting Through Fire and Smoke

Working with firearms in a smoke-filled environment is a fairly new concept for the officers of SCO19 at both ARV and CTSFO level. To my knowledge, SCO19 is the only specialist firearms command in the world to have developed viable tactics for working with firearms in such a hostile environment. Along with the ability to carry out their primary role of locating and neutralizing a threat, they also rescue hostages or persons trapped by armed criminals or terrorists within a burning building or a building full of smoke.

The need for this new skill set was first voiced after the devastating Mumbai attack in November 2008. What was particularly worrying about this attack was that after murdering many people in the Taj Mahal Palace Hotel, the terrorists then set fire to it. It prompted the question: how would we fulfil the public's expectation of a rescue should the building in which they are held be set on fire?

We realized that if we developed specialist training with the London Fire Brigade (LFB) we could carry out an entry into a burning building to neutralize any armed suspects and rescue persons who may be trapped, or are being held as hostages. At first glance this concept looks extreme, but history has shown us that these incidents have happened.

The biggest incident of this nature was the Waco siege in Texas in 1993. When the Bureau of Alcohol, Tobacco and Firearms suspected a compound belonging to the Branch Davidians sect near Waco was harbouring illegal weapons, it attempted to raid it and a gun battle commenced. The FBI stormed the building and so began a shootout leading to a fifty-one-day siege, which ended when the sect members set fire to the compound. Seventy-six Branch Davidians were killed, including their sect leader David Koresh. Many of the dead were women and children, with most consumed by the fire, while many were shot in mercy killings to prevent them dying horrible deaths in the flames. Four law enforcement agents were also killed and sixteen others wounded.

It was apparent that law enforcement officers could not safely enter the buildings due to the fires, and fire officers could not deal with the fires for risk of being shot at by sect members.

Another more recent incident, and one closer to home, was the fifteen-day Hackney siege in January 2003 when armed fugitive, Eli Hall, set fire to the house he was in, dying in the ensuing inferno. The LFB were prevented from dealing with the fire effectively due to the firearms threat.

Both these incidents demonstrate the need for officers to be trained, not only in how to survive in smoke-filled environments, but also how to deploy with their firearms, take on any armed threat, fire fight and rescue casualties before handing the building over, once safe from any firearms threat, to the LFB to carry out their role and deal with any other fires.

Above: The burnt-out Branch Davidians sect buildings in Waco, Texas following the fires and shootout which caused so many deaths.

Left: Breathing apparatus training of ARV officers during one of the first specialist entry and recovery team (SERT) courses. The team moves into a smoke-filled building. (*DL*)

FIGHTING THROUGH FIRE AND SMOKE

Although the idea was put forward in 2009, it was not until 2010 that it got the full backing and authority needed to put a training course together. The first course was run in 2010 and was made up purely of firearms instructors from CO19. From that course, two bespoke training courses were designed. Both were aimed at enabling CO19 officers to work in smoke-filled environments but each course had subtle differences.

The first course was a three-week long instruction aimed at ARV officers and held at specialist training centres in conjunction with LFB's Special Operations Group. It related to ARVs having an emergency search, rescue and fire-fighting capability and focused on training the officers in the use of all fire-fighting media, including breathing apparatus, along with teaching them the knowledge of fire science and behaviour. Completion of the course would qualify them to work as a specialist entry and recovery team (SERT) officer and carry out these tasks alongside the LFB. The aim of this training was not to replace firefighters but to enable SERT officers to deploy in extreme fire and smoke-related conditions.

The second was the smoke-filled environment course. It was one week long and deemed necessary to enhance the CTSFOs' capability for performing hostage rescue in such hostile environments.

Although the ARV SERT trained officers are capable of working independently, the CTSFO smoke-filled environment trained officers require the SERT officers to support them. In the

Above left: One of the training facilities on the SERT course, enabling officers to experience the choking effects of a building filled with thick black smoke. Not an experience for those who suffer from claustrophobia. (*DL*)

Above right: SERT officers training to use fire-fighting equipment to extinguish fires in buildings while providing firearms cover to neutralize any threat. (*DL*)

The fire room where SERT officers experience the immense heat in hostile environments. This is one of the most dangerous training exercises. (*DL*)

case of a hostage rescue operation the CTSFOs would carry out the initial assault supported by ARV SERT officers, who would use fire-fighting equipment to enable their progression and protect their egress. The CTSFOs would then perform a hostage rescue, using their ballistic protective equipment and fire-retardant equipment – including breathing apparatus – to take on and neutralize any firearms threat. The SERT officers would then assist in searching for and evacuating any casualties. The adage used is – if a door is hot, enter as a firefighter and if it's cold enter as a firearms officer.

This training and the operational application of this tactic is probably the most dangerous task a firearms officer will ever undertake. The training tests the officer's ability to work in a confined space filled with smoke and the claustrophobic fear is constant. The heat from a fire is debilitating and can induce panic. The training in conjunction with the LFB's experience in this field gives the officer the confidence to work through and complete the task.

National Aircraft Protection Officer Programme

Following the infamous attacks on 9/11, the ability to protect passengers and airliners became a priority for the British Government.

After 9/11, the US significantly increased its own Federal Air Marshal Service, which involved placing air marshals on domestic, as well as international, flights. However, the cost implications of a British programme delivered on the same scale as the American's was considered prohibitive. Instead, investment in ground-based security was considered key to strengthening safety on board aircraft.

This included investment in the improvement of airport security and infrastructure, such as the controversial body scanners and swabbing for explosives residue. Furthermore, the intelligence gained from both successful and failed attacks on aircraft led to additional security measures being implemented to prevent and deter the same style attack from happening again.

In December 2001, shoes were X-rayed after the failed attempt by Richard Reid to detonate explosives concealed in his shoe. In 2006, after an attempt to detonate liquid explosives on a

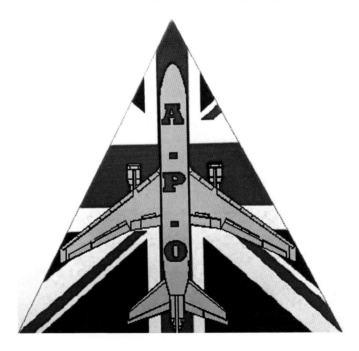

Badge of the National Aircraft Protection Officer. The programme began in 2001 with instructors from SO19 running the national courses.

Above and below: Two SFO sky marshal officers undergoing live fire refresher training on the range at Leman Street in 2003. (*Stephen Smith*)

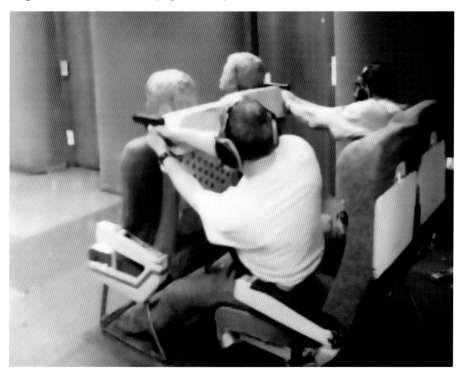

plane was foiled by UK police, restrictions on liquids in hand luggage were introduced as well as see-through bags in which to carry them. Later, attempts to conceal bombs in laptops and tablet computers led to the technology being more closely scrutinized at airport security.

Additional security was introduced on board the aircraft, with upgraded flight deck doors that could only be operated by the pilots, and CCTV of these doors. Mandatory security training for cabin and flight deck crews was improved and individual airlines implemented their own additional training to improve security awareness.

While the British Government was satisfied with these new security measures, the US Government was still concerned of the risk to its country from flights originating from key international airports, including those within the UK. These concerns, as well as a domestic need to provide a counter-terrorist option on British aircraft, led to the Met developing the National Aircraft Protection Officers (NAPO) programme.

SO19 was quickly identified as the ideal unit to develop this new capability. Late in 2001, under a veil of secrecy, a small training cell was selected from the SFO teams to research and develop a programme. The key areas of interest were how to deploy armed personnel onto the aircraft, including the carriage and storage of firearms and ammunition, and identifying the most suitable weapons and ammunition for the role. Several air marshal systems from around the world were examined and a model was developed that required superior, close quarter, unarmed combat and fast accurate shooting techniques in an aircraft cabin to safely and successfully overcome a hijack situation. The covert operators were to be known as Aircraft Protection Officers or APOs.

Visits to supportive UK airlines to discuss the development of working practices and how to educate flight and cabin crew on this new security concept were formulated and close working relationships developed. Excellent support was provided by the Civil Aviation Authority in the form of a technical course, which was part of the APO accreditation process. We would be working in a challenging new environment and it was important that the officers were knowledgeable about the highly regulated industry. Having developed a comprehensive training course, training sites were identified which were away from the public gaze. All that remained was to select the personnel. Applications were requested from all UK police forces with the initial selection criteria set to that of SFO level. This was due to the covert nature of the programme and the need for intervention skills, which these officers already had. In September 2002, the NAPO programme began training its first multi-police service students. This was the forerunner to the Combined Response Firearms Teams (CRFT) that were deployed at the London Olympics, and what has now developed into the CTSFO network.

It was a tough course, even for the SFOs, but they were well-suited to the role and took to the training well. The smaller Glock 19 and 26 pistols were selected for their concealability, along with the first UK deployments of the 124 grain hollow point ammunition. This was introduced for use on aircraft as it was a better performing bullet than the 95 grain JSP and less likely to over penetrate causing injury to other passengers or damage to the aircraft. It was the ballistic work undertaken by the NAPO team that led to the implementation of the hollow point bullets being authorized for national armed policing, which are still in use today.

The course concentrated on accurate close quarter shooting, mainly on small size targets. The accuracy required would have to be almost surgical, taking advantage of the element of surprise and maybe dealing with multiple targets both in front and behind where the APOs were seated. The APOs would work in teams dependent on the size of the aircraft and the assessed risk and threat.

The NAPO programme became operational in 2002 and, despite some reservations from certain pockets within the industry, went on to provide a highly trained, counter-terrorist capability flying on threat, risk and random routine flights. This collaborative success proved that a small covert team from multiple police units could deploy globally and protect UK assets anywhere in the world.

It is difficult to measure the value of such protection with no recorded incidents on UK aircraft during the time the NAPO programme was active but, of course, there is no price on the deterrent effect. This was not work for the faint hearted, as any response would require the APO to react from the position of a passenger hostage, which is wholly unique within the intervention world. There is nowhere to hide should the worst happen and nobody is coming to help you.

SO19 were founding members of the International In-Flight Security Officer Committee known as the IIFSOC. It was established to promote and help develop nations improve in-flight security as well as advise our own government on such matters. The committee continues to flourish with key founding members still playing an active role in the ongoing challenges that aviation security will continue to face.

The NAPO programme remains a viable response to aviation threats and can be called upon when required.

PART 6

MANAGING LONDON'S ARMED ASSETS

Fully kitted ARV officer fires his MCX carbine on the range. Note his SERT shoulder badge. (*AH*)

London's Armed Response Vehicles

As the role of the SFO changed and developed into the CTSFO following the 2012 Olympic Games, the ARV officer's role also changed. This happened almost overnight following the horrific attack on Lee Rigby in Woolwich, south-east London in May 2013. It soon became apparent that there were not enough mobile-armed assets available to support their unarmed colleagues and provide protection to the public who were feeling increasingly vulnerable to the evolving methods used by the terrorists.

Short of arming all the police, the next best thing was to provide more highly trained officers who could respond quickly when needed. This necessitated looking into where these new assets would be sent to patrol, and how they would support each other when called to attend a location where an attack was developing.

To accommodate the increase in ARV numbers, new bases were set up to augment the North London and South London bases already in use. There was also the need for all UK police forces to mutually support each other where required. This cross-border support, which would previously have needed permissions and authority on each separate occasion, would now be provided immediately, without any red tape or politics. The benefit of this was never more obvious than during the terrorist attack at London Bridge and Borough Market on 3 June 2017 when a City of London ARV crossed over the river following a call of support from the Met and BTP (British Transport Police) and found itself first at the scene and able to engage with and begin to neutralize the terrorists, thus preventing further deaths or serious injuries.

The response times of the Met ARVs continue to impress. They cannot always be right nearby, but they have endeavoured to get where they are needed within minutes of being called.

When I visited the SCO19 base while writing this book, I was impressed with the professionalism and pride from the officers I met, both ARV and CTSFO. Not only were they enthusiastic when showing me

Specialist Firearms Command ARV shoulder patch. (*Stephen Smith*)

134

Above: Fully-kitted ARV officer with short ballistic shield in front of a BMW ARV. (*Stephen Smith*)

Right: ARV officer's weapons carried on duty. Top: SIG MCX carbine with spare magazine. Left: Taser X-2 and Glock 17 pistol with spare magazine. (*Stephen Smith*)

The workhorse of SCO19's ARV fleet, the BMW X-5, an all-wheel-drive automatic sports activity vehicle. Used since 2013 when it replaced the BMW 530 saloon as the favoured vehicle. (*Stephen Smith*)

Crew of a 2018 ARV stand by their BMW X-5 with their kit set out. It includes, left-right: personal kit bags, personal body armour with ballistic plates, grab bags with extra rounds, stun grenades, X-2 Taser and cartridges, Glock 17 pistols and magazines, SIG MCX carbines and magazines, spare radios, portable main-set iPad, map book, acid burn first aid kit, ballistic trauma first aid holdall, ballistic bag for safe unloading of firearms, MOE equipment – Hooli bar and enforcer ram, ballistic blanket, back-to-back radios, balaclavas, cloth police baseball hats, ear defenders, ballistic helmets and short ballistic shield. (*Stephen Smith*)

the kit and how it had changed in the few years since I had worked there, but above all their morale was high. This gave me confidence to believe that we are at last going in the right direction in recruiting the best officers and equipping them with the right weaponry and protective equipment to do the job. Also, and more importantly, they were providing good leadership, which is hard to come by in many areas of policing.

136

Crew of a 1992 ARV stand by their Rover 827 with their kit set out. It includes, left-right: target indication board, personal body armour, .762 ballistic plates, torches, large seek-and-search torch, first aid box, clipboard, extendable mirror, portable main-set radio, folding stretcher, Heckler & Koch MP5 carbines with magazines, binoculars, Model 10 revolvers with jet loaders, ballistic bag for safe unloading of firearms, short ballistic shield, ballistic blanket, incident log. (*Stephen Smith*)

Recruitment and Selection for SCO19

Recruitment has always been one of the main topics of any police management meeting agenda. With SCO19 they have to retain, train and recruit for a unit, and also be extremely careful about who they place in these positions of high trust and responsibility. SCO19 has a duty of care to the public and to the police service it supports.

In a specialist unit that has, for decades, been among the best of its kind in the world, it would be easy to become complacent and just recruit in order to put bums on seats. However this has never been the case with SCO19 who have put a lot of effort into reaching out to the right personnel.

For an officer to be considered suitable to apply to join SCO19 and work on the ARVs, they need to be a serving police officer with a minimum of two years' service in the British police (they can also apply to transfer from Home Office police forces or other police services in the UK). It also helps if they are a qualified AFO, and a police advanced driver. While these skills are not essential, it means they already have some of the prerequisite capabilities required for becoming an ARV officer. Any officer without these skills would have to pass a basic firearms course, passing on both the pistol (currently the Glock 17) and the carbine (Heckler & Koch MP5, although they would then need to convert to the SIG MCX if they were successful).

The officer would have to complete a self-assessment form, evidencing their operational effectiveness and other criteria, to give the assessors an idea of what the candidate has been involved with in their police career. Many officers apply from other armed units such as the Diplomatic Protection Group or Royalty Protection. While these experienced firearms officers are very welcome, they still have to go through the same selection process as any other applicant. SCO19 actively advertise within the national police firearms community. Those wishing to apply have to pass a paper sift (to check eligibility and competency) before being invited to attend a two-day selection.

This two-day selection guarantees that each candidate has the same opportunities to succeed and it also gives the department a chance to look at the applicant and measure them against the required criteria.

Day One

Applicants are put through their paces at the National Police Firearms Training Centre in Gravesend, Kent. The first test is simple – they are instructed to attend in uniform. How a candidate dresses tells the assessors a lot about them. They look for self-discipline and personal pride in appearance as well as punctuality and general attitude and bearing. This is seen as an 'old school' ethos but still counts for a lot when someone will be representing your department. During the briefing by the senior lead trainer, every step is explained so they are under no illusion of what is expected of them.

Following this they are handed over to the physical training instructor for a job-related fitness test, which will include the dreaded bleep test (the candidate completes 20-metre shuttle runs in time with the bleeps until the bleeps get too fast). To achieve ARV standard, a recruit would have to run to a level of 9.4. They are then put through a physical circuit, which involves the officer demonstrating handcuffing and open-hand defence techniques. Each candidate is monitored and assessed and scored on every element. Once complete they go into a series of team-building exercises designed to test communication, teamwork and general attitude under pressure. Day one finishes with a knowledge check exam. If they have scored highly throughout the day they are invited back for day two.

Day Two

After a briefing, the candidate completes a series of scenarios, with role players acting as informants, victims and suspects. These are designed to give the assessors an idea of how the candidate reacts under pressure and in a confrontation situation. It also tests their communication skills and how they disseminate information, along with numerous important policing skills. Then comes the written map-reading exam, followed by a practical map-reading test based around a fictitious vehicle pursuit, which is done while being driven at speed in an ARV.

If the candidate has scored sufficiently well over the two days they are offered an ARV course. This is just the beginning of the journey, but hopefully one that can continue to bring the right standard of officer into the force firearms unit SCO19.

Taken from the top of the abseil tower at the National Police Firearms Training Centre, it shows the area the recruits will use for their assessments. (*Stephen Smith*)

The Firearms Reserve

Territorial Support Group Trained to Use Carbines 2016

The Metropolitan Police Territorial Support Group (TSG), which formed in 1986 to provide a police reserve across London, have borne the brunt of riots, demonstrations, public disorders and emergencies in the capital. They are trained to operate in the same way as their predecessors, the Special Patrol Group (SPG), to work in plain clothes targeting local and organized crime in support of the boroughs and divisions who may require extra help in those quarters.

In light of the recent security emergencies which have required additional armed officers, the TSG were considered the ideal choice to train up on the SIG 516 carbine. Initially selected officers were to be trained on the Heckler & Koch G36 carbine but when consideration was given to their function it was decided, rightly, that it would be prudent to train them on the SIG 516 carbine. The problem remained as to who would train these additional officers. Eventually it was decided to outsource the TSG training to the Police Service Northern Ireland (PSNI) who had the staff and facilities to do a good job.

By 2016 there were enough TSG officers trained on the SIG 516 to provide an effective firearms reserve for the commissioner of police to call on in times of need. However, during the next eighteen months, for reasons of conformity, armed officers on the TSG will convert to the SIG MCX weapons systems.

They continue to be a useful addition to the armed police reserve for London.

Firearms Training Contracted Out

2016

Following the increased threat of terror attacks in the UK, funding was made available to upgrade the Met armed response. It was decided once again to increase the number of ARVs patrolling London streets. These were to be deployed on an intelligence-led and risk-based system, hopefully placing these valuable armed assets in the locations they were most likely to be required.

This increase in ARV numbers led to a recruitment drive for more armed officers. Many came in from surrounding Home Office police and firearms units and they brought with them a

Met basic firearms students receive training in subject handling at one of the Civil Nuclear Constabulary training facilities. (*Stephen Smith*)

lot of experience. However, many still needed to be put through Met ARV courses to maintain the standard and confirm they were compatible with the force's operating methods.

The knock-on effect was to stretch the firearms training sites and the number of instructors who were available to carry out the training to the limit. During the recent cutbacks, experienced firearms instructors had been allowed to leave when their time was completed. Many joined other police forces, taking jobs as civilian firearms instructors. Some even went abroad. But by far the biggest employers of ex-SCO19 firearms officers were the Civil Nuclear Constabulary (CNC), responsible for providing protection to the UK nuclear energy sites – one of only a few fully armed police forces in the country. The fact that the CNC now employed a large number of ex-SCO19 firearms instructors made them the ideal candidates to conduct some of the training for new armed officers in the Met. There were mutual benefits to the CNC running the training – their skills base would improve by having a close liaison with the Met and their assistance would help the Met through a tough time where they were being stretched to capacity.

In April 2016, the first Met basic firearms courses were run by the CNC with ex-SCO19 instructors using training sites at Bisley and Aldershot. These worked well, with over 200 firearms officers trained within twenty-two months. Now there is greater cooperation between the Met and other Home Office forces and Northumbria and Cheshire are also running Met courses. This form of collaboration will be important to the future expansion in firearms assets and shows an increasing willingness to work with other police units around the country to get the job done.

Met Basic firearms students learning to shoot the MP5 carbine at one of the open-air ranges run by the CNC. (*Stephen Smith*)

Firearms Bases Open Across London

SCO19 Spreads Out Across the Capital

The Metropolitan Police Firearms Department began its life working from two bases. One was an operational base, from where the early PT17 level 1 and level 2 firearms teams worked, and as of 1991, the ARVs.

This base was housed in Old Street Police Station, next to what was Old Street Magistrates' Court in Shoreditch, (now the five-star Courthouse Hotel). The other base was a firearms

The Force Firearms unit's original base at Old Street Police Station in Shoreditch 1967-2001, which is now a luxury hotel. The unit had everything to the right of the first doorway and the magistrates' court used the rest of the building. (*Stephen Smith*)

143

Leman Street Police Station, the light grey building to the left of the Oliver Conquest Pub. It has been the main base for north ARVs and CTSFOs since 2001. (*Stephen Smith*)

training site at Lippitts Hill, formerly a Second World War prisoner-of-war camp complete with wooden huts and barbed wire (it would soon be sold for development). It was situated deep in Epping Forest in Essex.

Both these sites worked well for the firearms requirements of the times, but it was 2000 and 2001 respectively that saw the unit move to new bases. The operational base moved to Leman Street Police Station in the East End and a southern base was opened at Lambeth. The training department shifted out to a massive purpose-built site at Gravesend in Kent, which it shares with the Public Order Training Unit. Now, with the rising demand for specialist training and operations, it has outgrown these new locations.

The Met Police Firearms Training Centre remains at Gravesend but, as mentioned previously, has outsourced a number of its training courses, some to temporary sites and others to the training units of Home Office police forces and the CNC who run a Met initial firearms training course at one of their training sites in Surrey.

The operational requirements have grown the most in the past decade, necessitating a rethink on how best to serve the public and provide better response times.

Consequently, along with the north base at Leman Street (housing the CTSFO and ARV assets) and the south base at Lambeth (for ARVs), a west base at Lillie Road in Fulham was opened, (for ARVs) and an east base at Limehouse Police Station, (also for ARVs). These four bases work well at the moment providing ARV cover to all of London.

However, there are plans to build a high-security SCO19 superbase from where the CTSFO teams will work with purpose-built facilities allowing them to train onsite and expand, should further needs arise.

Duty of Care

How Health and Safety at Work Has Affected the Firearms Officer

Duty of care has long existed within British employment law. In 1974, the advent of the Health and Safety at Work Act ruled that an employer must take reasonable steps to provide a safe working environment for its staff and employees, and anyone who comes within their working environment.

However, since that date, and certainly within my working lifetime, employers have been slow to improve working conditions, with some merely paying lip service to the Act. I remember having to fight to get better protective equipment and most of the time we had to make do with old technology or the cheapest solution available. It was only after several legal challenges and police officers' deaths, which could have been prevented if the correct equipment had been available, that things began to change.

As a police officer, I always knew I had a duty of care to the public I served, and my colleagues, especially when planning an armed operation where there was a high chance of us being injured, or worse. My job was to minimize that danger and the better we got at doing this, the safer things became.

Over the years, welcomed changes in how we do business has seen major improvements in equipment including body armour, ballistic helmets, ballistic shields, torches on our weapons systems and better, more efficient weaponry. Officers now have the correct boots and protective Kevlar gloves and even receive training on lifting heavy objects.

Other protective clothing, which became standard issue within SO19, included flame-retardant coveralls in case an officer was required to use stun grenades; distraction devices or EMOE; respirators (gas masks) to prevent inhaling toxic fumes; glasses or goggles in case of flying glass or wood splinters; hearing protection to cushion the ear against loud bangs or explosions (a common injury) and sharp rescue knives in case an officer became snagged on an abseil rope during a descent and had to cut themselves from the rope.

All of these now appear to be common sense but lack of understanding – or funding – at that time made it a slow uphill struggle. Each of these items had come at a human cost and was a great improvement for officers using them. However, the biggest changes were by far those made in ballistic first aid. Following several court cases and inquests involving police-related shootings, it became accepted that the police had a responsibility to any injured parties, including those they had shot.

This juxtaposition of armed officers facing life and death situations against people attempting to kill them one minute, and being required to offer them life-saving first aid

146

treatment the next, became standard working practice. It was soon recognized that the basic 'first aid at work' training, that all police have to attain, was drastically insufficient for treating serious gunshot wounds. The other motivation for taking this seriously was the real possibility that one day the officers might have to use it to save a teammate's life.

Over the years officers were sent away on enhanced training courses in first aid. SCO19 officers received inputs from trauma doctors and battlefield medics from UK Special Forces. These inputs proved invaluable and were cascaded to all officers on the CTSFO teams, along with ARV officers.

Extra equipment began to be carried on operations, either in backpack form or in the gunships. These included defibrillators, oxygen cylinders, life-saving chest seals for gunshot wounds to the chest, blood-clotting agents and other wound dressings and equipment, such as tourniquets (at least 4 cm wide) and compression bandages. Officers were also duty-bound to carry smaller personal first aid kits about their person. They became expert in triaging casualties and getting down to skin level to help identify wounds.

These skills were used effectively to stabilize casualties, especially at the scenes of terrorist atrocities such as Westminster Bridge and Borough Market, where the officers were some of the first on the scene.

Some of these highly trained officers became specialist instructors in ballistic first aid, continue to train CTSFOs today and are considered to be among the best in their field.

An ARV medic tends to the wounds of a role player in a training exercise. They make the wounds as realistic as possible to prepare the medics for any eventuality. (*AH*)

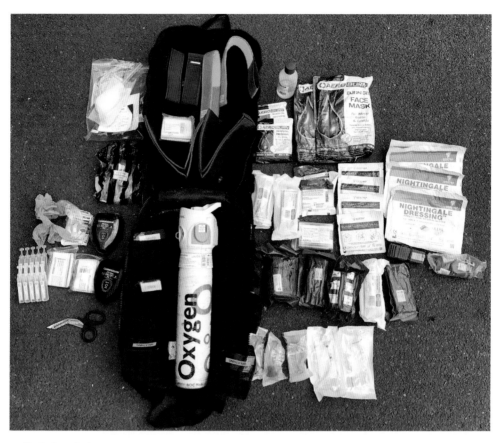

Ballistic first aid kit as carried by every ARV and CTSFO team on every single operation. (*Stephen Smith*)

The ballistic first aid kit along with an acid attack treatment bag. These are carried in every police vehicle following the increase in acid attacks in recent years. (*Stephen Smith*)

DUTY OF CARE

There is a saying: necessity is the mother of all invention. In the firearms world the frequent challenges posed to save life and resolve the criminal's commitment to crime makes this extremely pertinent. New and improving technology has allowed us to innovate, match and excel in the fight against crime. The kit officers wear, and use, is a balance between protection and manoeuvrability, and is now viewed more in terms of their multi-faceted role.

As laws evolve to assist police, and demands on policing increase due to budgetary constraints, the need to innovate has never been greater. The one thing that never changes is the officers' commitment to being the best they can in any situation.

Post-Incident Procedure

Post-Incident Procedure, or PIP as it is commonly known in police circles, can be a daunting process: I have experienced it on more than one occasion. It is initiated not only in fatal shootings but can be implemented when shots are fired or for death-in-police-custody cases. I will attempt to lay out the procedure that an officer will expect to be put through if he or she discharges a firearm or is involved in a death-in-police-custody. This procedure develops each time there is an incident and will continue to do so as different situations arise.

No other job, with the exception of the military, has its workers set out at the start of their day knowing that they may end it having intentionally taken a life. But that is the case with police officers, especially armed ones. Officers may have to do so legally, and with an exemption in law, to protect and save life by the carriage of lethal weapons.

Police shootings have always been investigated. Many years ago, this was with an internal investigation, which was open to allegations of police corruption and cover-up. Over the years, independent bodies were called upon to confirm the integrity of the investigation and, more recently, to represent the public interest and make sure the investigation was efficient and transparent.

Nowadays, the Independent Office for Police Conduct (IOPC) has a remit to carry out an investigation alongside the Met's investigators, known as the Directorate of Professional Standards. The perception is that these investigations have see-sawed between favouring the rights of the police and favouring the rights of the family and supporters of the person shot by police. Of course, this perception depends on which side of the fence you are on.

In 2018, Che Donald, Vice-Chairman of the Police Federation for England and Wales, and the firearms lead, was discussing investigations by the IOPC when he said: 'Nobody objects to an investigation following a death or serious incident, but it should be a fair, transparent and balanced investigation and not one designed to seek to apportion blame rather than establish the facts.'

In order to make things fairer and more transparent, the procedures followed by the police have been set out in the College of Policing's Authorised Professional Practice, which all forces adhere to.

The PIP Process

A PIP will be implemented when there has been any death following police contact. This includes anyone in police custody, a fatality resulting from a collision involving police vehicles or where shots have been discharged by police using conventional firearms or specialist munitions.

Primarily the PIP is there to ensure the transparency and integrity of the process of capturing evidence, but it also progresses ongoing crime matters by the submission of timely updates. Additionally, it ensures any possible learning takes place from what has happened and provides a start point for the welfare of all involved as it identifies those most affected.

It also extends to include police using less-lethal methods such as Taser, baton launcher, collapsible baton, or even CS irritant, which have resulted in death or serious injury. It also reveals any 'failings in command' that caused danger to officers or the public and which is in the public interest to investigate.

The PIP process may also be instigated in cases where an involuntary, accidental or negligent discharge occurs involving a police firearm. However, the full investigation will be implemented should death, injury or danger be caused as a result of any of the above.

Under the European Court of Human Rights, the state has to investigate all deaths caused by an agent of the state. This must be robust, independent, prompt, expeditious and be capable of determining whether force was justified and to be able to identify those responsible. This investigation will involve the next of kin to safeguard their legitimate interests and, to ensure accountability, it should be open to public scrutiny.

Key Police Witnesses

This procedure, however well practised and open, is daunting for the officer involved. Once an investigation is instigated, the officer will have access to a Police Federation representative. These reps – especially those from SCO19 – are trained in PIP and well-versed in the procedures and entitlements of key police witnesses (KPWs). A KPW is normally a person who used force or was responsible for the decision to use it. It could be an officer who gave first aid or restrained a person and may also be civilian staff who were involved in the passing of relevant information or part of the decision-making process.

All officers involved, including the KPWs, will go to a PIP suite where they will be allocated a trained post-incident manager (PIM) and a senior officer. They will be responsible for ensuring the integrity of the PIP process and making sure all parties know what they can and can't do. The IOPC is entitled to attend the PIP suite to observe procedures. These may involve police witnesses having their weapons forensically unloaded and the ammunition counted. The KPWs can ask if they are being treated as witnesses or suspects. This is an important question, as it will define how they are to be treated and the level of legal representation they may need from that point. The PIM will also liaise with the IOPC and the Fed reps and consider the welfare of all police witnesses. These processes can take many, many hours.

Frequently, scenes of police shootings are also crime scenes requiring their own investigation. You can imagine how complicated these can be with representatives from various investigation teams working to obtain and preserve best evidence.

Anonymity

There has been a lot of negativity around firearms officers being granted anonymity following a shooting incident. This is not given in every case and it can be reversed, as in the Azelle

Rodney case, when PC Long's anonymity was withdrawn once he was charged with murder, or in the Dean Joseph shooting (which I'll cover later) where the officer, PC Brown, was not granted anonymity in the first place.

Anonymity can be granted for a number of reasons. Firstly if, following a risk assessment, it is thought the officer and their family may be in danger. It may also be granted where the officer's anonymity is integral to the role they perform. However, nothing is hidden as the police service and IOPC always know the true identity of those involved. The courts will also be informed of an officer's true identity. At inquest, the officers will give evidence in front of the court and the family of the deceased using their code names. Sometimes, on the direction of the coroner, they may even be screened off so they're not visible from the public gallery.

Press Releases

The IOPC make the decisions regarding press releases. However they should provide any details of these to the PIM before they are released to the media. This went very wrong in the Mark Duggan case where the IPCC (now IOPC) press release contained incorrect facts, which inflamed the situation out on the streets, and were not changed even when the officers requested them to be.

The host police service can of course release their own press statements if they choose to.

Interviews by the IOPC

The IOPC can compel a KPW to attend an interview but cannot force an officer to speak. In all cases the officers will attend, having already made an initial account and a detailed statement.

Often the questions asked have already been dealt with in previous statements and officers have very little, if anything, to add. However, they do not say 'no comment' and will often assist with a written response to additional questions if it has been missed out in the original statements.

Officers' Accounts

An officer who has opened fire will be required to give an account of their actions. However this is done in a controlled way, in four stages, so as to safeguard their rights and, more importantly, so that they give best evidence.

Stage one is a brief account given at the scene, sufficient for the decision to be made to implement PIP. On most occasions this will occur immediately after an incident and is called a situational report or sit-rep.

Stage two is an account usually given at the PIP suite, probably within an hour or two of the incident but after the officers have received legal advice. It is normally from someone who was a witness but not a KPW and it should cover who was there and who fired shots etc. It is known as the PIM basic facts. In certain cases, it may be operationally necessary to give a more detailed update if suspects are outstanding or urgent details are required.

Stage three is the officer's 'personal initial account'. This is normally given on the day of the incident – subject to legal advice – and within four to six hours of the event. It should cover the officer's honestly held belief of their use of force and should consist of their independent recollection of events. If the officer has been told he or she is under investigation for criminal offences, this will not be done as they are suspects. However in most cases there will be the legal justification for the officer's use of force and so this should be a positive factor in the investigation for the officer.

Stage four is the officer's detailed account. Research from psychologists, backed up by practical application, shows that to achieve 'best evidence' two periods of sleep and forty-eight hours from the incident is required for the mind to remember and recall more facts. Most people's brains need time to digest and unravel the order of events and important detail.

This account is normally made in the presence of a solicitor. It will include why the officer felt the use of force or discharge of a firearm was absolutely necessary and their honestly held belief.

Again, this is not done if the officer is under criminal investigation. All these accounts will be given to the IOPC at the most within seven days of the incident, unless it is agreed by the IOPC, PIM and legal representation that more time may be required for a variety of reasons, such as welfare or technical or there are ongoing actions, which may require a delay to facilitate the process.

A fact often overlooked is that the officers are human and subject to the same emotions facing anyone who is involved in and exposed to the death or serious injury of a person. They are highly trained and skilled in how to react to a threat, but there is very little that can be done to prepare officers in how to deal with taking a life or being involved in such a case.

A family liaison officer is provided to KPWs to help them come to terms with the situation and there is a range of welfare support offered by the Police Federation, Police Firearms Officers Association and internal occupational health.

Conferring

Following some high-profile cases, it was felt officers could have colluded. Although this was not the case, in the spirit of openness and transparency, it was decided that a change in procedure was needed. Now, an officer can confer if there is an operational necessity, such as they need to pass on or discuss information relating to a real-time danger or threat or they have vital evidence relating to a serious crime. They may not, however, discuss or confer with another officer about their honestly held belief in the use of force.

If they do confer they must follow strict rules and record, in writing, the reasons and content of what was discussed, with whom it was discussed and when and where it took place.

At the onset of PIP, officers were given numerous reminders about conferring and an appointed officer overseeing the note-writing will ensure these rules are strictly adhered to.

Separating Officers

Many arguments have been made in favour of separating officers following a shooting incident. The main reason not to separate them is the fact they are witnesses not suspects. Unless it is believed they may confer inappropriately, or they are suspected of a criminal or disciplinary offence (in which case they will no longer have the rights of a witness) then there is no reason to split them up.

Keeping officers apart can have a detrimental effect, as there is human need for company following a traumatic episode.

Exhibits

Having their clothing taken for no apparent reason is a bugbear with officers. However, there is a good argument for taking officers' clothing as it may contain forensic evidence that could aid the investigation. If they do take an officer's clothing, suitable replacements must be provided, not a white paper forensic suit, as has happened in some cases, as this identifies the officer as the KPW to anyone who sees them, including the media.

The officer's firearms may also be taken as evidence. The remaining ammunition will be listed and checked against what they booked out with the weapon. Officers are not required by law to give blood samples.

Follow up

Senior management, or the 'Gold Group', will have a meeting to discuss the case every twenty-eight days. The officer's status will be discussed and they will be kept informed of developments through their Fed rep. An officer will only be suspended from duty in exceptional circumstances, although they may be temporarily withdrawn from firearms duties on a welfare basis.

I hope this gives a better understanding of what an officer will go through once they pull the trigger. In my experience, these procedures can be protracted and stressful.

There are moves afoot to pass legislation giving police firearms officers some form of professional legal protection. While this will not affect cases where an officer is clearly in breach of the law or their operating procedures, it should at least allow an officer to carry out their duty, for instance if instructed by a senior officer to take a 'critical shot' in a terrorist situation where they have information a subject is about to carry out an atrocity. Under current rules it is still ultimately the officer who makes the final decision for which they are responsible and may have to answer for in a court of law.

POST-INCIDENT PROCEDURE

Officers fully expect to have to justify their actions and account for their decision-making process when a weapon is discharged causing serious injury or a life taken. But people must understand that they cannot simply reel off a detailed account within minutes of taking such action and that it takes time to deal emotionally with the aftermath. Genuine mistakes may be made in the submission of evidence as the scenes are often traumatic and everyone copes with and reacts to them differently. They shouldn't be fearful of what will happen post shooting as it may affect their critical actions and lead to errors of judgement.

Any new legislation needs to be closely scrutinized, but I would welcome it if it afforded some protection and allowed the officers to do the difficult job they do without the fear of being sent to prison for life.

PART 7

A LESSON IN TERROR

CTSFOs carry out room combat training on the range at Leman Street. This training is critical when taking on terrorists in a building. (*AH*)

Terrorism in the UK: From the IRA to ISIS

2000-2013

All terrorist organizations – whether it be the IRA, Al-Qaeda, ISIS or one of the many others worldwide – share common features according to MI5. Their website has the following statement:

> 'Terrorism presents a serious and sustained threat to the United Kingdom and UK interests abroad. Terrorist groups seek to cause widespread disruption, fear and intimidation. They use violence or threat of violence as means of publicising their causes, motivating those who might be sympathetic to them and intimidating those who do not sympathise. They often aim to influence government policies and they often reject existing democratic processes, or even democracy itself as a means of achieving their objectives.'

The names may change over the years but the intention stays the same. The IRA conducted terrorist campaigns against the British Government in one form or another between 1969 and 2011 while Al-Qaeda, and its various strands, declared a jihad (holy war) against the UK in 2001, and are still carrying out atrocities.

If they were both attempting to achieve the same objectives, and we managed to coax the IRA to the negotiating table and eventual peace, why have we had such difficulty getting to grips with Islamic State (ISIS) and preventing such attacks as the London Tube bombings and the Birmingham Arena bombing? How do we seem to know so little about our latest enemy when, towards the end, we seemed able to thwart the IRA's every move?

The IRA had, on occasion, used warning phone calls to reduce casualties after leaving improvised explosive devices (IEDs) in bins and incendiary devices in shops, burning them to the ground. They sent small IEDs through the mail, laid down car bombs and set off massive lorry bombs, which nearly brought the City of London's financial district to a standstill. They carried out drive-by shootings and assassinations, targeted politicians and bombed the Conservative Party conference. They blew up soldiers playing music at the bandstand in Regents Park just hours after detonating a nail bomb that killed mounted troops and their horses on South Carriage Drive in Hyde Park. They were ruthless murderers, but we understood their tactics and became adept at arresting and stopping them because most of the time 'we knew who they were'.

The UK has officially been at peace with the IRA since the 1998 Good Friday Agreement. However, some splinter groups attempted to unravel this agreement by continuing aggressive acts. The final attacks on mainland Britain were in 2001. Known as the Real IRA, they had attempted to restart the Troubles by firing a rocket-propelled grenade at the capital's MI6 headquarters, detonating a series of car bombs in London – one at BBC Television Centre and another in Ealing – and finally in November that year, in Birmingham city centre. During these attacks, several people were injured.

Fortunately, the Real IRA were brought back in line and the fragile peace process held. The British people breathed a sigh of relief. There are still violent incidents related to sectarian violence in Northern Ireland, but nothing on the scale of the earlier IRA terror campaigns.

During the thirty or so years of the Troubles, the IRA murdered around 1,800 civilians and members of the security services, and injured and maimed countless more. It's a huge number but if you compare it with the deluge of current terror attacks, it puts them into perspective.

One of the reasons we became effective against the IRA was the mass of intelligence information that had been built up by our security services over fifty or so years. However, it seemed that no sooner had we made a form of peace in Northern Ireland, we were facing another peril, this time in the form of Muslim fundamentalist factions intent on bringing down our way of life.

It happened by way of a massive showcase attack, which must have been years in the planning, and it occurred a month before the end of the hostilities with the Real IRA. It was the worst terrorist atrocity of modern times.

On 11 September 2001, most of us looked on helplessly as our TV sets broadcast live the act of an Al-Qaeda-sponsored group of terrorists as they crashed commercial airliners into the World Trade Center in New York and the Pentagon in Washington killing thousands of innocent victims including sixty-seven Britons. This was clearly a declaration of intent and I was among those who was braced for attacks on our own shores from this new form of terrorism. It wasn't if, it was when.

Immediately following these attacks, the US demanded the Taliban – who now ruled in Afghanistan running the country under strict Muslim Sharia law – hand over the leader of Al-Qaeda, Osama bin Laden. When they refused, President George W. Bush initiated Operation Enduring Freedom. This was the war against Al-Qaeda and its allies, which included the Taliban. They called upon the UK to help, along with other nations. We agreed and were once again committed to a war, which we understood was necessary if we were to prevent attacks at home. However, hunting down and capturing Bin Laden would take considerably longer than expected and the so-called 'war on terror' would drag on.

For almost four years after the attack we now refer to as 9/11, our soldiers in Afghanistan delivered relative peace. There were no terrorist attacks in the UK during this time – some were attempted but none had succeeded.

But just as we were coming to terms with living in a society where we could go about our business without looking out for suspicious unattended packages or strange vehicles parked outside public buildings, a radical group, intent on disrupting and destroying the very fabric of our society, brought us back down to earth.

In this case it was the devastating attack on the London Underground and transport system by four Islamic extremist suicide bombers who, on 7 July 2005, detonated their vests so they exploded among commuters travelling to work or going about their business, killing fifty-two and injuring hundreds of others, leaving many with life-changing injuries. Two weeks later, another group attempted to copy this attack but failed, due to having the wrong mix of homemade explosive in their backpacks.

Two years later, on 30 June 2007, a lone Muslim extremist attacked Glasgow Airport in a car set to explode in a huge fireball. Thankfully, it failed to fully detonate but it still injured five and killed the perpetrator, a British-born self-radicalized doctor working in the UK. There followed a very serious game of cat-and-mouse as the nation's security services did sterling work foiling plot after plot by various grades of Islamic extremists inspired by preachers of hate who had travelled from Pakistan and the Far East to preach against the West and radicalize whoever would listen.

The problem grew from arresting suspects and stopping terrorist plots to preventing the message of hate from corrupting our young people and driving them into the arms of the Islamic extremists. This was no more prevalent than in our prison system, where many disillusioned black and Muslim prisoners saw this form of extremism as a path they wanted to follow. There was now a new drive to understand and counter this danger, which had penetrated deep into our society, focusing on large communities of second-generation Muslim settlers within the UK.

Our weaknesses in fully understanding and engaging with the diverse elements of our society had left our island nation further exposed, particularly in London and other major cities with large Muslim populations. These would bear the brunt of a new threat, which manifested itself as the war in Syria came to its endgame and saw hundreds of radicalized Muslim men of fighting age return to the UK intent on taking the fight back to their adopted home.

The role that the firearms unit would play in this fight was critical. They would be on the front line and needed to up their game.

Following the attack on the World Trade Center, contingency planning had gone mad. Having been 'geared up' to fight the IRA, and the way they conducted their terror campaigns, it would be wholly different to how Al-Qaeda conducted theirs. We went from terrorists who would make every effort to escape justice to continue their fight, to motivated suicide killers intent on murder and maiming as many people as possible and becoming martyrs in the belief it would lead them to heaven.

The tactics had to change to counter this threat and this could not happen overnight. For security services to operate effectively, they need good intelligence and good intelligence takes months or years to perfect and involves agents infiltrating and cultivating informants who have access to the people organizing and plotting these atrocities. It would be some years before this could be achieved. Having said that, the security services did a fantastic job with what they had.

SO19 also had to develop new tactics and train for worst-case scenarios and around 2004, a tactic called Operation Kratos (or just Kratos) was introduced to training. It was based around officers taking 'critical shots' at suspected suicide bombers or persons driving vehicle-borne devices into crowded big cities and involved firing to the lower head where the brain stem is located. The shot was to be taken either close up or from directed rifle fire. (The public was not aware of these tactics until the mistaken shooting of Jean Charles de Menezes at Stockwell tube on 22 July 2005.)

When used successfully, this is still one of only a few effective ways to stop a suicide bomber from detonating. It is still an option for armed officers within SCO19 who realistically could be the first to have contact with these suspects thanks to the close working relationship between front-line policing units and security services.

Following serious attacks in Paris and other European cities, the need for high-velocity weaponry and, in particular, the ability to engage terrorists over a protracted firefight or siege scenario would necessitate officers having access to large amounts of ammunition. It called for new thinking, with many reluctant senior police officers having to come to terms with the new order of things.

Large budgets were made available for new equipment, vehicles and weapons systems. Expertise from different and diverse sources was sought. A more open exchange of intelligence and debriefing on an international level, involving both the police and the military, was undertaken. Many good but painful lessons were learned from our friends in Europe from which we will benefit in times to come.

In the year ending 31 March 2018, 441 people had been arrested on suspicion of terrorist offences in the UK. This is the highest number of arrests since records began in 2001 and is a big increase on the previous year, which recorded 378 arrests. In 2017, the UK had the highest death toll from terrorist-related incidents in the whole of Europe.

We cannot afford to sit back, hoping the attacks will not happen on our shores. This was brought home in the most painful and unexpected way, not on the streets of Paris or Belgium, but on the streets of Woolwich, south-east London in 2013. Simply researching and writing about it was traumatic for me so I can only imagine how devastating it was for the public and emergency services that were present.

The Murder of Lee Rigby

Woolwich, 22 May 2013

Of all the terror attacks perpetrated in the UK in the name of Islam, the one that stands out for me as the most sickening is the savage murder of unarmed, off-duty, British soldier Lee Rigby. This was committed by two men who, from birth, had been nurtured and educated by the generous systems we have within the UK. They had then rejected their country in favour of a radical brand of Islam inspired by Al-Qaeda, which advocated hate and incited them to commit atrocities in the hope of provoking a war in the UK by pitching Christian against Muslim.

Because of the spirit of the people of this great nation, the ultimate aim of this act of terrorism was doomed to failure, but it would succeed in defining the cruel and callous nature of these recruits to Islamic extremism. It caused overwhelming sadness and anger to almost everyone who was unfortunate enough to see pictures and film footage as it unfolded on the streets of Woolwich, south-east London on that Wednesday afternoon in May 2013.

Fusilier Lee James Rigby, 25, 2nd Battalion, Royal Fusiliers who was stationed at the Royal Artillery Barracks Woolwich at the time of the attack in 2013.

Prior to this, the UK had been successful in foiling a number of terrorist attacks by Islamic extremists. It had been almost eight years since the London tube bombings of 2005, and six years since the attack on Glasgow Airport. During this time, terrorist attacks had been on the increase around the globe and the world had generally become less stable, with wars in both Syria and Afghanistan. These in particular were still high on the list of reasons to attack the West. British security services, along with Special Branch and the Anti-Terrorist Branch, had been working feverishly to keep tabs on the growing numbers of radicalized Muslim activists and returning fighters from the aforementioned hotspots of terrorist activity. Thrown into the equation was the increase of 'hate preachers' who encouraged action against the West and had a growing audience of young followers in mosques or out on the street.

A mixture of free speech and human rights legislation made it awkward for the authorities to stop their anti-West rants. There were moves afoot to change these laws but, as ever, it would be a slow journey.

Into this cauldron of hate-filled extremism two young men, Michael Olumide Adebolajo, 28, and Michael Oluwatobi Adebowale, 22, threw in their lot. They embarked on a path that would lead to the senseless murder of an innocent young man going about his business in the safety of his community, and finally into the sights of the armed officers of London's ARVs.

It is not certain how or when the two met, although they may well have had mutual acquaintances being brought up in the same area and converting to Islam at similar times. Both men were born in Lambeth, South London and were of Nigerian descent. They were brought up in Christian families and educated locally. Both were involved in crime at a young age and had spent time in prison – Adebolajo for assaulting two police officers and Adebowale for drugs offences. Adebolajo went on to attend Greenwich University and by the time he left, he'd converted to Islam. There are no records to support claims that Adebowale attended Greenwich with him.

Both were well known to security services prior to the attack. They had appeared on the radar due to their presence at meetings attended by hate preachers Mizanur Rahman and Anjem Choudary. Adebolajo had even spoken at some of these meetings, in which he promoted a desire for Britain to become an Islamic Khilafah state. Both men took active roles in counter-demonstrations against the English Defence league (EDL) and the British Nationalist Party (BNP). Adebolajo was arrested outside the Old Bailey during a violent protest against the arrest and trial of Rahman (later convicted of solicitation to murder British troops in Afghanistan).

In 2010 things escalated when Adebolajo travelled to Kenya. Kenyan police arrested him as he attempted to reach a training camp run by the militant group Al-Shabaab, which had links with Al-Qaeda. His movements were of great interest to the security services. He was released

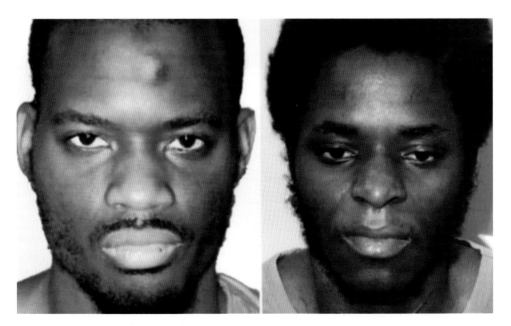

Lee Rigby's attackers: Michael Adebolajo on the left and Michael Adebowale on the right. (*Metropolitan Police*)

163

into British custody and, after an interview, released with no charges. He later alleged that they had attempted to recruit him as an informant.

At some point between 2010 and May 2013, Adebolajo and Adebowale got together and hatched a plan to commit an atrocity in the UK.

It later transpired that in December 2012, Adebowale had communicated on Facebook with a foreign-based extremist and discussed killing a soldier. Facebook later conceded that several of his accounts had been blocked by an automated service due to their links to extremism. This was apparently not known by the security services. Although their names had appeared in seven intelligence investigations, at the time of the attack neither was being closely monitored.

The level of help or encouragement afforded to them from other quarters is not known and is hard to prove but it is fair to say they were probably not working alone.

Their attack followed the pattern of similar incidents on the continent where low-tech weapons had been used to maim, injure and kill soldiers and police. These included knives and, increasingly, vehicles.

The day before the attack, Adebolajo dressed in the same clothes he would wear for the murder had purchased a five-piece knife set from Argos in Lewisham along with a knife sharpener. He also set aside a meat cleaver – the type used in butcher's shops – and two other kitchen knives, similar to those found in most domestic kitchens. At some point, much earlier than this, Adebolajo had obtained a ninety-two-year-old 9.4mm Dutch Model 91 revolver, which was popular with the Japanese during the Second World War. Although this weapon was tested later and proved to be viable, the ammunition was rare and hard to come by – Adebolajo did not have any at the time of the attack.

On 22 April 2013, the pair met up at Adebolajo's home in Lewisham. They left the address at 1pm in a blue Vauxhall Tigra with Adebolajo driving, and they headed off towards Woolwich where they were seen at 1.30pm cruising the streets near the Royal Artillery Barracks.

The rusty Dutch Model 91, 9.4mm revolver carried by Adebowale during the attack.

The two knives carried by Adebolajo which were among those used to murder Lee Rigby. (*Stephen Smith*)

Lee Rigby arrived at Woolwich Arsenal Station at 2.10pm and was making his way towards the barracks having completed duties at the Tower of London. At 2.13pm the men parked in the car park on Wellington Street and sat in the vehicle facing Artillery Place, watching for a suitable victim. They were probably drawn to Lee Rigby by his appearance, his tidy haircut and his rucksack, but most likely due to the fact he was wearing a 'Help for Heroes' hoodie and because he was walking towards the barracks. There is no intelligence suggesting the attackers knew Lee Rigby or that they had been targeting him. It appears to be a random attack based solely on his appearance and the location.

Fusilier Lee James Rigby, 25, was a drummer and machine-gunner in the 2nd Battalion of the Royal Regiment of Fusiliers and was based at the Royal Artillery Barracks. Originally from Middleton in Greater Manchester, Lee was a career soldier, joining the Army in 2006 and serving in Cyprus, Germany and Helmand Province, Afghanistan. He had also worked in the regimental recruitment unit, but at that time was posted to the regimental headquarters at the Tower of London. He was married with a 2-year-old son.

As he walked along Wellington Street and crossed the road at John Wilson Street entering Artillery Place, he again stepped into the road, crossing towards a shop on the other side. He would not have been aware of the Vauxhall Tigra driving in the other carriageway or the point when it accelerated, crossing the white lines towards him. Lee was halfway across the road when the car picked up pace, reaching a speed later assessed at being between 30 and 40 mph. It hit Lee hard, taking his legs away and knocking him onto the bonnet. He hit the windscreen with enough force to break it before being thrown off.

The vehicle continued at speed onto the pavement where it struck the base of a signpost, bringing it to a halt with debris from the car and the street sign littering the pavement. Lee Rigby lay motionless in the road behind – the high-impact collision would have caused serious injury to the fit, young man.

Both assailants leapt from the wrecked car clutching an array of weapons, which included four knives and the pistol. Adebolajo ran up to the helpless man and, as witnesses later stated, grabbed him by the hair and began to chop at his neck with the cleaver, striking him at least nine times. One cannot imagine what Lee's last moments must have been like – expecting help but instead receiving his death blows.

Adebowale casually walked over and joined in, stabbing at Lee's limp body multiple times with a long-bladed kitchen knife. They then dragged their victim towards the middle of the road where they dumped him temporarily.

On hearing the commotion and noise of the collisions, passers-by began to arrive and went over to the victim to offer help.

At 2.20pm, the first call was made to police stating that there was a 'male being attacked at the location.' The caller went on to describe that he was being hit with 'metal poles'. There was no mention of a firearm for another two minutes but the police information room was swamped with people calling in. Staff had difficulty deciphering what was happening as they received conflicting information, with some callers claiming 'there's a gang fight going down

The Blue Vauxhall Tigra hatchback used to run Lee Rigby over. Note the damage to the windscreen caused by the impact with Lee's body.

with people armed with knives and guns' and others saying 'there's been a road rage incident following an accident and the drivers are fighting.' Some callers were hysterical while poor English hindered others but one got it spot on when he said, 'two men have knocked a man down in a car; they are now trying to hack his head off with knives.'

The full horror of what had happened was not understood due to the confusion of the calls, but it was obvious that whatever it was, they needed to send armed units down there and on the hurry up.

Back at the scene, the old revolver was passed from Adebolajo to Adebowale who used it to threaten bystanders, keeping them at bay. Most ignored the two men. One woman even went over to Lee Rigby and stroked his body. This act of kindness undoubtedly prevented the pair from making further attempts to decapitate him.

At 2.24pm the first Trojan ARV unit acknowledged the call of 'men in the streets armed with guns and knives.' Moments later Trojan 561, which had been on patrol in the New Cross area, accepted the call and, being closest, began to make its way using the blues and twos. Sensing the urgency, two other Trojan units also began to make their way. The traffic was heavy and it would take TJ561 nine minutes to travel the five-and-a-half miles to Artillery Place.

The growing number of people gathering nearby distracted Adebolajo, who stood there bloodied cleaver in hand, ranting away in a feeble attempt to justify his actions, claiming among other things: 'This British soldier is one – he is an eye for an eye and a tooth for a tooth.'

One woman, scout leader Ingrid Loyau-Kennett, engaged the attackers in conversation asking them to put down their weapons. They refused but continued to use their public platform to call on the British Government to withdraw troops. The sickening image will haunt the nation for a very long time. Adebolajo later passed a bystander a handwritten two-page note, which laid out his warped justification for the attack.

Under normal circumstances, when responding to a call of this nature, two Trojan units would rendezvous nearby and arrive together to give them more tactical options. However, sensing this was no ordinary armed call, and having had reports of someone badly injured at the scene, they forewent this luxury making a decision to get there as soon as possible.

The officers found it unusual that not only were there so many calls of a conflicting nature but the suspects had not fled the scene. They were hanging around seemingly waiting for police to arrive. It was also rare to have live CCTV coverage of the suspects still on scene. This footage was sent to the Lambeth firearms control room who informed the Trojan units that the subjects were in the road between a white van (this later turned out to be a large lorry) and a bus.

Their initial thoughts were that the call might be a result of a road-rage incident or gang fight. Either way they knew there had been a casualty, that firearms and knives had been mentioned and it was near a bus stop, so they were concerned other members of the public may be at risk.

Local unarmed officers had arrived nearby but were firmly instructed that, because of the firearms information, they should try to maintain a cordon a safe distance away and await the arrival of armed units. On reflection, even with the criticism police received for standing off, it was the right thing to do. Any unarmed officer approaching the heavily armed pair could well have received the same fate as Lee Rigby. The next five minutes would seem like an age.

The Trojan control at Lambeth was now running the incident and coordinating the ARV response; it was relaying updates from the live CCTV link and providing tactical guidance to TJ561. The CCTV operator could see one of the suspects holding a firearm, along with knives, and gave frequent updates as to their location and actions. The sergeant in control warned his units to approach with 'extreme caution as there were now members of the public nearby'.

The crew of TJ561were aware that someone had been badly injured, but the extent of those injuries was not known. They had a description of both suspects and knew a firearm, along with knives, were in their possession. What they did not know was that someone had already been murdered and that the victim was a British soldier. They had no idea of the intention or motivation of the suspects. They would only learn that it was a terrorist incident some hours after the dust had settled.

The female driver of TJ561 guided the ARV through the outer cordon. One of the final updates put the two suspects approaching the bus parked at the scene and so, as they turned the corner into Wellington Place from the South Circular Road, the two officers in the front of the vehicle were drawn to the big red bus looming to the left in front of them. They were seriously worried that these armed men may have boarded the bus and be threatening passengers or that a hijack situation might arise. They were scanning the people near and on the bus for any sign of the subjects. However, due to the delay in relaying the CCTV updates, they were unaware the men had walked back across the road only moments earlier.

From the moment the ARV had turned the corner into Wellington Place and moved towards the bus, the officer in the rear was scanning the street. While his two colleagues were focused on the bus, he noticed two men loitering in the road in front of a large white lorry 20 to 30 metres away to the right. Their description matched that of the suspects and then, as the ARV came to a halt angled in front of the bus, he noticed that one of the men, Adebolajo, was holding a large knife in his right hand.

The two men appeared to react to the arrival of the ARV and Adebolajo began moving towards them at a fast walk. The ARV officer was focused on this male and very concerned at the glint of steel in his hand. As he shouted to his colleagues: 'Over there to the right!', the killer's pace changed from a fast walk to a run. The driver of the BMW X5 ARV was now alerted to someone approaching the car fast to her right side. Adebolajo was picking up pace, running in a kind of long curve towards the ARV driver and he had a meat cleaver in his right hand. He'd dropped the smaller chef's knife, swapping it for the heavier meat cleaver, which he now brought above his head as if ready to chop down hard. Both the driver and rear passenger knew they were in grave danger but were confined to the car. They could tell by his demeanor and his aggressive hate-filled expression that they were under attack.

Within three to four seconds of arriving on scene, Adebolajo had charged to within 2 metres of the ARV. The officer in the rear seat levelled his MP5 carbine and fired two shots at him through the open rear offside window. Adebolajo was hit in his right arm, his humerus bone (upper arm) smashed by the hollow point 9mm round. He threw up his arms and appeared to jump sideways to his left, before smashing to the ground writhing in pain.

The officer in the front passenger seat had already left the vehicle as it came to a halt and was making his way toward the bus. He had not seen Adebolajo's charge towards the car. The driver, meanwhile, fearing she was about to be hacked at, was unable to draw her pistol from her thigh holster due to the confined nature of the driver's seat. Instead she took the only option open to her and drew her X-26 Taser from its cross-draw pouch on the front of her body armour. As her colleague behind fired two shots at Adebolajo, she flung open the driver's door and quickly exited the ARV. She closed Adebolajo down, followed by her colleague who shot him as he lay on the ground making efforts to get back up.

Still considering him to be a threat, she fired her Taser. The two sharp barbs found their mark delivering 50,000 volts. The effect of being tasered would have been extremely painful as the barb placement was at its optimum spacing. Adebolajo was now overcome and would make no further attempt to attack the officers.

On hearing the sharp crack of a firearm being discharged, the officer who had exited from the nearside front seat and headed toward the bus, spun around looking for the source of the gunfire. He immediately picked out Adebowale wearing a green jacket, who was up to this point unseen by his colleagues who were focused on Adebolajo. He was standing on the opposite pavement at a distance of about 8 to 10 metres away, pointing a revolver at the officers. Initially the officer thought he was firing at Adebolajo as he saw him crash to the ground in front of him and heard two gunshots ring out. But no, Adebowale was pointing the revolver at the ARV crew and needed to be neutralized quickly. The officer brought his MP5 carbine up and fired four shots. Adebowale was hit at least once at this point as a round passed straight through his leg, causing him to buckle and collapse to the ground only metres away from his fellow killer.

The first two officers had been so focused on Adebolajo that they only now became aware of Adebowale as he collapsed onto the pavement. The three officers came together at the rear of the ARV, weapons up they moved forward almost as one towards the two now prostrate attackers. The female officer discarded her Taser and drew her Glock pistol levelling it at Adebolajo who remained writhing on the ground. As they drew near, Adebowale, now lying on his left side, raised his right arm, still clutching the revolver, and pointed it directly at the officers. He was shot twice more by the third officer, one round of which passed through the thumb of his gun-wielding hand. Since arriving on scene, the ARV crew had neutralized both killers in around fourteen seconds.

The officers began carrying out first aid to the pair they had shot as per their training. They fetched the ballistic first aid kit and began locating and treating wounds. At the same time, local plain-clothes officers arrived and assessed Lee Rigby but there was nothing that could be done for him. The public now began to close in, phones in hand, filming the aftermath.

Moments later, another ARV arrived and gradually the scene was controlled, people were moved and the full horror of what had happened became apparent.

The London Ambulance Service attended and removed the two murderers to hospital. Both had life-changing gunshot wounds – Adebowale lost his right thumb and had been hit in the abdomen and thigh, Adebolajo had shattered bones in his arm. But neither was as life changing as the wounds they had so needlessly and cruelly inflicted on Lee Rigby.

Who knows what might have occurred had TJ561 not driven straight to the scene? Normally ARVs can respond anywhere in London within twenty minutes so it is commendable that the first police ARV arrived within nine minutes from receiving the call, and fourteen minutes from when the attack began.

LONDON'S ARMED POLICE UP CLOSE AND PERSONAL

The police arrival at this incident was caught on camera, as was the subsequent shooting of the two subjects. The video showed the ARV stopped in the middle of the road, sparking an immediate response from the two men who attempted to engage it. Adebolajo charged at the officers with a meat cleaver and Adebowale pointed a firearm (it later transpired that he believed the gun given to him by Adebolajo was loaded and he thought that the breech had exploded as he was firing at police, thus causing his injury).

It is a credit to the armed officers that they engaged and neutralized both subjects so quickly. Anyone who has handled a weapon will know how difficult it is to hit a moving target, especially in moments of high stress.

The full horror of the attack was beginning to dawn on everybody as the video and witness reports began filtering through. Before long, there were TV clips featuring the rants of the attackers standing with blood-stained knives. Some media sources were later criticized for the tasteless coverage.

Following the attack on Lee Rigby there was an expected anti-Muslim backlash, which included physical and verbal assaults on Muslims, attacks on mosques, the spraying of anti-

Cleaver at the ready, Adebolajo charges at the ARV moments before he is shot.

Adebolajo appears to jump back as the officer in the rear seat engages him with two shots.

170

The officer on the left shoots Adebowale in the groin and thigh as he points a pistol at the officers. He is already collapsing to the ground.

Two officers disarm Adebowale after he is shot twice more in the hand and arm, while their colleague covers Adebolajo.

Muslim graffiti and demonstrations by the now-outlawed EDL and BNP. The police and government feared revenge attacks and further civil unrest and called for calm. However, although shocked by events, the feeling of the general public was one of consolidation. Many reflected on how it could be that homegrown British subjects could become so radicalized and capable of committing such an attack, and how it could be stopped from ever happening again.

The post mortem found that Lee Rigby died from 'multiple incised wounds'.

On 12 July 2013, the fusilier was given a full military funeral attended by Prime Minister David Cameron and the Lord Mayor of London along with several thousand mourners. A monument was installed in his honour at The Valley football stadium by Charlton Athletic fans – less than a mile from the scene of the attack – and over £600,000 was donated to the Help for Heroes charity.

Adebolajo spent nine days in hospital with bullet wounds to his left arm. Adebowale spent six days being treated – his right thumb was amputated, his liver was damaged and he had an entry and exit wound to his thigh.

On 27 September 2013, both assailants appeared via video link at the Old Bailey and pleaded not guilty to the murder of Lee Rigby and attempted murder of police officers.

In December that year, following a short trial, they were both found guilty of murder and firearms offences. On 26 February 2014 they were sentenced to life imprisonment. Adebolajo, the more dominant of the two, was given a 'whole life order' while Adebowale was ordered to serve at least forty-five years in prison. The judge, Mr Justice Sweeney, said, 'Adebolajo was the leader of the joint enterprise, but Adebowale played his part enthusiastically.' He went on to

The National Monument Arboretum in Staffordshire where Lee Rigby is remembered alongside others who have been killed in service. (*Stephen Smith*)

Lee Rigby's name on the monument.
(*Stephen Smith*)

add that their extremist views were a 'betrayal of Islam' to which Adebowale shouted: 'That's a lie!' and Adebolajo shouted: 'Allahu Akbar'. After a brief struggle with guards, the convicted murderers were removed from the court to begin their life behind bars.

An appeal against their long sentences, at taxpayers' expense, failed to change the ruling. The combined cost to the British taxpayers for defending the two murderers had spiralled to £212,613.

On 19 December 2013, the IPCC report concluded that the officers who had used force had 'acted entirely appropriately' and had shown 'skill and professionalism'.

Adebolajo continues to be disruptive in prison. Staff have stated that 'he is volatile, manipulative and fixates on staff, particularly female members. His devotion to radical Islam is total, and all-consuming. He still believes he is an active terrorist.'

The question of how young British Muslims could be radicalized was asked in parliament. The government reacted by setting up a task force to look at ways of preventing the growth of Islamic extremism in Britain and identifying persons vulnerable to radicalization in mosques, prisons and universities.

On 6 September 2016, the hate preachers Mohammed Rahman and Anjem Choudary were found guilty at the Old Bailey of inviting support for ISIS and each was sentenced to five-and-a-half years' imprisonment.

Lee Rigby's name has been added to the National Memorial Arboretum in Staffordshire to those who have lost their lives in the war on terror.

Active Shooters, Spree Shooters and Mass Killings

The term active shooter has been around a while, having been coined in the US to identify the phenomenon that began there around 1966. Since then it has plagued the US with regular occurrences that seem to grow in magnitude, with each one causing deaths, injuries and destruction and heaping misery on the victims, their families and the survivors of these attacks.

In more recent times there have been incidents outside the US – no continent, country or region has been spared – with many copycat cases seemingly trying to outdo the other.

The US Department of Homeland Security (DHS) defines an active shooter as 'an individual actively engaged in killing or attempting to kill people in a confined and populated area.' It adds: 'In most cases, active shooters use firearms and there is no pattern or method to their selection of victims.' Most incidents of this kind occur against so-called 'soft targets', such as schools, colleges, nurseries, or on occasion in the workplace or locations related to the active shooter.

The most notorious examples are the 1999 Columbine High School massacre in Colorado, where two teenage shooters, Eric Harris and Dylan Klebold, killed thirteen and wounded twenty-one others, and the attack on Sandy Hook Elementary School in Connecticut when 20-year-old Adam Lanza murdered twenty children aged six and seven as well as school staff and his mother.

An FBI study from data gathered between 2000 and 2013 found that contrary to popular belief, only twenty-five per cent of these shooters appeared to be suffering from mental health issues and the incident was normally the result of a long-standing dispute or grudge against individuals. It also found they purchased the weapons legally but specifically for the task, and the shooting was planned over a long period with the assailant usually posting a desire to kill or hurt people on social media long before the event took place.

The following statistics are taken from incidents in the US as they offer the best picture of the size of problem. Although we have far fewer instances in Europe, we cannot sit back and do nothing.

In 2017, the FBI categorized thirty-three active shootings across the US – excluding gang and drug-related violence – and at each one, three or more people (excluding the shooter) died. The worst of these occurred in Las Vegas in October 2017, when a lone shooter opened fire on a crowd at a country music festival, killing fifty-eight and wounding more than 500.

Between the years 2000 and 2017, there were 799 deaths (not including the shooters) and 1,418 wounded from active shooter incidents in the US.

We are fortunate in the UK to have mostly escaped this phenomenon, which is probably due to our tough firearms legislation and the difficulty in sourcing viable firearms and ammunition.

ACTIVE SHOOTERS, SPREE SHOOTERS AND MASS KILLINGS

Or it is just something we British don't do? Either way it is hard to understand why we have had only two recorded cases of active shooters in recent times.

The first occurred in August 1987, and would now be redefined as a spree shooter due to the fact it was not confined and occurred over a larger area in the market town of Hungerford in Berkshire. Michael Ryan ran amok in the town killing sixteen people, including an unarmed police officer, and wounding a further fifteen.

He used mostly legally held firearms, which forced through changes to our already strict laws, banning fully automatic weapons from public ownership.

The second occurrence would be classified as an active shooter incident and occurred at Dunblane Primary School near Stirling in Scotland in March 1996, when Thomas Hamilton shot sixteen pupils and a teacher dead before turning the gun on himself. Once again, the government came down on gun owners, banning the possession of any pistol with the exception of muzzle-loading and historic pistols along with certain sporting pistols.

Other spree shootings have occurred in the UK. The first was in October 1978, in the Midlands towns of West Bromwich and Nuneaton, when Barry Williams shot and killed five people in a spree lasting over an hour. He was arrested following a high-speed car chase and was convicted of manslaughter due to diminished responsibility.

In Monkseaton, North Tyneside in 1989, Robert Sartin shot fifteen people, one fatally, with his father's double-barrelled shotgun during a twenty-minute shooting spree. Sartin was detained indefinitely under the Mental Health Act.

There were two spree shootings in 2010. The first in June involved Derrick Bird who killed twelve people and injured eleven while driving through several villages in Cumbria. His spree finished when he shot himself dead. Then, just one month later and following a six-day manhunt, Raoul Moat shot three people including a police officer, one fatally, before also shooting himself dead. Sadly, the police officer, PC David Rathband, who had been shot in the face and blinded, took his own life twenty months later.

The final category of mass killings in the UK can be placed firmly on the actions of terrorists. The aim of each terrorist attack – from IRA bombings to the ISIS-inspired suicide bombings on the London tube in 2005 and Manchester Arena in 2017, plus the vehicle-ramming attacks and knife-spree killings – is to kill as many people as possible.

It is essential that we monitor the trends of these attacks to allow us to better prevent them. It is also important to develop tactics and training for our armed officers, and the public, so we can react and deal with any threat as it happens. We are fortunate that in the grand scheme of things these terrible instances are relatively rare.

The advice on how to survive an incident should you find yourself mixed up in one varies. The Met advise the public to 'Run, Hide and Tell', which could save your life. However the advice endorsed by the FBI and DHS in the US has a sting in its tail. I have copied the following from one of its advisory papers:

Option 1. Run
Running should be your first choice. Take note of the two nearest exits in any facility you enter, and make sure you have an escape route in mind. Leave your belongings behind, and take anyone who is willing to go with you. Don't let anyone's indecisiveness slow you down.

Option 2. Hide

If running isn't an option, look for a safe hiding place. Your hiding place should protect you if shots are fired in your direction, and it should not trap you or restrict your movement. Lock the door or barricade the entry, silence your cell phone and turn off radios, televisions and other sources of noise.

Option 3. Fight

As a last resort, fight the shooter, but only if your life is in imminent danger. Active shooter situations are no time for passive responses. If you choose to fight, commit to your actions. The DHS recommends you act aggressively by yelling, throwing items at the shooter and trying to incapacitate them.

Option 4. Tell

Call the police, as soon as it is safe to do so, give your location, any landmarks or buildings.

Please remember these options and see how they worked out in the Borough Market attack in 2017, which I cover later. They may save your life should you be unfortunate enough to get caught up in an incident. I would advocate always having a plan and, where possible, identifying the threat and reacting quickly.

The Atlas Network

Strength in Numbers

Cooperation between specialist police units around the world is a major tool in the fight against international crime and, more importantly, terrorism. This cooperation is based on mutual trust and informal contact with other units in the same field.

The idea of a Europe-wide network to utilize and combine the member nations' special intervention units (SIUs), help gather cross-border intelligence, share developments and consider new policing methods and tactics, originated in 1996. This is when the European Union Council created a directory of specialized counter-terrorist competencies, skills and expertise to facilitate cooperation on special interventions between EU member states.

It was not until October 2001 – a month after the attack on the World Trade Center – that the heads of the SIUs first met. The main objective was 'protecting and saving lives' and it focused on the rescue of hostages, rapid response in crisis situations and the cooperation and enhancement of capabilities. The ATLAS Network was born.

Since then there have been regular meetings, along with joint counter-terrorism exercises across Europe, every year. In 2003, this involved a four-day international training incident held in Germany to increase competencies to handle assault and hostage-taking from boats. In 2004, a large-scale exercise took place in the harbour of Rotterdam. There have been exercises in Italy looking at enforced entry into high-speed trains, along with a joint study in Spain of the effect of explosives on different types of doors to improve entry techniques. To date there have been over fifty joint training events.

SCO19 has been an active member of the ATLAS Network, frequently hosting visiting units, proffering ideas and suggestions, sending officers to learn new techniques and bringing back innovative ideas from SIUs across Europe.

There are currently thirty-eight SIUs formed from the twenty-eight member states as well as Norway, Sweden and Switzerland.

ATLAS recognizes that a member state may not have the means, resources or expertise to deal effectively with all crisis situations, in particular large crisis situations, and therefore provides a framework for a member state to request assistance from another member.

A permanent support office for the ATLAS Network is planned for 2019, which will strengthen the network's capabilities.

I am assured that the UK's involvement in the ATLAS Network will continue past Brexit and well into the future.

Operation Temperer

Troops Deployed to Assist Police 22 April 2015

In April 2015, following an increase in terrorist attacks, including in Paris and Tunisia, the National Police Chiefs Council (NPCC) met in Leicester to discuss contingency planning in the event of further attacks in the UK. Billed on paper as 'Counter Terrorism, Post Paris, and Large Scale Military Support to the Police!', it was no surprise that the plans, otherwise known as Operation Temperer, found their way into the press and were reported in detail.

The plans revealed that in the event of the UK's terror threat going from 'severe' to 'critical' (meaning an attack was imminent rather than highly likely) certain actions would be initiated.

Firstly, up to 5,000 soldiers and military personnel would be mobilized. These would replace armed police officers guarding installations and buildings, such as our nuclear power

Armed British Transport Police officers ready for patrol outside St Pancras Station, London. They carry the LMT .556 carbine fitted with the Leupold Mk4 Tactical Rifle Scope, fold-down, tactical fore grip and tactical illuminator. (*Mark Williams*)

stations and facilities (currently guarded by the CNC), along with military and government establishments (some guarded by the Ministry of Defence Police) and some other locations guarded by armed Home Office police. These armed officers would be released to assist in securing possible terrorist targets such as transport hubs, shopping malls, large sporting events and popular tourist and religious locations within the UK.

At the same time, MI5 and the security services would be working hard to track down and prevent the attack from taking place.

Many saw the plans as controversial. Certain politicians believed the public would think the police had lost control, which may, in turn, result in public unrest as well as a major security alert. Some of the reluctance to accept the plans stemmed from 2003 when the British Army assisted police by positioning armoured vehicles at Heathrow Airport following a terrorist threat to blow up aircraft as they took off. This caused a public outcry, although many felt it was justified, reassuring, gave an added feeling of security and might help bring the perpetrators into custody sooner.

Operation Temperer was activated in May 2017, following the Manchester Arena bombing. Seeing military personnel take up posts around the country and work closely with armed officers was a great success and the public viewed it as a reassuring boost to their feeling of security.

Operation Temperer worked and remains one of the nation's emergency contingency options.

Officers from the CNC on patrol in Cardiff during the first Operation Temperer deployment in May 2017. They are armed with the Heckler & Koch G36 carbine fitted with the ACOG TA31 RM-CNC advanced optical gun sight, along with the Glock 17 pistol.

Anti-Terrorist Exercise in London

Operation Strongtower 30 June 2015

At the end of June 2015, the Met's anti-terrorist command, along with SC&O19, put on a show for the UK's media. Reporters and photographers were invited to witness a staged exercise across London. The exercise was performed to showcase CTSFO and ARV ability to respond to a series of terrorist attacks.

The training department of SC&O19 spent six months planning a series of rolling mock terrorist attacks that would test the capability and reaction of their assets and resources. Over 1,000 people were involved, including police officers, staff and volunteers who acted as members of the public, victims and terrorists.

CTSFOs deploy over a gate wearing their new grey kit and equipped with the SIG carbine during Operation Strongtower. (*Metropolitan Police*)

ANTI-TERRORIST EXERCISE IN LONDON

Other agencies included the London Ambulance Service, the London Fire Brigade, Transport for London, and the NHS.

A two-day training seminar took place in secret so that everyone, except the emergency services taking part, knew the script. This was done to test the reaction and training of the personnel and give them the maximum challenge. The scenarios were based on the 2008 Mumbai attack, the stabbing attack on two police officers in Australia in 2014, and the *Charlie Hebdo* attacks in Paris in January 2015. It was given the code name Operation Strongtower.

Police commissioner Sir Bernard Hogan-Howe said: 'We intend first of all to stop them from getting to attack. But should we not stop the terrorists in their planning, it's essential we disrupt them in any of the attacks that may take place.'

The exercise was a success and showed once again that our emergency services could work together effectively, given the right training and equipment. The exercise also showcased for the first time the new 'grey kit' of the CTSFOs and the SIG-516 carbines.

Superintendent Chris Nelson of SCO&19 said: 'Whilst Strongtower was the first large-scale exercise, SC&O19 continues to test and exercise all of its tactical capabilities both internally and as part of continuation training as well as with partners on larger scale exercises at sites across London, such as the Royal Mint, Heathrow Airport, and others in the Home Counties.'

A role-playing terrorist opens fire with an automatic weapon to simulate a Mumbai-style attack during an exercise. (*Metropolitan Police*)

Leytonstone Tube Knife Attack

5 December 2015

On Saturday, 5 December 2015, shortly after 7.10pm at the busy underground station at Leytonstone in East London, former mini-cab driver Muhiddin Mire, 29, and originally from Somalia, terrorized members of the public.

Mire, armed with a short-bladed bread knife, had travelled from Stratford to Leytonstone and was walking towards the ticket hall before he pulled out the knife and shouted: 'This is for Syria!' and 'All your blood will be spilled!' He was a terrifying figure, wearing a grey button-up top and a black hat, as he attacked people who were trying to leave the station. He stabbed one of his victims, 56-year-old Lyle Zimmerman, in the neck. Mire had travelled with Zimmerman from Stratford to Leytonstone before the attack. Fortunately, although Mr Zimmerman's wounds were serious, they were not life-threatening. Two others, including a police officer, were injured as they bravely attempted to disarm him.

There were no armed officers at Leytonstone Underground Station at that time, but thankfully officers near to the station were armed with the X-26 Taser. These officers quickly made their way into the station and confronted the tall and aggressive Mire. One officer managed to deploy his Taser but the first cartridge failed to work, possibly because one of the barbs missed. However the officer stuck to his training and reloaded a second cartridge. This time both barbs successfully struck Mire and 50,000 volts brought him to the ground, where police were able to disarm and secure him.

Part of the incident was recorded on passengers' mobile phones and clearly showed Mire with a knife. It highlighted the bravery of members of the public who were prepared to take on the attacker. One man fended off Mire's knife thrusts by using his backpack as a shield and other passengers threw bottles at him. One person was recorded shouting: 'You ain't no Muslim, Bruv.' Thankfully no one was killed in the attack.

Mire was later convicted of attempted murder and given a minimum prison term of eight-and-a-half years. Owing to his diagnosed schizophrenia, it was declassified from terrorism to an attack by a man suffering from mental illness. However, it was clear that Mire had been self-radicalized from the internet as he had Syria-related material on his mobile phone. Frustratingly, his family had previously sought medical attention for him in a bid to get him sectioned under the Mental Health Act.

It is interesting to note how easy it seems for ISIS to prey on people with mental illnesses and how difficult it is for the authorities to monitor and assess the risk those people are to themselves and the public.

Above left: CCTV shows the moment an unarmed officer deployed his X-26 Taser against attacker Muhiddin Mire after he had injured two.

Above right: A tube traveller attempts to fend off attacker Muhiddin Mire using his backpack as a shield at Leytonstone Underground Station.

It seems inevitable that these types of attacks will continue, but it also begs the question of how we should arm our police. Clearly, Taser is not the safest way of dealing with a violent attacker armed with a knife intent on killing (terrorist or not), as it can fail or might not deploy properly due to myriad reasons. However, it is certainly better than nothing.

In most other countries, police would have shot this attacker. Thankfully he survived and we were able to put him through the due processes of law. However, it was a miracle that no one was killed.

PART 8

HEROES AND VILLAINS

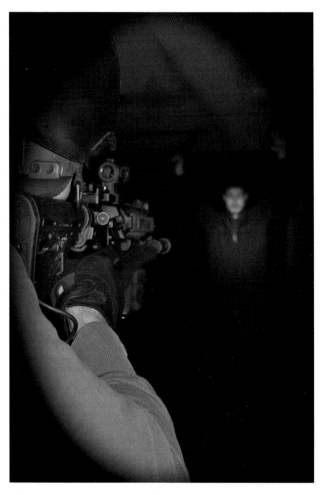

The surrender of an armed subject is taken by torchlight in this 'subdued light' training scenario. (*Stephen Smith*)

NCA Officer Wins George Medal

First Non-Home Office Police Shooting Incident 23 May 2014

For some years there have been security and law-enforcement agencies who are not affiliated to the Met, but who have been authorized by the Home Office to carry firearms in London on armed operations. There have been no recorded instances of these officers discharging their weapons in London, until now.

On 23 May 2014, at 10.45pm, members of the National Crime Agency (NCA) were conducting a surveillance operation in West Green Road, Tottenham. They were following gang members who they believed to be involved in serious offences including firearms and drugs. The day's observations had finished at a pool bar near West Green Lane and during the surveillance it became apparent that the subjects were involved in a feud with another gang. After a time of inactivity, the operation was stood down for the day and one of the officers, Martin Finney, who was armed for his own protection, started to return to his vehicle.

He noticed a vehicle pull up containing four black males and thought something didn't look right. One of the men in the car got out, walked towards the pool bar, calmly drew out a handgun and fired three shots through the window into the bar, which contained around thirty people.

Finney was alone and not wearing body armour due to the nature of the surveillance. He later said: 'I could not walk away and do nothing. I had to act.' He drew his Glock 17 pistol from the covert holster on his belt and identified himself as an armed police officer by shouting 'Armed Police!' The shooter, Sedat Meric, turned and opened fire at the officer, narrowly missing Finney's head. He started running and Finney returned fire and gave chase. Later in court, the officer stated: 'I wasn't going to cower behind a car. I wanted to arrest him. I just tried to make myself as small as possible and get a good shot back. He went around the corner and I moved for cover. I could see his eyes looking at me and the gun come up.' He went on to say: 'At the back of my mind I didn't know if he had already killed someone. His firing was totally indiscriminate – he had no regard for life. I was terrified somebody might have been hit.'

The ensuing shootout moved down the street with both combatants ducking and shooting round parked cars. Both Meric and Finney exchanged shots but the shootout ended when Meric's self-loading pistol ran out of rounds, at which point he put the gun on the ground and raised his hands in an act of surrender.

Finney was reluctant to go forward at first, believing it was a ploy to draw him out of cover and maybe the man's associates would be waiting to open fire on him. Cautiously, he approached Meric and arrested him for possession of a firearm, with intent to endanger life.

Above left: Grainy CCTV image of Sedat Meric as he points his pistol and opens fire at the window of a busy pool hall in Tottenham.

Above right: Here you can just make out Martin Finney begin to give chase while returning fire with his Glock 17 pistol.

The incident was partially captured on CCTV and before long posted on social media. It is unbelievable that no one was hurt by Meric's indiscriminate firing.

Sedat Meric was sentenced to fifteen years' imprisonment. Martin Finney, who had been a firearms officer for twelve years, was awarded the George Medal for his tenacity and bravery. Finney had displayed the kind of courage we can admire and celebrate and I applaud the issue of this medal. Sadly many other officers' bravery goes unrecognized due to the public reaction following some shooting incidents.

Murder in Edmonton

ARV Officers Overpower Suspect 4 September 2014

This account demonstrates not only the bravery, determination and restraint of our armed police officers but also shows how, on rare occasions, peaceful communities can suddenly be turned into scenes of complete horror.

On Thursday, 4 September 2014 at 1pm, the residents of a suburban street in Edmonton, North London, were stunned by an apparently motiveless attack on an 82-year-old woman as she put out the washing in her garden.

Residents called police following sightings of a man armed with a curved-bladed machete, who was terrorizing people in the street. The man, later identified as Nicholas Salvador, had tried to attack two people by their homes but they managed to escape and run to safety. Salvador, who was stripped to his waist, then decapitated a cat in the street.

Due to the violent nature of the incident, police assigned ARVs to the scene along with a helicopter, which quickly arrived overhead, and which captured the horrendous events that followed on its CCTV.

Before the ARV arrived, Salvador moved around to the rear gardens where he came across elderly Palmira Silva, who was oblivious to the danger she was in. She went over to the bare-chested man at her fence but after a short exchange he attacked her with the machete. She stood no chance and after stabbing her repeatedly he decapitated her. The crew of India Nine

Above left: Topless Nicholas Salvador, who is armed with a machete and a pole, goes on a rampage after killing and decapitating 82-year-old Palmira Silva.

Above right: Armed and deadly, he walks down the street terrorizing residents before returning to the rear gardens where he encountered armed police.

Nine (the police helicopter) were shocked by the brutality of the attack. The radio operator put out an urgent call to the officers attending: 'Any units down on Nightingale Road, get to as many premises as you can and get people away from this location.' He continued: 'He has decapitated a woman…he is agitated and lethal. He needs taking out.' The commentary to those officers en route was far from the calm, unflappable radio voice they were used to hearing.

Salvador went through some gardens and back out in the street where he struck at people in cars with his machete, before moving back into the rear gardens to continue his forty-five-minute rampage.

The radio operator of India Nine Nine told the officers in the street that there were two children playing in one of the gardens and that they needed to be rescued. The officers wasted no time finding them and getting them to safety.

Other officers worked feverishly, evacuating residents in the houses that backed onto the gardens and forcing front doors in an effort to alert people to the crazed knifeman crashing through fences like a human bulldozer. People climbed out of windows and escaped over flat roofs to the safety of the police in the road.

Former ARV officer Bernie Hamilton who attended the scene told me: 'You could hear the distress in the radio operator's voice as he told us about the two kids in the garden of the house he had broken into.'

Salvador had kicked in the back door of a house, which was divided into flats. He was now in the front room of the ground-floor flat. Bernie recalled what happened next:

'As we deployed I could see him through the window in the front room, soaked in blood – it was literally dripping off him. He was hitting things in the room with the machete. I brought my G36 carbine up and entered the flat through the open UPVC door. I went down the hallway, all the time hearing him smashing things up. It was imperative that we stopped him before he killed anyone else.

'I attempted to kick the door in, leading into the living room so we could get vision on him. It was one of those things I instantly regretted as my foot went through the door panel and the door stayed shut. I had the situation where there was a man in the room with a machete and my foot was temporarily stuck in the door. I thought I may have to shoot through the door to stop him from chopping my foot off. Thankfully that didn't happen, my colleague behind me managed to pull me free and we forced open the door.

'We entered the room and my number two immediately fired his Taser. The man went down. It did its work for five seconds but as soon as the shock wore off, he began crawling across the floor and the barbs became dislodged. He made it to the meter cupboard and crawled in. I managed to get my foot on the machete, my colleague managed to get one cuff on him. He was slippery with blood and wanted to fight us.

'We repeatedly tasered him, but each time we pulled him out, he fought us. He even bit through my trousers into my calf, it was very painful. This fight went on for what seemed like an age, I think we tasered him six times in total. All the while he was hanging onto the gas main and trying to pull it off the wall.

I was worried the Taser might ignite the gas if he succeeded but thankfully that was never put to the test. There were other officers helping us now but there was Taser wire everywhere, it was like a spider's web so most of us kept getting residual shocks every time it was applied. I noticed his arm was cut down to the tendons, probably from where he had punched through windows.

'It was an epic battle, but in the end we managed to get the Taser deployed effectively and got him out and cuffed.'

But this wasn't the end. Even handcuffed, Salvador continued to kick and bite, so much so that the ambulance crew, with the help of the officers, found it necessary to roll him in carpet to protect them from injury.

It was reported that Salvador had trained as a cage fighter. If true, this would explain some of his determination and resilience to resist the officers, one of whom fractured his wrist during the struggle.

Once the crazed murderer was secured, officers located the body of Mrs Silva. It was a terrible event, which shocked everyone there. Initial news coverage reported it as some kind of terrorist attack. However, it turned out Salvador was local to the area and it was soon ascertained that there was no link to terrorism and the man was suffering from a serious mental disorder.

Further enquiries revealed that there was no connection between the suspect and his victim, Mrs Silva, who was a widow of five years and a popular local lady whose family owned and ran the local café.

Detective Inspector John Sandlin said of the arresting officers: 'They put themselves in extreme danger to protect the public.' Mayor of London Boris Johnson said: 'London is a safe city and incidents like this are very rare. I'd like to commend the bravery shown by the officers involved in keeping other members of the public safe during a very volatile situation.'

Two days later, 25-year-old Nicholas Salvador, originally from Nigeria, who had lived in the UK since he was 14, appeared at Highbury Magistrates' Court charged with Mrs Silva's murder and assaulting a police officer.

In June the following year, Salvador stood trial for murder. Recorder Nicholas Hilliard QC told him: It is established beyond any doubt that you killed Mrs Silva in an attack of extraordinary brutality and ferocity. You thought you were encountering a demonic force…you could not have been more deluded. Nobody who saw it could forget the mild and trusting way Mrs Silva approached you over the wall while you were brandishing a knife.'

The court heard how Salvador stabbed her repeatedly before cutting off her head. CCTV footage also showed Salvador killing two cats before targeting Mrs Silva. The court heard he had lost his job three days before the incident and was a heavy smoker of skunk cannabis. They also heard evidence from two psychiatrists that he was suffering from paranoid schizophrenia and had been staying with friends just three doors down from Mrs Silva at the time of the attack.

Nicholas Salvador was found not guilty of murder due to diminished responsibility and was detained indefinitely in a psychiatric hospital.

Paranoid schizophrenic Nicholas Salvador, who was found not guilty of murder due to diminished responsibility.

Once again, this case displayed the courage of the police officers, some of whom were unarmed as they arrived on scene. The arrival of the ARVs was decisive in maintaining the safety of the public and they exercised great restraint by deploying less-lethal measures to arrest him. The ARV officers quite rightly received the Commissioner's Commendation Awards for bravery. Other police at the scene were also commended for their actions that day.

The Dean Joseph Shooting

Man Killed in Flat Armed With Knife 4-5 September 2014

Julie Moyses, a 54-year-old teaching assistant and mother of two, lived alone in the basement flat of a mid-terraced Georgian house in Shepperton Road, Islington, North London. She had previously been in a relationship with 40-year-old Dean Joseph, but had ended it due to his violent behaviour towards her. Joseph, who had difficulty accepting her decision, made several attempts to change her mind and, as Julie grew more fearful of him, she had no option but to take out a non-molestation order, banning him from going anywhere near her or her flat.

Contemporary photo of the front of the premises in Shepperton Road, showing the window through which Dean Joseph was shot and the small area in which the officers had to work. (*Stephen Smith*)

THE DEAN JOSEPH SHOOTING

Shortly after 11pm on Thursday, 4 September 2014, local residents heard a commotion and the sound of breaking glass coming from outside Julie's flat. Neighbours called 999 claiming a man appeared to be breaking into the address.

Local unarmed officers from Islington Police Station were assigned and PC Clark was one of the first on scene. While his colleague went around the back to cut off the escape of any burglar who may still be in the premises, he made his way to a position just outside the broken basement window, set half below and half above ground level. A narrow, restricted passage separated the outer wall of the building and the front garden, where there was a small parapet wall. He could hear noises coming from inside the room and some sort of struggle. He reached through the broken window, pulled back the curtain and illuminated the dark bedroom with his torch.

What PC Clark saw, and the events that followed, will probably stay with him for the rest of his life. His torch picked out two people; a man dressed in dark clothing with short dark hair brandishing a 7-inch, bladed kitchen knife and a terrified woman in night clothes. The man immediately turned towards the officer and shouted, 'Stay where you are. If you even try and come in, I will kill you.' Worried for the safety of the woman, PC Clark remained where he was but kept his torch shining into the room.

Joseph had smashed out the bottom panels of glass of the sash window leading into the bedroom of the apartment. He had forced Julie Moyses into the rear corner of the room between a cupboard and the doorway. Julie was sitting with her knees drawn up to her chin, cowering from Joseph who faced her. He had hold of her arm, pinning her into the corner, and was holding a knife to her neck and waving it around, threatening to slit her throat. There was a second knife close to Joseph on the bedroom floor. PC Clark had no option but to remain outside the window and would be there for the next ninety minutes.

It was accepted later in court that Joseph had come prepared, bringing two 7-inch razor-sharp kitchen knives with him. They were believed to have come from shared belongings that Joseph had taken when Julie had split from him. He had kept these possessions with him at the hostel from where he was currently being evicted due to unreasonable behaviour. Julie later described how Joseph had come through the window with the knife shouting: 'You're going to get it tonight, bitch.'

Because of the threat to life, ARVs were dispatched and a police negotiator was called out from home and began making her way. Local officers continued to contain the premises and do their best in what was now a hostage situation. At 11.30pm, armed officers from SC&O19 began to arrive and the control of the incident fell to them.

The ARV officers quickly came up with a plan. It was decided to put a covert armed containment on the premises (so as not to identify themselves as armed officers in case the hostage-taker reacted adversely). The focus was on the bedroom, now known as the 'stronghold' (a term used in police and military circles to describe a location where hostages are being held).

PC Clark would continue talking with Joseph – as he seemed to have established a rapport and was making some headway in calming him down – until the negotiator arrived. Meanwhile some officers would prepare for an emergency entry into the premises should the need arise to save life.

As further SC&O19 assets began to appear, they were briefed by an officer from the first ARV to arrive. He would remain running the control for the duration of the incident. Paramedics also arrived and were held on standby.

One of the ARV officers, PC Stuart Brown, went round to the rear of the building. He gained access through other flats to have a look for any other entry points at the rear or points where the suspect might escape. Having concluded his reconnaissance and finding it covered, he joined onto the rear of the entry team.

PC Brown understood how these incidents could go from relative calm to extreme violence in the blink of an eye. He noticed that the two officers who were standing either side of the basement window next to PC Clark were out of sight of the couple in the room. They were armed with Glock pistols and Tasers but no rifles. He felt relieved when the officer in charge of the incident directed him to provide firearms cover into the room with his G36.

He was aware of the plan and understood that they were still attempting to remain covert as far as firearms were concerned as the situation might escalate if Joseph was confronted with a firearm. If Joseph had any intention of harming himself, or his hostage, he might see it as an opportunity to force what is known in armed police circles as a 'suicide by cop', and this could end very badly for Julie Moyses.

It was 12.20am when PC Brown moved across the front of the premises in the dark, trying not to make too much noise on the stone chippings in the small front garden. The basement window was relatively small – about 3-feet wide by 4-feet high – but big enough for Joseph to have forced his way through into the bedroom. PC Brown quietly lowered himself into the sitting position on the raised edge of the parapet, next to PC Clark who had, by now, been talking to Joseph for forty minutes.

He thought that if he positioned himself beside PC Clark, he would not be seen by the people in the room, owing to the beam of light from Clark's torch that he was holding out in front of them. The officer made his presence known to PC Clark then settled down into the tight space they now shared. He was able to place his feet on the windowsill and quickly brought his G36 carbine up, placing the selector to fire, and resting his elbows on his knees.

PC Brown looked into the room and assessed the situation. As well as the light from the torch, there was ambient light from a wall-mounted TV to the couple's right. It was tuned to a late-night casino channel, showing roulette. He could also make out that the room was a good-sized double bedroom and the bedhead was against the wall to their left.

The two people were approximately 15 feet away from him. He had a clear view of Joseph, who was sitting facing Julie with his back at an oblique angle to the officers.

There was a 2-feet high drawer unit obscuring the lower part of Joseph's back. This helped rule out the use of the X-26 Taser as the spread of barbs would not be able to deploy without one of them hitting the unit, rendering it ineffective – that along with the fact the Taser would not be ideal to use in a hostage situation where the hostage-taker was armed with a lethal weapon.

Brown saw Joseph was holding a large knife in his right hand, which he now held against his own neck, confirming the officers' earlier worry that he might self-harm if police attempted to intervene. He was gripping Julie's right forearm with his left hand close to her wrist, preventing her from getting up.

What troubled PC Brown was the close proximity of the two people to each other. If he had to engage Joseph, the bullet or even part of the bullet – if it fragmented – might over penetrate and injure or even kill Julie. He aimed his G36 between Joseph's left shoulder blade and spine, hoping that if he were forced to shoot, the round would exit from the right side of the chest thus missing

Julie. Although it would be a narrow margin of error, he was determined to afford this petrified lady the best chance of survival should things get nasty. He settled down for what might be a long night.

With some help from the officers either side of him, PC Clark continued the stressful job of calming Joseph down, although Joseph continued to threaten to slit Julie's throat.

The other two ARV officers were huddled either side of the window relaying updates to the police firearms control and their fellow officers on the containment. They were doing what they were trained to do, which was to wait patiently. Only one person would have the final say in how this played out and that was the unpredictable, armed and violent Joseph. Time moved slowly for the officers, but each painful moment must have seemed like an eternity for Julie Moyses.

Her ordeal had now been going on for ten minutes short of two hours. It's hard to imagine the fear and tension in that room, with Joseph not budging an inch despite the noble efforts of PC Clark to make him see reason. They were still awaiting the arrival of the police negotiator.

During this time, Joseph had been holding Julie's arms in front of her, forcing her to remain sitting in the corner of the room, the veiled threat of the knife (although still held against his own neck) ever present. PC Brown was fully aware that in most cases 'action beats reaction', and so he was watching for any signs that Joseph was about to harm Julie. He knew that he would have to interpret Joseph's intentions should he move the knife from his own neck. Was he intending to put it down, or was he intending to stab or slash at Julie's throat? He had been tracking Joseph through the Aimpoint sights of his Heckler & Koch G36 carbine and every few minutes he would look over the sights to give his eyes some relief. He still hoped PC Clark could talk some sense into this man.

As an experienced ARV officer, PC Brown understood the possibility of firing as a reaction to any sudden movement. He had the presence of mind to place his finger alongside the trigger guard of the weapon, and not on the trigger, until he was ready to shoot, thus giving him that extra split-second of thinking time before opening fire.

It was now 12.55am on 5 September and the standoff must have felt like a lifetime to all those involved. Later, at St Pancras Coroner's Court, PC Brown would describe what happened in the following few moments:

'I don't recall any words being said by either party. I just recall, all of a sudden, the knife went from his neck. He thrust his arm out to Julie Moyses' neck and the blade went in contact with her. He thrust it really hard into her neck. He pinned her physically in the corner with the blade of the knife on her neck and at that moment in time I believed he was going to kill her and that was what was happening in front of me – he was about to kill Miss Moyses.

'I knew at that moment he was intending to kill her and I was the only person in that whole siege scenario who could do anything at that moment, and the only thing I could do to stop it was to fire a shot at him.'

Julie Moyses also gave a statement, which was read out in court: 'The policemen [PC Clark] was saying, "Let her go". Dean was shouting, "There's nothing to live for. One of us is going to die tonight." At one point Dean put the knife tight to my throat and I really thought Dean was going to kill me then. That was when I heard the bang. I heard a loud bang and a flash. I saw Dean's face in front of me and I saw him sinking like something had happened to him.'

PC Brown had fired a shot from his G36 carbine, aimed at Joseph's central body mass and couldn't understand why Joseph had not fallen down. He told the jury: 'He still had the knife in his hand and was moving back towards Miss Moyses, but I still believed he intended to kill her. I thought everything that's happened and he's still hell bent on doing it. I had no other option but to fire a second shot.'

This time Joseph fell backwards and away from Julie. At that point two distraction stun grenades were tossed into the room, one through the window Joseph had climbed through and the other through a window at the rear of the premises. The front door was broken down and the officers made their entry into the smoke-filled room, trying to pick out the hostage and the hostage-taker. They needed to be sure there was no longer any threat to Julie Moyses or themselves.

To add to the confusion, the stun grenades had activated the smoke alarms, which continued for a while until the smoke had cleared.

Dean Joseph was critically wounded on the floor of the room. Julie Moyses was crouched in the corner where she had spent most of her ordeal, clearly shaken and terrified. The entry team gathered her up and led her from the room.

Other officers began first aid on Joseph. The two bullets had struck him from the left side of his body. The first entered between his shoulder blade and spine, the second – fired as he had turned side-on and twisted towards Julie – through his tricep, entering his torso through the armpit. After a brief survey of the wounds the officers commenced CPR.

Once he saw his colleagues make their entry into the room, PC Brown placed his selector to 'safe' and lowered the muzzle of his carbine. He remembered feeling a reassuring tap on his shoulder from a colleague. He got up from his cramped position and was directed to sit in one of the ARVs and another officer sat with him. He saw Julie Moyses being led towards an ambulance by local officers. He later commented that 'seeing her safe was a tremendous boost'.

Sadly, the hostage negotiator arrived too late and was receiving a briefing when the shots were fired. Whether her intervention would have changed the outcome remains unknown.

The ambulance crew, who had been on standby, were led into the room. They allowed the officers to continue doing CPR as they put drips in and hooked Joseph up to the ECG. Unable to get a trolley into the confined space, they placed Joseph onto a canvas stretcher and helped the officers evacuate him to the ambulance.

Their journey to hospital was no easy matter. They soon came to the conclusion that if they carried on, he would not survive the journey. Their only option was to stop the ambulance and meet the doctors from the Helicopter Emergency Medical Service (HEMS) as soon as possible. The HEMS crew were on their way from the Royal London Hospital to join them (they travelled by road as there were no suitable landing sites for the helicopter close to where the ambulance had stopped). The ambulance was on the forecourt of Shoreditch Fire Station. The doctors opened up Joseph's chest and began to massage his heart but at 1.20am, after the medics had fought hard to save his life, he was pronounced dead.

At the coroner's court, the senior coroner Mary Hassell, asked PC Brown, 'When you look back, do you think you were right?' PC Brown replied, 'Yes I believe I saved Miss Moyses life that day and if I hadn't acted we'd all be sitting here for an inquest into Miss Moyses. I had no other option than to prevent death.'

The jury returned a lawful killing verdict. But they also concluded that there may have been other contributory factors, including inadequate communication and the fact that Joseph was never made aware armed officers were present, or warned that he might be shot. They believed that because there was already a uniform presence, the police could no longer be covert and should have announced the fact that firearms were present. PC Brown had argued that they remained covert with the firearms as announcing they were armed police may have risked Julie's life or forced Joseph to react in a negative way. The jury also made reference to the fact there was no guidance from specially trained negotiators.

This was the first fatal police shooting since Mark Duggan in August 2011 and the IPCC were keen to do a thorough job. Their findings were released following the inquest and, after considering several aspects of the case, concluded that the officer who shot Joseph did so after believing the hostage was becoming distressed and Joseph was becoming a greater threat to her and him. The IPCC cleared the police for not explicitly warning Joseph about the presence of armed officers and validated the police decision not to deploy the less-lethal Taser first.

During the inquest, Leslie Thomas, the lawyer representing Joseph's family, claimed the officers had conferred over certain points prior to making their statements. Although this was within the permitted rules regarding conferring, the IPCC looked into the matter and cleared police of any 'deliberate attempt' to mislead investigators. They also found no evidence that any officer involved acted criminally or in a way that would justify disciplinary proceedings.

In August 2018, the family of Dean Joseph were in court claiming damages against the Metropolitan Police. They stated that there were shortcomings with the planning of the operation, that PC Brown had lied in his evidence, and that the shooting was unnecessary.

On 9 August 2018, judge Alan Saggerson found against the family stating that 'the officer should be commended rather than criticized' and that the challenges to PC Brown's integrity were 'without justification or adequate foundation and are to be deplored.' He went on to say:

> 'The fatal shooting of Dean Joseph has, in my judgment, been proven to have been absolutely necessary, justified and proportionate in these extremely difficult, dangerous and volatile circumstances.
>
> 'The officers, and in particular PC Brown, honestly and genuinely believed that Mr Joseph was within a second or two of stabbing Ms Moyses in the throat, cutting her throat or stabbing her in the upper torso. The imminent threat did not change after the first, apparently ineffective, shot. PC Brown had no other option open to him but to shoot on each of two occasions where there was a real risk of a fatality, without warning. Had he not done so, the only result would have been the probably fatal stabbing or cutting of the throat of Ms Moyses.'

This verdict spelled the end of a long and stressful period of allegations and unfair criticism of the officer's integrity.

The incident sadly ended in the death of Dean Joseph, but he had gone out that night intent on terrorizing or causing harm to Julie Moyses. His actions ultimately forced the officer into firing those two shots, which fatally wounded him. PC Stuart Brown's actions saved a life that night.

Trident Officer Wounded in Hackney

15 October 2015

At around 12.45pm on Thursday, 15 October 2015 in Scriven Street, Hackney, East London, officers from Operation Trident (a Met Police unit set up to tackle gun crime in the capital's Afro-Caribbean communities), supported by SC&O19 officers from the ARVs, attended an address following intelligence-led information that there was a firearm hidden there.

This operation had followed a spate of gang-related violence in the local area, culminating in a fatal shooting in Hackney three weeks earlier, when a 25-year-old man was shot dead in a busy high street.

Owing to the geography of the estate, it was difficult identifying and containing the rear of the premises but the officers did this as best they could.

As police gained entry at the front door, a man appeared at the rear window. A neighbour said: 'A black man appeared at the window opposite. They ordered him to remain inside but he threw something out of the window. The next thing I know I see him running over the rooftops. I then heard a loud bang, a single bang coming from Scriven Street.'

The containment had failed and a suspect, who was possibly armed, was escaping onto the estate. Things were going horribly wrong. The suspect, 31-year-old gang member Tyrone Henry, had escaped leaving his shoes behind and was desperately trying to evade police. He was now running from Scriven Street towards a busy junction with Lovelace Street and Haggerston Road that came out opposite a row of shops. Under his arm, rolled up in kitchen paper inside a Tesco carrier bag, was a loaded Beretta pistol.

SC&O19 officers were quick to give chase and had managed to catch up with him by the shops. According to Henry later at his trial, he was tripped by one of these officers and his gun went off. Either way, the round hit a detective who had gone to assist the officers to cut off Henry's escape. The bullet had entered just below his left shoulder and exited out his back. He collapsed in the middle of the street.

Henry was quickly overpowered and arrested for attempted murder of a police officer. The wounded Trident officer was treated at the scene by police, then taken to hospital by air ambulance where he was stabilized and later made a good recovery.

Henry was later charged with attempted murder of a police officer, possession of a firearm with intent to endanger life and being a prohibited person in possession of a firearm. He pleaded guilty to possession of a prohibited weapon and appeared at the Old Bailey to answer the charge of possessing a firearm with intent to endanger life. The other charge of attempted murder had not been proceeded with.

TRIDENT OFFICER WOUNDED IN HACKNEY

The jury acquitted him for this offence as police could not prove beyond doubt that he had deliberately fired the gun at them. Forensic officers had examined the pistol and found that the weapon's safety catch was in the 'safe' position when police recovered it but as it had discharged a round it was defective.

Henry admitted that he had taken delivery of the pistol the day before the raid so he could 'sort out a beef between his friends'.

He added that he jumped from the window as the police raided the flat, and he had picked up the gun from beneath his son's pushchair in the garden where he had hidden it, then he had climbed over the roof 'to get away from the missus' house'. Detective Chief Inspector Kevin Baldwin said: 'Tyrone Henry may not have pulled the trigger of the gun that shot the officer, but had he not been in possession of an illegal firearm it would not have been on the streets. It was fortunate that no officers or members of the public were killed by this defective pistol.'

With two previous firearms convictions, Henry was sentenced to seven years' imprisonment for possession of a prohibited weapon.

Commander Duncan Bell said: 'It shows the tireless actions of police, which demonstrated the officers' selfless dedication to duty. This incident recalls the very real risks our police officers face on a day-to-day basis while protecting the safety of Londoners.'

Moped and Scooter Gangs

If asked which types of crime are having the biggest impact on Londoners right now, I would say moped and scooter gangs. I don't know anyone who has not either been directly affected, knows someone who has been the victim, or witnessed these criminals in action. In 2017, in London alone there were 16,000 reported scooter or moped attacks.

These criminals are generally youngsters who steal scooter-type bikes or small motorcycles then go hunting for victims to rob, or perform high-speed snatches of phones or handbags. Their mode of transport means they're highly mobile and hard to catch. They are opportunists and will think nothing of using extreme violence to achieve their purpose. In July 2017, one such gang stabbed Danny Pearce to death in Greenwich and in October that same year Abdul Samad was killed in Maida Vale.

Never a week goes by when these gangs aren't mentioned in the local or national press. In 2018 there were over sixty moped-related robberies per day. It is becoming an epidemic.

Group of two bikes with both pillions preparing to rob a woman with a small child of her handbag. These robbers were chased off by scaffolders from a nearby lorry. (*Amanda Holden*)

MOPED AND SCOOTER GANGS

The perpetrators use hammers, knives, machetes and sometimes acid, and usually the pillion passenger threatens and robs. They target mobile-phones users, snatching the phone out of an unsuspecting victim's hand as they ride past slowly. They often stop outside cafés, walk in and snatch laptops from tables or handbags from the backs of chairs and make their escape on the back of the bike.

The moped gangs sometimes work as a pair on one bike, but mostly they work in groups of two bikes, riding up to victims on either side to trap them, or using the bikes to shepherd their victim until they're trapped between the two bikes and have nowhere to go. Occasionally, up to eight bikes with pillions will come together for big robberies on high-end shops. These methods have been used in several high-value robberies in Oxford Street and Regent Street where they smash their way in with sledgehammers while others keep guard outside.

In June 2018, moped robbers attacked comedian Michael McIntyre, smashing his car window with hammers as he waited outside his children's school, and grabbing his expensive watch from his wrist.

Many of these attacks are filmed by onlookers who post the footage on the internet, underlining how vulnerable we all are to this form of attack. From a civilian standpoint, I can understand the anger at the fact that police cannot always chase these moped riders if they remove their helmets, for fear the suspect may fall off and become injured! However, recent changes to police tactics means they can now use their vehicles to knock them off their bikes, whether they are wearing a helmet or not.

We must look at the law around these crimes and find a way of combatting this modern-day menace, which has become the favoured method of street robbery.

Murder and Highway Robbery in Maida Vale

Moped Robbers Hunted Down by ARVs 16 October 2017

On Monday, 16 October 2017, Nathan Gilmaney, 19, and 18-year-old Troy Thomas, both young career criminals with convictions for robbery, drugs and other offences, were out on a stolen moped doing knifepoint robberies. Their aim was to steal mobile phones to sell, as well as cash and jewellery. Both believed it was their right to take whatever they wanted from anyone they cared to rob.

Their trail of violence was partly tracked on local council and private CCTV footage and was described by a crown court judge as 'chilling'. Thomas, the driver – at the time on bail for

Left, Troy Thomas, 18, the moped driver and right, Nathan Gilmaney, 19, the knifeman. (*Metropolitan Police*)

robbery – and Gilmaney, the pillion passenger and knifeman, were out on a robbery spree that would end in murder.

They robbed their first victim in Maida Vale with Gilmaney stabbing the man in the back, puncturing his lung. An hour later they attacked another man in Paddington, who was with his elderly aunt. They stole jewellery and money at knifepoint before Gilmaney stabbed the man in the stomach.

Their next victim was charity youth worker Abdul Samad, who was returning home to his parents' address in Maida Vale just before midnight. As he was walking along the pavement towards the house, they rode up on the moped and demanded his iPhone. Gilmaney had a large lock knife in his hand. Abdul Samad handed over his phone and the pair rode off.

When they realized they needed his PIN to unlock the phone, they spun the moped round and pulled up next to Abdul a few yards further down the road. What happened next was captured on CCTV. Abdul apparently told them his PIN and they unlocked the phone. He was then seen handing over his wallet. He offered no resistance at all during these two encounters but, for no apparent reason, Gilmaney lunged forward at him striking him in the chest.

CCTV footage of charity youth worker Abdul Samad handing over his wallet just moments before being fatally stabbed in the chest by Nathan Gilmaney.

Abdul Samad who was murdered following a moped robbery.

Gilmaney was heard to shout, 'Let's go!' and the pair, who hadn't even got off the moped to carry out the robbery, rode off down the road leaving Abdul Samad, to stagger to his parents' doorstep where he collapsed in a pool of his own blood.

A Trojan ARV was on patrol some way away and answered a call on the radio to a man in Maida Vale needing urgent first aid. The ARV had a comprehensive first aid kit and all the crew were trained in advanced first aid. When they arrived, local officers were already on scene and an ambulance with paramedics was just arriving. The paramedics performed emergency surgery in the street but could do little to stop the bleed. Abdul Samad had been stabbed in the heart and died a short time later.

The local sergeant told the ARV crew that the man was possibly the victim of moped robbers, who had carried out a series of knifepoint robberies earlier that evening. The local officers had already dealt with some of the victims of Thomas and Gilmaney and had gleaned good descriptions of the pair, which they gave to the ARV crew. The driver was wearing a light top and had a white helmet, and the pillion wore dark clothing and had a black helmet. The officers noted down these descriptions and left to patrol the local area.

Unbeknown to the officers at the time, after murdering Abdul Samad the pair had tried to rob a man in nearby Golborne Road but he had managed to escape. Undeterred, they saw their next victim further down the street and trapped him between two parked cars. He threw them his bag and phone before managing to flee.

Most likely, while the ARV was with the murder victim and talking to the police sergeant, the pair were making a visit to a block of flats in Maida Vale, where they sold Abdul's phone. It was now 1am and they donned balaclavas to hunt for more victims.

After twenty minutes of searching, they attempted to rob a man in Porchester Road. Gilmaney stabbed him in the stomach after he refused to let go of his phone. A short time later they followed a man who was talking on his phone and Gilmaney stabbed him in the arm before snatching it. The pair rode down Portobello Road where they snatched the phone from a woman's hand before riding off, then at 2am Gilmaney punched a 16-year-old girl in the face after she had handed him her handbag.

It was now shortly after 2am and the pair were targeting what would be their final victim, a man walking home. The man handed over his wallet but true to form Gilmaney stabbed him in the stomach.

The Trojan ARV had remained in the area and was doing a search of popular moped haunts when they saw two men, who matched the description, sitting on the kerb near to a moped. As they drove towards them, the pair got on the moped and shot off. The moped drove down a number of back streets with the ARV in hot pursuit. The pillion, Gilmaney, removed his helmet and waved it at the officers (he believed that this action would usually mean police would have to abandon the pursuit for fear of causing injury to the riders) but, owing to the seriousness of the crimes and the risk the riders posed, the police were having none of it. Officers in the police operations room had authorized the continued pursuit.

In an act of desperation Thomas drove the moped down a dead-end street and attempted to mount the pavement to drive back up. However, due to the weight of rider and pillion, the bike would not get up the kerb. The ARV pulled up almost on top of the bike, but as the crew began to deploy the two murderers ran back up the street.

MURDER AND HIGHWAY ROBBERY IN MAIDA VALE

The driver of the ARV remained and secured the moped, while the two crew members gave chase on foot. One officer fired his Taser twice during the foot chase but, as happens frequently when firing at a moving target, the barbs did not deploy effectively. As the two officers continued the chase, they gained ground on Gilmaney and one rugby-tackled him to the ground. During the brief struggle Gilmaney received a black eye. He was arrested on suspicion of murder and handcuffed.

Thomas, meanwhile, had managed to run off down a side street. The police helicopter, which was already airborne over London and had been assigned to help with the chase, picked him up on its night vision camera. He was seen taking his helmet off and looking for a place to hide, dumping the helmet in the road and crawling under a big 4X4 car parked nearby. The helicopter passed the information on to the original ARV, which had since picked up one of the officers who had detained Gilmaney. They were now in the same street, and with the police helicopter's help, were guided to the car that Thomas had crawled under. The officers unceremoniously dragged Thomas out from his hiding place and arrested him on suspicion of murder.

The suspects had property in their possession belonging to seven robbery victims. Three of those were stabbing victims. A trained police search team was brought in to search the streets for the murder weapon and found the lock knife used in the murder of Abdul Samad. Statements were taken from all the surviving victims and these would be used to build a watertight case against the two would-be highwaymen turned ruthless murderers.

It had been a successful night for the Trojan unit and the Met, but a sad one for the family of Abdul Samad. Thankfully all the other victims of Gilmaney's savagery survived.

At the trial, the jury was shown CCTV footage of the arrests, along with their four-hour robbery spree, during which they had stabbed and assaulted most of their victims with callous disregard for their lives.

Judge Richard Marks QC sentenced Gilmaney to life with a minimum of twenty-seven years and Thomas to a minimum of twenty-two years. In sentencing the pair he added: 'Abdul

Above left: Troy Thomas, who is fleeing from police attempts to hide under a parked car, unaware the police helicopter is watching his heat source. (*Metropolitan Police*)

Above right: Two ARV officers drag hapless murderer Troy Thomas out from under the parked car. (*Metropolitan Police*)

Samad was an outstanding young man in his twenties, engaged to be married with his whole life ahead of him. Your wicked stabbing of him has left his family understandably utterly devastated.' Gilmaney shouted obscenities after he was sentenced and the public gallery had to be cleared after his repeated outbursts.

Gilmaney's barrister, Dexter Dias QC, stated that his client had attention deficit hyperactivity disorder and an IQ of barely sixty. After the verdict, Detective Inspector Shaun Fitzgerald said of the pair: 'The teenagers believed they had the right to threaten and rob wherever they wanted, often stabbing their victims for no other reason at all but to prove they could.'

Once again London's ARVs had proved their worth by removing two highly dangerous murderers from its streets and displaying the trademark skills of SC&O19 – determination, tenacity and teamwork.

PART 9

THE AGE OF FILM

Officers talk down an armed suspect. From now on all encounters will be captured on body worn video. (*Bob Owen*).

Shootout in Hendon

Mark Bryan shot by ARV Officers 14 February 2015

Valentine's Day is normally seen as an opportunity to declare your love for someone special. However, for those involved in the arrest of Mark Bryan on 14 February 2015, it was a day they would just be happy to survive.

In the run up to that date, Mark Anthony Bryan's life was going from bad to worse. His marriage was failing, which resulted in his wife throwing him out of the marital home. Then he foolishly agreed to do some unofficial debt collecting, which involved travelling outside London and threatening a client. Having completed that job, Bryan returned home unsure if the police were after him but hoping he could make things good with his wife. Unfortunately this was not to be.

In a fit of depression, he went round to an associate's first-floor flat at Franklin House in Hendon. The associate was Arnold Mpanzu, who had a history of violence and was known to be schizophrenic. Mpanzu wasn't there and Bryan proceeded to drink himself stupid, consuming a whole bottle of whisky before starting another.

During this drinking binge he started firing a shotgun he had in his possession, shooting at objects around the room before firing from the balcony of the apartment onto wasteland and buildings it overlooked. It was reminiscent of the Chelsea siege of May 2008, when alcoholic lawyer Mark Saunders began taking pot shots at his neighbours' flats from the window of his apartment, which resulted in him being shot dead by police.

At 6.14pm, the police information room began to receive calls from neighbours, stating that they had heard loud bangs coming from the tower block. One of them said they had heard 'pings, as if whatever was being fired was hitting things'. The police operator could hear the bangs in the background. Trojan 304 was dispatched to attend the scene.

To put this in perspective, London's ARVs receive dozens of calls every night to the 'sounds of gunfire', and take each call seriously. Most of the time it's fireworks or a car backfiring.

TJ 304 spoke to the informants but couldn't identify where the shots had come from. They were pointed in the direction of wasteland behind the block but after carrying out an area search, and finding no obvious signs that a crime had been committed, they closed the call and returned on patrol.

At 7.50pm, a neighbour living opposite Franklin House heard loud bangs and saw flashes coming from the flat at the bottom right of the block. She heard a man's voice in a cockney accent shouting: 'Whoever wants it is going to get it' and 'I'm going to blow everyone's heads off.' After telling a neighbour to watch from the balcony she called the police.

SHOOTOUT IN HENDON

By 8.13pm, there were several more calls to the police, one stating that they had counted twenty-two bangs. Many more had heard the shouting and seen gun flashes. A close neighbour told police a man was shouting: 'Do you fucking want it?' followed by more shots. This neighbour believed the shots were coming from Flat 3 Franklin House. Another neighbour reported hearing 'three loud bangs…and like something hitting the wall directly in front of me. I believe it was pellets that hit the wall.'

ARVs were reassigned. They now had an actual source for the gunfire and enquiries into who lived there were made. Arnold Mpanzu's name came up, and due to his history of violence and mental issues, alarm bells rang.

Four ARVs were assigned, including the kit car, which is an ARV with additional equipment, mainly MOE and shotguns. The operational firearms commander, code name N81, was given a briefing over the radio by Trojan control. Concerns were raised regarding the danger of the suspect firing the weapon from the balcony at people on the street. They agreed the weapon appeared to be a viable firearm and they would be facing an individual who had immediate possession of that firearm.

The tactic chosen was to contain the premises and try and establish contact with the occupant of the flat to identify them and find out why they were firing a gun. For example were they emotionally or mentally distressed? Once contained, the address would be entered by the door being forced open, then officers would talk the occupant from the premises. A dog handler was assigned as was the ambulance service.

N81 confirmed that his officers had effectively contained the premises, preventing the possibility of the subject escaping. He briefed his entry team. One officer would carry the ballistic shield, another would provide support and cover over the top with a carbine, the MOE officers would breach the door using the enforcer ram followed by the searching officers. N81 would make sure they all carried out their allotted tasks and would make decisions needed for any contingencies, at all times using the national decision-making model to justify his course of action.

Four armed officers made their way up to the first-floor hall where they identified the front door of Flat 3 Franklin House. One officer listened for any noise coming from the flat but it was silent. The shield officer placed the ballistic shield on the floor in front of the door, being careful to leave enough room for the MOE officer to swing the enforcer ram against the door. They waited, listening for any noise from the premises or any communication such as a light coming on or curtains twitching. At this point N81 ordered the dog to be brought up to the landing and waited until it arrived.

On a nod from N81, the MOE officer swung the enforcer. The loud bang echoed round the hallway; the noise was usually enough to wake up any occupant. In this case the first hit put the front door in and the door swung against the wall. The shield officer covering the premises with his pistol shouted: 'Armed police! Come to the front door with your hands empty.' He then added: 'If you do not come out we're sending the dog in. Come out with your hands empty.' There was no response. Because of the possibility of the occupier being emotionally or mentally distressed, the officer added: 'Arnold can you hear me?' and 'Arnold it's the police. We are going to have a dog come in the house.' Again, there was no response.

Above left: The 'stick' of ARV officers form up around the doorway to No 3 Franklin House, ready for the door to be breached.

Above right: The shield officer and covering officer shout into the flat, calling for 'Arnold' (Mark Bryan) to 'come to the front door with your hands empty.'

The dog handler brought her specialist dog forward on a very short leash to the front of the stick. She pushed the eager dog forward into the flat saying 'Find him! Find him!' The dog padded around with its tail wagging, sniffing the air and then came out. The handler wasn't happy and sent the dog in again. This time it pushed a door open with its nose and went into the room.

There was a pause, then a bark, then the sound of someone shouting 'Arrrgh! Arrrgh!' The dog returned, tail wagging, job complete.

The shield officer shouted into the flat: 'Arnold come to the front door with your hands empty,' and Bryan responded shouting, 'I don't want anyone hurt.' 'Neither do we,' replied the officer.

At 9.09pm, there was the unmistakable noise of a gun being fired. Lead shot punched through the door leaving a large hole and hundreds of lead pellets hit the wall by the front door. Officers felt the rush of air from the shotgun blast and the wadding from the cartridge grazed an officer's leg.

Although every firearms officer on a live operation can expect to encounter hostile reactions from an armed suspect, this still came as a shock. The officers realized they were in a situation which could end in someone being killed. N81 asked if anyone was hurt. Relieved that his team was uninjured he considered his options. They could not return fire as the shotgun had been fired through a door and there could be innocent people in the room with the shooter.

They held their positions and the shield officer shouted: 'Arnold, put the weapon down and come out with your hands empty, mate.' Again, Bryan replied, 'I don't want to hurt anyone.'

N81, an experienced officer recently promoted from the CTSFOs, instructed the shield to move back to the edge of the door. Negotiations continued for around ten minutes with Bryan saying he 'didn't want to hurt anyone' and 'go away.' Then a second shot was fired through the door from inside the room. This time the pellets hit near to where the shield had moved from moments earlier.

SHOOTOUT IN HENDON

An officer reported hearing what he believed were shotgun cartridges being ejected and more being loaded. Although N81 feared for his own safety and that of his colleagues, he knew they had to remain in position and try to end this in as safe a way as possible.

He requested a further shield be brought up along with a box of stun grenades and notified the on-call CTSFO inspector of developments. He then moved forward to the side of the front door and looked around the edge of the door. It was now 9.20pm. Inside, the hall was illuminated by his fellow officers' torches. N81 later said:

> 'I saw the barrel of a gun, which I believed to be a shotgun pointing at me. From its position I thought he must be crouching down. I could hear my officers shouting at the subject, I thought: "Oh my God, he's going to shoot us." As I was thinking this I was bringing my Glock up, thinking he's going to kill me.
>
> 'At this point there was an exchange of fire from myself and the subject with the shotgun, I remember clearly seeing the muzzle flash from his weapon. I fired a number of shots towards him, instinctively without taking aim, until he started to slump down to the left of the door. I moved slightly to my right to obtain a better angle of view. I saw him move up again and I could see the shotgun coming up again. I was thinking: "He's going to shoot again" and I fired two aimed shots into his torso until he slumped back and the shotgun was out of view. I could tell by the noise that my colleagues must have fired as well.'

Bryan had discharged both barrels of the side-by-side sawn-off shotgun. N81 had fired five shots at Bryan, the shield support officer at the side of the shield had fired three times with his SIG-516 carbine and the shield officer had fired once with his pistol.

Bryan was now on the ground but still moving and still a threat. The officers kept their guns trained on him. During the exchange of gunfire he had received wounds to his hands, arm, stomach and groin. Officers called for paramedics to be sent up.

The officers tried to persuade him to give up but he held onto the shotgun, refusing to show them his hands, and they believed he was still attempting to reload it. After two minutes, N81 decided to deploy stun grenades by way of a distraction to allow them to enter the flat and disarm him. They were also concerned that Bryan needed urgent medical aid. He called for officers to 'prep stunnies'.

Under the cover of the blinding flashes and loud bangs, the officers made their entry, quickly removing the shotgun from Bryan's hands. They searched the flat for possible innocents and then commenced life-saving treatment on him, plugging the wounds and stopping the bleeding. The officers continued until paramedics

The plywood door of the room through which Bryan fired his shotgun twice at police.

arrived and took over, eventually removing him to hospital. Thanks to the initial treatment by the officers who had shot him and the expert treatment from the paramedics, Bryan was eventually able to recover from his wounds.

Officers found forty-seven discharged shotgun cartridges in the flat, along with one-and-a-half empty bottles of whisky. One of the officers in the doorway had received slight wounding, consistent with shotgun pellets grazing his arm.

The IPCC took over the investigation and was able to use the body worn video (BWV) footage from eight of the officers present to help understand what had happened.

Although helpful to the IPCC's investigation, the visual imagery captured from this incident was poor due to the shoulder mountings on the officers' body armour which allowed the camera to move about. This was to prove a persistent fault until it was rectified later that year following two further police shootings.

One valuable point that came out during the investigation was how the audio can sometimes be misleading when used out of context. When played back, it was of such good sound quality and so loud that it over-emphasized certain speech and noises.

This was the first police shooting investigation to utilize BWV. The footage bore out the officers' accounts of the incident. Operation Guster – as the IPCC's investigation was known – concluded quickly. Both the officers who had opened fire were returned to full operational duties and the officers present at the scene rightly received commissioner's commendations for bravery. N81's decision to wait for the support dog had probably saved lives.

The incident was also the first recorded use of distraction stun grenades by the ARVs, and their use provided the opportunity to disarm the suspect at a point where he may well have forced the officers to shoot him again.

One could surmise that owing to Bryan's depression and the amount of alcohol he had consumed, he may have been attempting to engineer a suicide-by-cop scenario. But whatever way you look at it, he endangered the public and the police and how no one was seriously hurt by Bryan's actions defies belief.

Mark Bryan was charged with possession of a firearm of less than 30cm, possession of a firearm with intent to cause fear of violence and making use of a firearm with intent but not the attempted murder of police officers. On 8 December 2015, at Woolwich Crown Court, Bryan pleaded guilty to these offences and was sentenced to ten years' imprisonment.

The Nathaniel Brophy Shooting

Lambeth 21 August 2015

Nathaniel Brophy, 34, lived in a rented flat in Tilson Gardens, Lambeth, between Brixton and Clapham in South London. He had worked as a delivery driver until 2010 when an apparently random attack by a man armed with a hammer left him with some brain damage, partial paralysis of one hand and difficulties speaking. Since then, he had struggled to pay his rent. Refusing to seek help, he was given notice of eviction and was finally evicted from his flat.

On Friday, 21 August 2015 at 9.45am, local police accompanied housing officials to the flat as they feared Brophy might return and cause trouble.

Their fears were realized as when they entered the flat Brophy was already there. The landlords had failed to change the locks and he had let himself in with his key. He emerged from one of the rooms holding a pistol and told police and housing officials to leave immediately. They did as instructed and left the flat.

SC&O19 were called out, along with police negotiators and the ambulance service. ARVs arrived and contained the block and the balcony that accessed Brophy's flat. Police evacuated local residents and began negotiations. This would be the beginning of a seven-hour siege.

Eventually, at 4.45pm, Brophy opened his front door and came outside. There was some sudden movement and, perceiving a lethal threat, two officers opened fire. Each officer fired twice and Brophy was hit three times.

Although not fatal, his wounds were serious. One round struck him in the right femur, another in his lower abdomen and a third in his back as he twisted away. He was immediately given first aid and received emergency treatment from an ambulance on site.

Brophy was taken to King's College Hospital under armed guard and following three operations was taken off the critical list. The IPCC was notified and invited to take over the investigation into the shooting. The incident was filmed from both CCTV cameras on the estate and from BWV. Including the local officers, there were thirteen police BWVs from which the IPCC could piece together a picture of events leading up to the shooting.

A non-police firearm was recovered. This proved to be an imitation firearm that fired air gun pellets.

The principal officers involved in the shooting began their PIPs. This was to be the first time the IPCC would be present to oversee the writing of the officers' notes. Apparently, this was to provide proof that the officers had not conferred about their honestly held belief or any fact that may have influenced that belief.

It had been normal for officers to confer only on facts such as times, street names, or other details where there is no dispute, and there had always been a third party present when officers wrote their notes. However, from now on the IPCC wanted one of its officers to take on this role. The IPCC has long pushed for the practice to change.

Superintendent Mark Welton of SC&O19 commented on this following the Duggan Shooting in 2011. He said: 'You can't have a process the cops are confident in and the people of London are not. You are trying to defend something nobody else likes apart from yourself. These processes do not support the officers or make them appear truthful witnesses. I'm not surprised the family and the public don't like it, as it is administered by the police.'

When Brophy was well enough, he was arrested for suspected firearms offences and later appeared at Southwark Crown Court where he was sentenced to sixteen months for two counts of possessing an imitation firearm with intent to cause fear of violence.

The IPCC released a statement which said: 'Our investigation examined all of these issues in great detail. It concluded that armed police responded to a member of the public (a housing officer) and a police officer being threatened by Mr Brophy with what appeared to be a firearm in the course of their normal duties. The IPCC investigator was satisfied that the officers' actions were appropriate in the circumstances and it was a justified use of force.' It also concluded that shots were fired in response to a genuinely perceived escalation in the threat posed by Brophy.

The IPCC recommended the Met review mounting positions for BWV after poor quality images were recorded during the siege.

The key police witnesses were all returned to full operational status within a reasonable time frame.

Above left: Nathaniel Brophy, who was seriously wounded after keeping police at bay in a seven-hour siege in Brixton.

Above right: The Walther-style imitation pistol used by Brophy to threaten police and housing officials.

The James Fox Shooting

First fatal shooting captured on body worn video
Enfield 30 August 2015

James Kerry Fox, 45, had a history of mental health issues aggravated by a family bereavement, anxiety, depression and heavy drinking. This led to him having frequent contact with the mental health services and, on one occasion, to him being sectioned under the Mental Health Act.

Fox lived alone in his flat at Picardy House, Enfield, North London. On Sunday, 30 August 2015 at around 9.35pm, armed police from SC&O19's ARVs attended a premises in Barnet following reports that Fox was at the address with a gun making threats against his father, who was not at home at the time.

In a recording of the emergency call, a child was heard saying, 'He had a gun and was pointing it at me. He was pointing it at my head.' When police arrived, Fox had already left.

The informant, Fox's stepmother Mary Bourke, stated that before her stepson had arrived he had made phone calls to her, threatening to burn his father's house down and kill members of the family. He had then turned up at the house with a gun, which she said was wrapped in a blue plastic bag and tucked into his waistband. Other family members described it as a long-barrelled pistol.

Due to Fox's recognized mental state, he fitted into the category of being emotionally or mentally distressed, which flagged him up as being unpredictable and in need of special consideration so long as this didn't put the public or the police in any additional danger.

When asked about his possible whereabouts, Mrs Bourke said he would probably have gone back to his home address using a local bus. This information was passed back up the command chain and over the radio, although ARV officers made a search of the area just in case he was still in the vicinity.

The tactical firearms commander made the decision that officers would go to Fox's home address in order to arrest him. Prior to leaving, officers were reminded of the

James Fox, shot fatally by police after pointing a firearm at officers who came to arrest him at his flat in Enfield.

circumstances in which they could use force and were made aware of Fox's potential state of mind and the need to give him extra consideration if at all possible. They were to take the X-26 Taser with them.

Just before 11.40pm, the ARV officers attended the base of the block of Fox's flats. Some officers were positioned on the lower level, while five officers made their way to his address on the sixth floor to arrest him. They ascended in two groups, stopping at the fourth floor to regroup and check equipment before a final move up.

They carried additional equipment in the form of a ballistic shield, as well as an enforcer ram and a stainless-steel Halligan 'Hooli' bar. Both pieces of equipment are used for breaching doors.

They reached the sixth floor and remained in single file. The officer at the front of the group, code name M27, was carrying a half-length ballistic shield with the words 'POLICE' clearly marked half-way up. Directly behind her was D29, who was armed with a SIG-516 carbine. M27 stopped just short of the door.

Two of the five were wearing BWV cameras. These cameras were still in their trial period within SC&O19 and, as such, were not issued to every officer. They were a different specification to the ones used by local borough police teams but it was hoped that the department would soon adopt them for everyday use.

Each of the officers was armed with their issue Glock 17 pistol and all – with the exception of a female officer who was carrying the ballistic shield – carried a SIG-516 carbine.

Above left: Film taken from the officers' BWV showing the muzzle of James Fox's gun protruding out of the door and pointing at the officers.

Above right: BWV showing the moment officers opened fire on James Fox.

Left: This one from another angle shows the shield officer firing her Glock pistol during the incident.

THE JAMES FOX SHOOTING

The officers notified control that they were in position and about to initiate contact by breaching the front door of the flat. As they were doing this, M27 heard a noise coming from behind the front door, which sounded like a key being inserted in the lock. She moved position slightly to offer protection to the front door of the premises behind her. No sooner had this happened and, without warning, the front door was flung open.

Both officers were positioned no further than 1 metre away and as the door was opening they responded with shouts of 'Armed Police!'

James Fox brought his handgun up from waist height in one fluid movement, punching it out in front of him. He pointed first at the head of one officer and then swept across to point it at the second. Both officers believed they were about to be shot and, fearing their lives were in immediate danger, opened fire.

This incident was caught on camera, which proved it had lasted no more than one second and clearly demonstrated that the officers shouted their warning prior to opening fire.

Fox suffered five gunshot wounds, including one to the head. During the inquest that followed, the wounds were described by a medical professional as 'non-survivable'. He slumped to the ground.

With the main threat neutralized, officers were still required to search the premises in case there were other armed subjects inside. They then changed roles from armed police officer to police medic and attempted to save the life of the man who had just threatened them. They administered first aid and worked to resuscitate him until the arrival of doctors from the air ambulance, which had been called by Trojan control.

Sadly, it was in vain and Fox was pronounced dead at the scene. A non-police firearm was recovered close to his body.

As this was the first fatal police shooting to be captured on BWV cameras, all those involved were interested to know if the cameras would help the investigation uncover the truth of what was a fast-moving incident.

Although the footage captured by the two police BWV cameras was integral to the investigation, it was not without its faults. One of the cameras – worn on the left shoulder of one of the two leading officers – was recording for the entire incident but the mounts supplied for the trials left a lot to be desired. The camera had become slightly dislodged and was only able to record Fox throwing open the door and coming up with the gun in his hand, with the finger on trigger. It missed him pointing the gun at the leading officer's head.

However the second camera, worn by an officer positioned further down the corridor, had caught the weapon protruding from the doorway and being pointed head height towards the officers.

The combination of the footage from both cameras and the officers' accounts gave an accurate, undeniable picture of events and clearly showed that the officers who opened fire had no option but to react as they did.

One of the issues surrounding BWV evidence is whether the officers should be allowed to view the footage of the incident prior to making their notes. In this case the IPCC decreed that officers were not allowed access to footage until six months after the incident.

In a later meeting with the IPCC, the officers had the opportunity to explain how, in their opinion, this lengthy delay had a negative impact on all concerned. It had caused undue distress to the officers who were left for months wondering if it had captured the truth of the matter or was being used to build a case against them.

The rules about viewing footage have since changed and officers are now normally permitted to view it after they have made their 'personal initial account', which includes a statement of facts giving their honestly held belief justifying their actions. This concession represents a major step in helping officers recover from traumatic events and gaining some peace of mind.

If the IPCC (now the IOPC) hopes to regain the trust of the officers it investigates, it must be in a position to justify its actions and be held to account when it steps outside the line. In this incident, it was accused of failing the officers under investigation for a second time when it mistakenly released personal details of the key police witnesses, who had been granted anonymity to members of the press. Thankfully this damage was contained and the details were not put out.

James Fox's family were understandably upset by his death and complained that when the door was opened he had no opportunity to give himself up.

However, the IPCC investigation concluded that: 'Both officers were entitled to believe there was an immediate threat to life and were justified in their decision to fire their weapons. [Fox's decision] to come to the door of his address with the weapon in his hand was the primary reason he was shot.'

Questions were asked at the inquest as to why police could not have taken a mental health professional with them but it was accepted that on a Bank Holiday Sunday evening this would have been difficult.

The jury found that it was a lawful killing. The court commended the officers for their efforts to give first aid and for the quality of their evidence, which fully supported the footage retrieved from the BWV.

The shooting of James Fox was clearly tragic for all concerned although neither the officers' actions nor the tactics of the Met were found to be at fault. It was the first fatal police shooting to involve a female officer from SC&O19 and also the first to use footage from officers' BWV to help corroborate police evidence in a fatal shooting.

It gave a rare insight into how little time an armed officer has to react to perceived life or death situations. Undoubtedly the presence of BWV helped the case come to inquest quicker than most previous police shooting incidents.

When Desperate Measures Fail

Firearms Expert Takes His Own Life 30 January 2016

I have chosen to cover this tragic story because it shows how difficult, sometimes impossible, a task we give our armed police. We expect them to protect us from armed and dangerous criminals and terrorists but show restraint, empathy and compassion when dealing with armed people who are emotionally or mentally distressed. On many occasions they have to make instant judgement calls – like playing God with people's lives – and live with the consequences. Sometimes all there is left for these officers is to pick up the pieces.

I will avoid touching on any of the mitigating factors or recriminations that may have contributed to Tony Hanley's state of mind at the time of his death, as they are not the points I wish to make and I do not wish to cause further upset or distress to his family or work colleagues.

On Saturday, 30 January 2016, while most people were enjoying a relaxing weekend, 51-year-old Tony Hanley was finding it impossible to put thoughts of work out of his mind.

Tony worked for the Metropolitan Police. He had been recruited as a forensic analytical specialist but had gone on to work in the Personal Protection Group. His work involved testing protective equipment, such as stab-proof vests and making recommendations on issues such as which ammunition the Met should use in their firearms.

Unbeknown to many, Tony had been struggling with mental issues, including depression, for many years. It also transpired that he had been a high-functioning alcoholic, often drinking up to a bottle of whisky a day. When he stopped drinking three months before his death he became even more depressed. It coincided with him having a breakdown and threatening to harm himself. He was signed off sick from work.

By 30 January, Tony had been off work for three months and was not getting any better. He attended his doctor's surgery the day before, complaining of anxiety and depression, saying that he felt suicidal and fearing he would 'take others' with him. He later told his girlfriend he had asked the doctor to section him under the Mental Health Act but was refused.

Tony's girlfriend had visited him at his address in Wallington, south-west London at 6.20pm that evening. She said she found him 'sitting in a chair holding a handgun.' She added: 'He told me he was feeling really depressed. I told him he would get through it, but he said "you don't know what's going on in my head."'

For some reason, Tony blamed himself for the shooting of Mark Duggan in Tottenham in 2011. He felt he was responsible for recommending the type of ammunition used by police in the shooting and the subsequent rioting that swept the country. He couldn't sleep at night and kept seeing dead people, including the ghost of Mark Duggan.

At around 7.55pm, police received a call to his address from a neighbour claiming they had spoken with Tony's girlfriend who had left in tears saying he had a gun and she was concerned for his safety. At 8.02pm, the operator received a call from Tony himself saying, among other things, 'Get the firearms officers to me now.' He claimed to have a gun to his head and asked for help. The operator traced the call to Tony's address and, because of its nature, ARVs were dispatched.

An ARV attended the address and attempted to make contact, only to find that Tony had left the premises. Meanwhile, a local unarmed officer posted on the outer cordon had spoken with a member of the public who 'stunk of alcohol'. The male, who turned out to be Tony Hanley, showed him a police identification card and said, 'I am the one you are looking for.'

After telling Tony to take his hand out of his pocket, the officer attempted to restrain him but Tony broke free. He then withdrew a pistol from his right pocket and waved it from side to side.

He walked along Bridge Road, away from the officer who followed and radioed this information in.

Before long, armed officers arrived on foot. At this point, Tony's pistol was lowered down and by his thigh. the ARV officers pointed their carbines at him and shouted: 'Tony, we are armed police. Put the gun down, we don't want to hurt you.'

Tony raised the gun slowly and pointed it at his own temple. The officers increased their efforts to persuade him to put the gun down but he ceased to be communicative.

There followed a tense standoff during which time further armed officers arrived, two with baton guns and one with an X-26 Taser.

An unsuspecting member of the public walked on the pavement nearby and was told to move away. Tony was temporarily distracted by this and, fearing he was about to harm himself or others, the two officers fired their baton guns.

Tony was hit by two projectiles within seconds of each other. He made a winded 'oof' noise as each one struck. Usually this would have knocked a person down but strangely this did not happen. Instead, Tony moved the pistol away from his head, allowing the third officer to discharge his Taser. However, this method also failed. The barbs deployed and sparked but not sufficiently to deliver an incapacitating charge. Nevertheless, the officers used the distraction to move forward hoping to restrain and disarm him. Seeing their intention, Tony moved backwards and sideways, raised the pistol to his head and shot himself.

He fell to the ground and officers were quick to begin giving first aid. At this point he was unconscious but still breathing. In a bid to deliver medical treatment, they removed some of his clothing, which revealed he was wearing Met police body armour. This explained the ineffectiveness of the baton rounds, and possibly why the Taser barbs failed to engage.

Paramedics were quickly on scene and Tony was taken to St George's Hospital in Tooting where he died of his injuries. Toxicology results revealed that – along with alcohol – ketamine, diazepam, citalopram and sertraline were found in his blood.

He had shot himself with a Walther PP 7.65 self-loading pistol. He had two fully charged magazines with the weapon, which was in perfect working order. It is still not clear how he came to have it.

Tony Hanley was an expert in his field and had the respect of many within the police firearms community, including specialist rifle officers with whom he worked closely. This case highlights the problems of undiagnosed stress and mental illness in the workplace and, as always in these circumstances, what a needless waste of human life.

An investigation by the IPCC concluded that: 'The officers used reasonable and appropriate force to try and protect Mr Hanley and themselves in what must have been incredibly difficult circumstances.'

PART 10

A YEAR OF TERROR

CTSFOs move through a building in subdued light, weapons ready. The officer on the right has night vision goggles and a short ballistic shield.

Westminster Bridge and Parliament Attack

Lone terrorist attacks the seat of British Government
22 March 2017

The Palace of Westminster (known to most as the Houses of Parliament) has been a target for terrorism since it was built in 1016.

It was the scene of the Gunpowder Plot in November 1605 when English Catholics attempted to assassinate King James I. In January 1885, a bomb was left in St Mary Undercroft, Westminster Hall by Irish extremists, which wounded a police officer after it exploded while he attempted to remove it. During the Second World War, the Nazis targeted it three times, completely destroying the lower house. In June 1974, the IRA left a bomb in the entrance to Westminster Hall which exploded injuring eleven people, and in March 1979 the Irish National Liberation Army planted a car bomb in Northern Ireland Secretary Airey Neave's car which detonated, killing him as he drove up the ramp of the underground car park into New Palace Yard. More recently it has been the target of cyber terrorism.

All these incidents drew massive public interest and made politicians, and all those who worked in the seat of government, feel vulnerable to attack.

Westminster Bridge and The Palace of Westminster: the seat of government in the UK and the most attacked building in London. (*Stephen Smith*)

WESTMINSTER BRIDGE AND PARLIAMENT ATTACK

Security services had long feared attacks by so-called lone wolf attackers who had become radicalized by extremist groups. These people allegedly operate on their own and, for this reason, are harder to discover and gain intelligence on. In truth, it is unlikely the terrorist who attacked the Houses of Parliament in March 2017 was a lone wolf, as there is a strong likelihood he had direction and help from others, although to this day no other person has been charged in relation to this attack.

Adrian Russell Elms was born in 1965 and grew up in Tunbridge Wells in Kent. He had an unremarkable childhood, attending the local school where he excelled at football and rapped in a school band with his friends. He was a popular boy with no apparent interest in religion, and even complained when the local pub was turned into a mosque.

Adrian Elms changed his name to Khalid Masood after becoming radicalized in the UK by hate preachers including Anjem Choudary.

He left school at 16 but, after struggling to get work, became involved with using and selling cannabis and mixing with petty criminals. He had his first stint in prison during the 1980s for criminal damage.

In 1991 his fortunes changed and he married, moving in with his wife to her expensive house in Rye, East Sussex. She made him the manager of her business and they had three children together. All looked to be going well until 2000 when, following an argument in a pub in Rye, he attacked a man and slashed him across the face with a knife. The wound was deep and needed twenty stitches and Elms was charged with grievous bodily harm and possession of an offensive weapon.

It was while serving a two-year sentence for this crime that Elms became radicalized, changing his name to Khalid Masood. He also became interested in bodybuilding and developed a taste for steroids and cocaine.

In 2004 he remarried, this time to a Muslim woman, Farzana Malik, but this marriage only lasted a matter of weeks as Masood beat her badly, causing her to leave the country for her own safety. She later described him as a violent psychopath.

He moved between several locations including Birmingham, Eastbourne and Crawley in West Sussex, making at least two trips to Saudi Arabia to fuel his increasing interest in Islamic fundamentalism. He even spent time in Jeddah, working as an English teacher, although records show he had never qualified as a teacher in the UK.

In 2010 he was living in Luton, a location frequently visited by radical preacher Anjem Choudary, and living with an African woman, along with his eldest daughter from his first marriage who had converted to Islam.

The signs were there. Security Services had looked into his links to violent extremism but he was considered a minor threat among a list of 300 other suspects at that time.

In the days preceding the attack, Masood was seen on CCTV and identified – after the event – casually walking over Westminster Bridge on a route almost exactly the same as the one he would take on the day of his attack. He saw how he could move into the cycle lane to get past the security measures near the boundary fence of Parliament. He was observed walking in Parliament Square and spending time watching the activity around the main gates leading into New Palace Yard.

LONDON'S ARMED POLICE UP CLOSE AND PERSONAL

On 22 March 2017, at around 2.20pm, he drove his rented 4X4 Hyundai Tucson SUV onto the south side of Westminster Bridge. The bridge was busy with foot passengers and vehicles – it was after all one of the more popular crossings over the River Thames.

Masood timed his approach, waiting for a gap in the traffic that would allow him to accelerate onto the pavement for maximum effect. Having got to a speed of around 40 mph, he deliberately swerved the 4X4 onto the wide pavement crammed with human traffic. People screamed and shouted – at first they thought it was an accident or even a drink driver before realizing what was actually happening.

What he was thinking as he mowed down men, women, children, the elderly and the infirm, no one can know but he continued to drive down the remaining length of the pavement. The people he did not hit, run over or drag underneath his car were forced to dive out of its path. Some threw themselves into the road, others climbed or jumped up onto the parapet wall of the bridge – anything to avoid being hit by the big SUV. One victim, 31-year-old Romanian tourist Andreea Cristea, was knocked clean over the wall, falling into the murky river below (sadly dying of her wounds two weeks later in hospital).

The Hyundai continued along the pavement for hundreds of yards, killing 75-year-old retired window cleaner Leslie Rhodes, American tourist Kurt Cochran, 54, mother-of-two Aysha Frade, 43, and injuring twenty-nine people including PC Kris Aves who had attempted to stop Masood in the vehicle. PC Aves was left with life-changing injuries, as were many others that day.

When the vehicle reached the end of the accessible pavement, it swerved. There was just enough room for the vehicle to access the pavement on the north side of the river and then the boundary wall of New Palace Yard, which stands in front of the House of Commons. In this building the house was sitting, with Prime Minister Theresa May in attendance.

The wrought-iron railings into which Masood finally crashed his car following a killing rampage on Westminster Bridge. Officers and paramedics are seen giving medical attention to some of his victims.

Masood once again mounted the pavement at speed, hitting further victims before ramming his car into the heavy wrought-iron fence. Intent on further killing, he climbed from the wreckage, grabbed two large kitchen knives and moved towards Parliament Square. His new goal was to get into the grounds of Parliament itself.

As he turned the corner there would have been groups of people milling around, walking and chatting and taking photos of Big Ben. There would have been confusion as some people were aware of the carnage he'd caused and others weren't.

Some police officers would have left the gates at the Houses of Parliament to get to the scene of the crash and help the victims, possibly passing Masood as he rounded the corner.

He ran through all the confusion to get to the gates, where one person stood barring his entry into New Palace Yard. That person was PC Keith Palmer, an officer whose responsibility that day was to facilitate the unobstructed entry and exit of MPs and their staff in their vehicles. He was also responsible for making sure there was no unauthorized access into the grounds. It was common practice at that time to leave the gates open at busy times.

Acting Commissioner of the Metropolitan Police Craig Mackey was being driven back to New Scotland Yard from a meeting with ministers at Parliament. He was in the front passenger seat of his unmarked police car, which was slowing down to exit New Palace Yard. As the vehicle blockers lowered to allow his car to leave he, along with his fellow passengers, were shocked to see Masood stabbing PC Palmer almost next to where the vehicle had stopped. What he saw resulted in him being classed as a significant key witness to the attack.

Masood was strong and fit for his fifty-two years, and knew how to use a knife. He had also studied online how to defeat police body armour. Yet however imposing and frightening Masood was, PC Palmer would not have hesitated for one second in doing his duty and stopping him from entering New Palace Yard. He was an extremely brave and conscientious police officer of fifteen years, an ex-soldier who had seen active service with the Royal Artillery.

PC Keith Palmer was wearing his 'Met vest', which was stab resistant, and afforded protection to his upper abdomen and chest area, as well as his beat-duty helmet. He would not have had time to draw his police baton, and would have grappled with Masood, trying to deflect the knife blows and disarm him. It is likely that Masood would have stabbed the officer early in the scuffle and he clearly knew where to attack as most of the wounds were above and below the stab vest.

Despite this, the officer fought on bravely until he was eventually pushed aside, bleeding profusely from several stab wounds and left for dead by a man intent on attacking the politicians in Parliament.

Masood continued into New Palace Yard. The yard had been busy but the fight at the gate had caused MPs and staff to run to safety away from him.

The wounded PC Palmer was not ready to give up, as he was aware of the threat this man caused to the people he was there to protect. He went after Masood, grabbing at him and shouting at him to stop. Masood turned and stabbed PC Palmer, wounding him again. This time the officer went down and stayed on the ground.

Keith Palmer's efforts had not been in vain. He had delayed the attacker long enough for people to get to safety, and caused a commotion which drew the attention of two plain-clothed

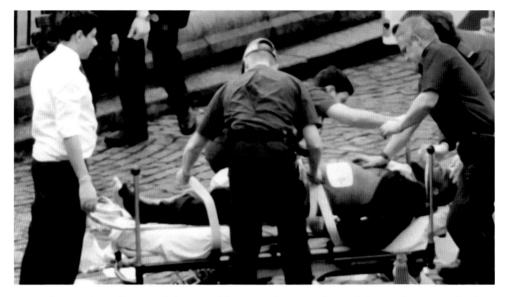

New Palace Yard. Fatally wounded, Masood is removed to a waiting ambulance after being shot by a personal protection officer.

close protection officers who were waiting by their vehicle parked by the cloisters next to the House of Commons. They were waiting for Defence Secretary Michael Fallon to leave. The officers were unaware that their colleague had been stabbed but did know there was a commotion about 100 metres away at Carriage Gates. After hearing a crash and seeing people running towards them, they started to make their way towards the gates.

Both of these officers were highly trained bodyguards – known in police circles as personal protection officers – and would have passed intense training programmes run by specialist instructors from SC&O19.

As they approached, they became aware of a tall, thickset, black male who was armed with two large knives and moving quickly in their direction. Both officers drew their Glock 19 pistols (slightly smaller than the Glock 17 by about half an inch, and with a smaller magazine capacity of fifteen rounds it is favoured by protection officers for its extra concealability). They were trained to react quickly and decisively. The closer of the two officers came into a combat crouch and, after shouting at the man to drop the knives, at a closing distance of about 5 to 10 metres opened fire. The officer fired three shots, hitting Masood in the upper torso. Masood went down on the cobblestones under the shadows of the Norman towers of Westminster Hall.

Confusion reigned. Were there multiple attackers? Was this attack just a diversion? Rumours abounded as information was assimilated from differing reports, one of which stated that two further subjects had leapt from the boot of the attacker's vehicle after it had hit the railings of New Palace Yard. Even uncorroborated this had to be taken seriously. If these other subjects had made their way into Westminster Hall, they could be anywhere in the building.

A lockdown was declared. Following protocols, the prime minister was evacuated and MPs were shepherded to safe areas. Officers were scrambled to all quarters of the grounds. One can only imagine how they felt as they learned one of their colleagues had been stabbed and was on the ground.

ARVs were on London Bridge in sixty seconds and their crews were busy giving first aid to the multitude of injured people (following previous incidents ARV officers had been given extra trauma training). They were now calmly triaging the injured onto ambulances.

It was quickly apparent that PC Palmer was seriously hurt. MP Tobias Ellwood, a former Army officer with medical training, had refused to go to the safety of the chamber, choosing to stay behind with the stabbed officer who he, along with others, battled to keep alive. Alas it was in vain.

As ambulances arrived, doctors and medical staff ran on foot from St Thomas's Hospital on the other side of the river to give help. There was a fantastic team effort with emergency services working with members of the public to help the wounded, some of whom sustained life-changing injuries. It was a credit to those who laboured that the fatalities were kept to just five (not including Masood who was also afforded first aid treatment, not only by the officer who had just shot him, but also by the colleagues of the officer he had just killed. He died later in hospital).

Armed officers flooded the area. CTSFO teams from SC&O19 coordinated an armed search of Westminster Hall and other buildings for additional suspects. Eventually, after all the pieces had been threaded together, it was understood that there was only one attacker, and thanks to the swift action of the police protection officers, he had been dealt with.

As the emergency services slowly regained control of the incident, the full horror became apparent. In just eighty-two seconds, Masood had engineered a 'low-tech' onslaught. Lessons would have to be learned and relearned, and once again London would have to pull together and find a way of understanding this, and preventing it from happening again.

In the days and weeks that followed, twelve individuals were arrested in connection with the attack. Some were associates or relatives of the perpetrator while others were known to him. All were released without charge.

On 10 April 2017, around 5,000 of PC Keith Palmer's colleagues joined members of the public to line the funeral route that stretched for two-and-a-half miles. The service was held at Southwark Cathedral and as well as his family, and 5-year-old daughter, Commissioner Cressida Dick, senior police officers, politicians and the Lord Mayor of London also attended.

In June 2017, after much public support, the Queen recognized the bravery shown by PC Palmer and posthumously awarded him the George Medal, the second highest award for bravery that can be bestowed on non-military personnel.

Masood killed and injured people from eleven separate nationalities and ISIS soon claimed credit.

Questions were asked in the House as to why were there were no armed officers on the main gate as up until six months earlier there had been. As far back as 2003, the Diplomatic Protection Group (DPG) provided four armed officers who were stationed permanently at the gates. However some MPs

Hero PC Keith Palmer, killed while attempting to stop Masood. He was later awarded a posthumous George Medal for his bravery.

Two armed officers on duty at the main gates of Parliament in 2018, giving it the protection it lacked on that day in March 2017. (*Stephen Smith*)

had claimed that armed police were off-putting, unwelcoming, and created a bad atmosphere. Eventually complacency won the argument and the armed cover was reduced to officers from the DPG attending at random times in vehicles and patrolling the perimeter.

That incident would change the way Parliament viewed its security measures and it changed how we protect pedestrians on London's bridges and in large pedestrian areas. Large concrete barriers, bollards and specially reinforced street furniture were put in place to prevent vehicles mounting the pavements. Sadly, they're there to stay.

On 3 October 2018, Chief Coroner, Mark Lucraft QC, said: 'Keith Palmer's death on 22 March last year could possibly have been prevented if armed officers had been nearby.' He praised the 'great dignity of the families' throughout the process and also the 'quite overwhelming response from medics and members of the public'.

Nine days later, at the inquest into the death of Khalid Masood, the coroner directed the jury to a verdict of lawful killing. Assistant Commissioner Neil Basu said the two police protection officers 'acted with great courage…they undoubtedly prevented others from being injured… I pay tribute to their tremendous professionalism and bravery.'

Female Suspect Shot in Raid

All Girl Terror Squad Arrested 27 April 2017

MI5 work round the clock to protect our society from terror attacks. It's no secret that they snoop on social media, listen in on phone calls and use other forms of covert surveillance against those who would do us harm. Some liberal-minded people might think their methods infringe human rights, but without them we would be a much easier target and suffer many more devastating attacks. As a result, we would see more grieving families, more vigils for the dead and more sadness in our communities.

We must also consider how terror attacks affect our economy, tourism, and our attitudes towards using public transport and flying. Terrorism affects us in so many negative ways, which, after all, is one of its aims.

So when MI5 set a trap to catch would-be terrorists, I applaud it, as long as they stay within the law and government policy and have the correct warrants.

The following story touches loosely on the important work of MI5 but also gives an insight into how many young Muslim women are easily drawn into a perverted brand of Islam, which subjugates them into a form of slavery, and in many cases turns them into murderers.

The case of 18-year-old Safaa Boular, along with her mother, Mina Dich 44, her sister Rizlaine, 22, and 21-year-old family friend Khawla Barghouthi, is unusual and, I believe, unique in the UK in so far as they appear to be the only all-female terrorist cell.

In order to investigate the causes of Safaa Boular's radicalization, we don't have to look far for possible role models. Her mother, Mina Dich, was a hardline Muslim fundamentalist. She raised Safaa to be strict Muslim, made her observe the Muslim codes and to wear a full burka. It appears Safaa initially resented and rebelled against these restrictions, looking jealously on at her school friends who had the freedom to wear fashionable clothes, listen to music, go out and talk to boys. She apparently suffered bullying because of her religion and her clothes. Her mother used this to alienate her from her peers, making her turn inwards to find other answers.

At Safaa Boular's trial, Britain's top counter-terrorism officer Dean Haydon said: 'As a family unit they are pretty dysfunctional. On the evidence we can see they had access to a vast amount of extremist material.'

The second of the role models was her older sister Rizlaine, who had already been radicalized (not surprising in a home where every bad thing was blamed on the sins of the *kafir* or non-believer). Rizlaine had flown out to Istanbul intent on joining ISIS but was stopped and promptly flown back.

It was around the time of the Paris attacks in November 2015 that Safaa became more interested in 'why people do the things they do'. She established contact with a woman in Syria nicknamed 'Mother of America', who painted a picture of a rosy life for those in the caliphate, where everyone was equal. She was passed over to female ISIS recruiter Umm Isa Al-Amriki who specialized in persuading young women from around the world to join their cause and become fighters and mothers of a new generation of jihadists.

The ISIS recruiters knew what they were doing and Safaa was introduced to a British-born Pakistani national from Coventry, Naweed Hussain. Hussain was 30 and had joined ISIS in Syria in June 2015. He declared his love for the then 15-year-old Safaa and led her to believe that when she was 16 she could come to Syria and marry him.

Hussain sent photos of himself posing with guns, looking every part the ISIS soldier and a pin-up figure to many vulnerable young Muslim girls. He also sent pictures of himself at scenes of executions. She, in turn, sent him intimate pictures of herself.

The couple spent an increasing amount of time on social media, discussing subjects that included wearing 'his and her' suicide vests, holding hands and together achieving martyrdom. On at least three occasions, Hussain urged her to commit atrocities in London.

Safaa was now fully committed to the cause and at 16, the couple underwent a form of marriage online.

Hussain continued trying to persuade her to carry out attacks and it was around this time the British security services began to work on their elaborate sting.

Hussain was fooled into believing MI5 officers were Eastern European ISIS converts in the UK. So taken in was he by these undercover officers that he revealed his intention to cause murder in London and gave them details of his 'wife' in the UK.

Naweed Hussain posing with his AK assault rifle to encourage his teenage girlfriend, Safaa Boular, to commit atrocities in London.

FEMALE SUSPECT SHOT IN RAID

MI5 discovered Safaa's plans to travel to Syria and join ISIS and she was arrested and her passport seized.

While in custody she underwent an antiradicalization programme and began wearing Western clothes. Eventually she persuaded the authorities that she was no longer a risk and was granted bail on the understanding she would not have contact with Hussain or her sister.

Once out on bail, and accepting that she was never going to meet her husband, she turned her attention to planning attacks in London. She re-established contact with Hussain online and he instructed her to stab strangers outside popular tourist attractions. They discussed various plots, including an attack on the British Museum. Safaa even took a selfie of herself, wearing a burka, outside the MI5 headquarters.

On 4 April 2017, Hussain was killed in a US drone strike. Agents masquerading as Hussain's ISIS commander in Syria made contact with Safaa, breaking the news of his death. She was devastated and vowed to join him. She told the officers that Hussain had talked of attacking the British Museum with a Tokarev (a Russian pistol) and pineapples, which was code for hand grenades.

Police arrested her and Safaa was remanded in custody. However, while locked up at the Medway Secure Training Centre, she persuaded her mother Mina and sister Rizlaine into taking over the planning of the attack. They devised a way of communicating using Alice in Wonderland as a code. Her sister was given the codename 'the Mad Hatter' owing to her 'mad' hair. Together they planned a 'tea party' but instead of cake and sandwiches they would bring knives.

Mina and Rizlaine were seen purchasing a pack of knives and a rucksack in Sainsbury's, with the intention of attacking Westminster. On the way home, Mina threw the small knives from the car, keeping only the large kitchen knives.

They conspired with Khawla Barghouthi, a female friend of the family. They were recorded at her house discussing the planned knife attack and practising with the knives. Meanwhile, Safaa continued to plot along with them.

A decision was made to arrest Mina, Rizlaine and Khawla, and on the evening of 27 April 2017, following a pre-planned briefing from the Anti-Terrorist Squad, CTSFO teams from SC&O19, dressed in grey kit, moved off in their covert vehicles. The target address for this armed operation was a mid-terraced house in Harlesden Road, Willesden, north-west London, home of the Boular family.

The premises had been under observation prior to the raid and the occupants were believed to be in the advance stages of planning an attack on the capital.

Armed containment was put on the premises and CTSFO officers moved up to the front of the house. Officers used shotguns to fire gas through the windows into the upstairs rooms, then the front door was breached and entry made.

As the first officers entered the premises, Rizlaine ran towards them from the kitchen armed with a large knife. She was shot once in the lower torso.

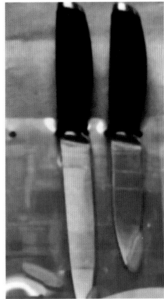

The kitchen knives purchased by Safaa's mother, Mina Dich, which she intended to use in an act of terrorism in London.

Above: CTSFOs remove the wounded Rizlaine Boular from her home before sending in forensic officers and evidence-gatherers.

Below: Filled with hate. Left to right: Safaa Boular 18, her sister Rizlaine, 22, and their mother Mina Dich, 44.

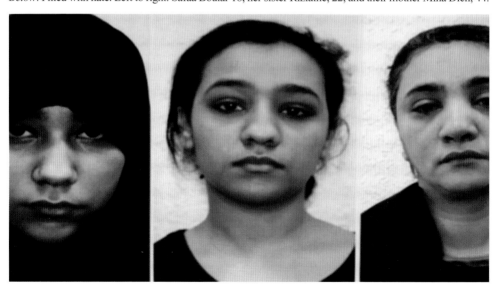

She was arrested and led from the premises to the waiting ambulance (she was to make a full recovery). Khawla Barghouthi was also arrested inside the premises. Later that same day, Mina Dich was arrested as she visited her daughter Safaa at the detention centre.

At court, Mina and Rizlaine pleaded guilty to preparation for terrorist acts, while Khawla pleaded guilty to failing to disclose information about an act of terrorism.

On 4 June 2018, Safaa Boular was found guilty of planning an act of terrorism in the UK. Rizlaine received a life sentence, her mother Dich six years and nine months and Barghouthi two years and four months. Safaa Boular was remanded for sentencing at a later date. At the trial, counter-terrorism officer Dean Haydon said: 'All three women were filled with hate and toxic ideology and were determined to carry out a terrorist attack. We can't say who was the ringleader in the family, there are a lot of different strands to this.'

He went on to describe Safaa as a 'calculated' and 'devious' teenager who was committed to her cause, emphasizing that she had reached out to individuals in Syria and that Hussain encouraged her, or inspired her thereafter.

He concluded that: 'If we hadn't arrested her and intervened when we did, I'm without doubt she would have carried out an attack here in London, causing injury and death.'

Following an investigation by the IOPC into the shooting of Rizlaine Boular, there was no evidence of any wrongdoing by police. The officer who shot her was returned to full operational duties within a fairly short time frame.

On 3 August 2018, Safaa Boular was sentenced to life imprisonment with a minimum of thirteen years.

Second Terror Plot Foiled in One Day

Man arrested with three knives outside Parliament 27 April 2017

On Thursday, 27 April 2017, just five days after the deadly attack on Westminster Bridge and the Houses of Parliament, ex-Taliban bomb maker, Khalid Ali was stopped and arrested by ARV officers in Whitehall not far from the gates of Downing Street. He was armed with three knives and intended to attack police officers and politicians.

Khalid Mohammed Omar Ali, 28, was born in Saudi Arabia as one of seven children. His parents of Ethiopian and Somalian origin brought their family over to the UK in 1992.

Ali was brought up in Edmonton, North London and trained as a gas engineer and plumber. During his teenage years, he became increasingly interested in religion and politics although he managed to keep any extreme religious and political views hidden, and in 2010 worked with aid convoys to Gaza.

In 2011, after telling his family he was moving to Birmingham to work and that they would not hear from him for five years, he travelled to Afghanistan to fight for the Taliban.

His family reported him missing and, in a subsequent search of his rooms, police found a laptop with extreme Al-Qaeda material on its hard drive.

On arrival in Afghanistan, the Taliban sent him to a training camp to learn bomb-making skills. The following year, Ali's fingerprints were found on component parts of explosive devices handed over to the American forces. Over the next five years he helped the Taliban build hundreds of explosive devices, including some used to kill and maim British and allied forces.

In October 2016, he resurfaced at the British consulate in Istanbul claiming to have lost his passport. He landed at Heathrow Airport and was questioned under terrorism laws. There was no lawful reason to hold him at that time but, as a matter of routine, his fingerprints were sent to the FBI, who checked their database and identified him as a prolific bomb maker. However, because this information was not declassified by the FBI, the UK could not legally act on it.

Ali soon began planning an attack in the UK and, as he was under surveillance, was seen carrying out hostile reconnaissance on New Scotland Yard and the MI6 building. In March 2017 he was seen on camera behaving suspiciously near police officers outside Downing Street.

On 25 April he bought a set of knives and a sharpener. The following day he was observed buying a mobile phone and that night he was seen disposing of the packaging for the knives and phone.

SECOND TERROR PLOT FOILED IN ONE DAY

Meanwhile, Ali's mother had become suspicious of her son's behaviour and while he was out of the house she looked in his room. Upon finding the knives and, worried he intended to harm other family members, she removed them, hiding them in another part of the house. Ali returned and finding the knives missing, argued with his mother who called the police saying she wanted him out of the house.

Ali played down her allegations, claiming he knew nothing of what his mother was saying. He left the property as instructed after midnight, still intent on carrying out his attack.

Early on the morning of 27 April 2017, he travelled to Ealing where he purchased three more kitchen knives from Wilko. One of these was 8 inches long and the other two were small paring knives.

Ali was picked up on CCTV at his gym, unpacking the knives and throwing away the packaging in preparation for their use. He then made his way to Victoria Station where he took the underground to Westminster.

He walked round Parliament Square before walking down by Westminster Bridge where he dumped the mobile phone in the river. It had apparently been used to take pictures of police officers wearing stab-resistant vests and was believed by security services to have been used to contact the Taliban for final authorization for the attack. It has never been recovered.

Ali was making his final approach, but as he moved into Whitehall and towards Downing Street an ARV was called forward.

Khalid Ali being arrested by ARV officers in Whitehall before he could follow through on his intention to carry out knife attacks in central London.

The ARV had been on standby for some time, waiting to be called in. It pulled up and officers quickly deployed onto the pavement taking control of the bearded terrorist.

Ali was wearing a blue jacket and tracksuit bottoms. A search revealed the three knives, one secreted in his waistband, the others in his jacket pockets. He told officers he did not care about the safety of the public, and said: 'You lot are carrying weapons, so you must know you are in danger.'

It was only following the arrest that permission was released to use the evidence of Ali's bomb making, which meant he could be prosecuted in Britain for those offences. During his interviews under caution, Ali boasted he had pressed the button over 300 times. The jury at his trial were later told: 'He had returned from a five-year stint making bombs in Afghanistan to "deliver a message".'

He was found guilty of preparing terrorist acts and two counts of possession of an explosive substance with intent.

Once again, we ask the question, why would someone like Khalid Ali, who was taken in by the UK, turn against his adopted country?

I think we have to accept that we cannot judge these people by our rational way of thinking and we must understand there will always be someone similar to Ali waiting to take his place. We have to work hard to support our security services and hope to catch them before they strike.

Ali seemed to have been under the control of the security services for a reasonable amount of time and they were able to spring the net before he could attack, even though it looked like a close-run thing.

On 20 July 2018, Old Bailey judge Nicholas Hilliard QC sentenced Khalid Ali to a minimum of forty years for making bombs for the Taliban. He also sentenced him to twenty-five years for his terror plot in Westminster. In passing sentence the judge said of Ali he 'had no doubt whatsoever there is a considerable risk of him committing violent acts in the future.'

This was another successful operation by the security services, supported by SC&O19, which prevented another atrocity in the heart of London.

Three knives purchased by Khalid Ali. He intended to target police officers and politicians in and around Parliament with these weapons.

Manchester Arena Bombing

Plus Parsons Green attack – Both Activate Operation Temperer
22 May and 15 September 2017

On the evening of Monday, 22 May 2017, pop singer Ariana Grande had just performed live to 14,200 mostly young female fans at the Manchester Arena, when a large homemade bomb, packed with nuts and bolts, was detonated by Islamist suicide bomber Salman Ramadan Abedi.

The bomb, carried by Abedi in a backpack, was detonated in the foyer area just as the crowds of young fans were leaving. It killed twenty-three (including the attacker) and injured 500 others. The blast was so great that it caused structural damage to the train station situated below ground, underneath the foyer.

The bomber was a 22-year-old Manchester-born Muslim of Libyan descent. He attended his local mosque and was described as a regular kid who used cannabis and alcohol when out with his friends.

His family had fled to the UK to escape the Gaddafi regime in the early 1990s. Abedi, who was believed to have self-radicalized, was known to security services but not considered to be a high risk. It was later reported that he had used his student loans to travel abroad to Libya where he learnt about terrorism and bomb making. Shortly after returning from one of these trips he made the bomb he would use at the Manchester Arena.

Police believe Abedi acted mostly alone – he certainly constructed the bomb himself – although it is fair to assume others were aware of his intentions.

The dreadful effect the bomb had on the nation as a whole was compounded by the number of children and young people killed or maimed by the explosion, and the long-term effect it had on those injured, and their families. It was believed this attack might be the beginning of a series of similar assaults on the UK. Prime Minister Theresa May called an emergency meeting of COBRA before announcing the raising of the UK terror threat to 'critical', which is its highest level. It was to remain at this level for five days.

Operation Temperer was activated for the first time following its inception in 2015 in response to the Paris attacks. It would release over 5,000 British service personnel to assist the civilian police and they would replace the officers in non-critical roles, such as guarding the UK's nuclear power stations. Thus, hundreds of firearms-trained officers could be sent to patrol and provide armed support to vulnerable areas, such as shopping malls, sporting events, transport hubs and any busy area that may be considered a soft target for a terrorist attack.

This first deployment was heralded as a great success. The additional armed officers provided a feeling of security to the nervous public and acted as a deterrent to further attacks.

Sadly, just one week after Operation Temperer was stood down came the attack on London Bridge and Borough Market. There was to be no respite and no let up.

Later that year, on 15 September, a bomb was detonated on a District Line tube train at Parsons Green Underground Station, which was packed with commuters and schoolchildren. The bomb was described as a crude 'bucket bomb' made up of homemade explosives. Thankfully it failed to explode properly, although up to thirty people were treated for burn injuries. Police arrested 18-year-old Iraqi refugee Ahmed Hassan in the ferry departure lounge at Dover. It was not known when or where Hassan had been radicalized – he had been in the country for around three years and had apparently lived happily with his foster parents at Sunbury-on-Thames.

This attack also triggered Operation Temperer and, once again, the additional armed officers were welcome reinforcements to back up police around the country.

If any good has come from these attacks it is the ability to mobilize large numbers of firearms-trained officers to be deployed where they are needed most.

London Bridge and Borough Market Attack

Three Terrorists Shot Dead By ARVs 3 June 2017

On a typical Saturday evening in June, hundreds of people were enjoying a night out in the popular Borough Market area of Southwark in South London, which boasts quirky pubs, restaurants, wine bars and cafés.

Always popular with Londoners as well as tourists from all over the world, it is a stone's throw from one of the busiest River Thames crossings, London Bridge, and surrounds the historic Southwark Cathedral. It is accessed by steps from the bridge's west walkway or by alleyways and small side streets and is just minutes away from busy London Bridge Station.

The market is mainly vehicle free, although there is access for deliveries and slow-moving vehicles when you reach Stoney Street on its west boundary. At weekends and busy times, drinkers and smokers crowd the walkways and people eat al fresco at tables set on the pavement or within roped-off areas on the cobbled streets. Steeped in history, Borough Market has been trading at this site for over 1,000 years.

Just after 10pm on that Saturday night, terror would be unleashed there and in the moments that followed, eleven people would be dead (including the murderers) and forty-eight injured.

This attack would come only two weeks after the terrible bombing at the Manchester Arena. But these perpetrators would not use a body worn device to kill and maim. Instead – having possibly been inspired by the attack on Westminster Bridge and the Houses of Parliament three months earlier – they would use the low-tech weaponry that had appeared so successful on that day back in March.

Following these previous attacks, the security threat level in the UK had jumped to critical, meaning an attack is expected imminently. At the end of May, this had been downgraded to severe, which meant an attack is highly likely – and it was.

That Saturday, events began to unfold in Harold Hill in the North London borough of Havering, when 27-year-old Khuram Shazad Butt, a Pakistani-born British citizen, attempted to hire a seven-and-a-half-tonne lorry. Thankfully, due to recent legislation the hire company was required to obtain additional identification documents, which he was unable to produce. Having been refused permission, he went to a builders' merchants and hired a large white Renault van on an hourly basis as fewer checks were needed. Several bags of ballast were loaded into the van to give it more weight.

Butt had two conspirators, 30-year-old Rachid Redouane, a failed Libyan asylum seeker, and Youssef Zaghba, 22, an Italian national born in Morocco, who like Butt were

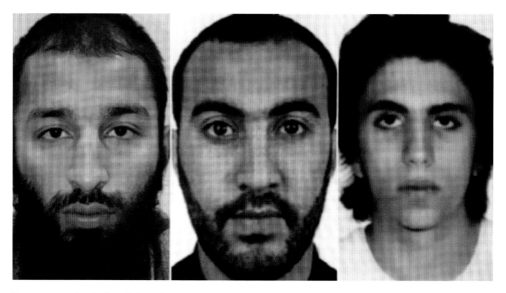

Intent on murder. Left to right: Khuram Butt, Rachid Redouane and Youssef Zaghba. (*Metropolitan Police*)

ISIS-inspired Islamists. Together, they set about preparing for their attack. They made fake suicide vests, wrapping plastic water bottles in grey gaffer tape and attaching them to belts and webbing – simple but effective even to the trained eye. They also obtained several 12-inch long, razor-sharp, ceramic kitchen knives. These they strapped to their wrists with leather straps and tape.

The group filled thirteen wine bottles with flammable liquid and inserted rags to make petrol bombs. They also obtained blowtorches with which to ignite them quickly. Thankfully none of these would be used in the attack.

At 9.58pm Butt drove the hire van south across London Bridge. It was seen six minutes later travelling back the way it had come. It is possible they may have been intending to attack a bigger target, maybe Oxford Circus or Covent Garden.

Purely by chance, a City of London ARV was carrying out a vehicle stop on the north side of the bridge and was stationary in the road with its blue lights on. Maybe they thought this was a police road block. In any case they quickly performed a clumsy U-turn, which sent them south back over the bridge. It could not have been easy for Butt to control the van with 12-inch knives taped to his wrists and wearing a fake suicide vest, but there was no question about it – their minds were made up and the attack was on.

The three terrorists accelerated back over the bridge. First they swerved up onto the east pavement, ploughing into as many pedestrians as they could, killing or injuring all in their path, dragging and crushing without mercy. They repeated this rampage at least another three times, zigzagging onto the road and then back up onto the pavement, each time aiming for knots of pedestrians one of whom – Xavier Thomas – was knocked over the parapet and into the cold waters below (his body would be recovered much later further downstream). After leaving a trail of death and destruction in its wake, the van reached the junction of St Thomas Street where it swerved one last time, across the pedestrian crossing and over towards the west footway where it mounted the pavement just past the Barrow Boy & Banker pub. Again, the murderers aimed at a group of pedestrians, crushing several of them against the cast-iron railings, tossing one over the railings and onto the paving 15 feet below. The van then came to a final stop.

Not satisfied with leaving three dead and scores of people lying on the bridge, the three men leapt from the cab of the van, the razor-sharp knives strapped to their wrists. Their fake suicide vests succeeded in causing fear and panic in all who saw them. They immediately began stabbing those around the van, including any who lay injured and helpless on the pavement.

Right: The van used by the three terrorists to kill three people on London Bridge and injure many. Having smashed it into the railings, they jumped out and began their knife attacks, leaving a further five dead and many more injured.

Below: The iron railings left of the Barrow Boy & Banker pub, near to where the van came to a halt. In the background is Southwark Cathedral and the walkways leading to Borough Market. (*Stephen Smith*)

LONDON'S ARMED POLICE UP CLOSE AND PERSONAL

The screams of the victims alerted British Transport Police (BTP) officer Wayne Marques, who was on patrol at London Bridge Station. At first he thought the fracas was a pub fight that had spilled out onto the pavement, but as he got nearer he realized people were being stabbed. Despite the threat to their lives, he observed that people nearby were standing and staring like deer caught in headlights.

PC Marques withdrew his extendable baton and flicked it out to its full length before charging at the men. He aimed his first blow at an attacker's head. The man looked round and threw up his arms in an effort to deflect the blow. PC Marques later stated that he put all his strength into the strike and was going for a knockout blow. He heard the man cry out in pain but he now had the attention of all three attackers who wasted no time in turning on him and stabbing him. This brave officer received stab wounds to his head, left leg and left hand. The wound to his eye left him temporarily blinded. Although seriously wounded, he managed to hold his ground, refusing to give up. The three attackers stood shoulder to shoulder, each in turn making moves to stab him, while he fended them off with his baton. He later said the 'short one on the left had bulging eyes and repeated "Allahu Akbar" over and over again.'

To his surprise, the three men suddenly turned and ran off in the direction of Borough Market. As colleagues arrived, PC Marques told them to 'Go get 'em' as he lay bleeding on the pavement, fully believing he was about to die. There were to be many more individual acts of heroism that day, some big, some small, which undoubtedly saved many lives.

Seeing what was happening from his position on London Bridge, a London black cab driver told his passenger to 'hang on, I'm going to ram him.' The driver span his taxi round but his intended target sidestepped out of the way. He later told the *Independent* he stopped as 'three police officers came running towards them with batons drawn. They didn't know what was happening. There was a guy with a really long blade randomly stabbing people. I told people to turn around and run away.'

As the three murderers moved towards the market in search of easier prey, off-duty Metropolitan Police officer Charlie Guenigault ran after them and rugby-tackled one of them to the ground. He fought with his bare hands, only to be rewarded with several stab wounds from the other two terrorists. He continued to fight but the attackers, cowards that they were, did not want to stand and fight and instead went looking for less-troublesome victims in the covered market area. It was here that many of the victims were attacked and stabbed, some unaware of what was occurring until they were set upon. Instead of running away, Spanish banker Ignacio Echeverria fought the attackers, using his skateboard to strike them and fending off blows until he was overpowered and stabbed to death. Nurse Kirsty Boden, was killed as she ran towards the danger in an attempt to help the wounded. Baker Florin Morariu, shepherded people to the safety of his baker's shop before managing to fight the three men off using empty bread crates.

Witness Gerard Vowels later told the BBC: 'I saw a geezer on the floor saying "I've been stabbed, I've been stabbed." He had blood all down him. Then I saw these three Muslim guys come up with knives.' He saw the men set about a young woman in the market under the railway viaduct, stabbing her some fifteen times and shouting 'This is for Allah!' Vowels followed shouting 'Run! Run! Run!' as he threw bottles, glasses, stools and chairs at them. He added: 'I tried to help as many people as I could. I was defenceless. If I had fallen over they probably would have stabbed me.'

A daytime scene of the covered market area where the terrorists passed through, killing and maiming as they went. (*Stephen Smith*)

A Met ARV kit car was first at the scene on the bridge by the crashed van. The officers made their way into the market where there were bodies and bleeding victims, as well as revellers drinking in the bars and dining in restaurants oblivious to the danger they were in. Drunken groups were wandering about, unaware of what was happening.

The terrorists were by now working their way down Stoney Street by the side of the railway viaduct under which stands Borough Market. On the left of the street are several pubs and restaurants. They entered the Boro Bistro wine bar and stabbed four customers then walked towards the Mexican bistro, El Pastor, and the customers sitting outside narrowly escaped harm when the quick-thinking waiter shepherded them inside. The knife-wielding attackers quickly followed them but were met with a hail of bottles and chairs. The next port of call was the Wheatsheaf pub next door, but as the attackers entered, the doorman, Ozzie Gandaa, fought them with a bar stool. Despite noticing the men were wearing what appeared to be suicide vests, he led a charge against them with customers, preventing them from getting into the pub and forcing them back out onto the street.

There were many other reports of drinkers taking the same action, defending themselves and attacking the three men with anything that came to hand.

The attackers stayed together, working as a team. They moved on through the market area to The Black & Blue steakhouse, which is popular with tourists. After seeing the puzzled look on the diners' faces through the large glass-panelled windows, they attempted to enter. Seeing the impending danger, a female member of staff had locked the door shut, gaining several valuable seconds allowing many diners to flee out of a rear door, this action undoubtedly saved many lives as the attackers managed to force open the door. Many drinkers in the restaurant bar were still oblivious to the threat that the three men posed. The men burst in shouting at them to get on the floor.

The terrorists spent no longer than two minutes in the restaurant immediately stabbing one man near the door as they entered, he threw punches at his attackers despite being stabbed twice in the stomach. Butt, who had ditched his jacket outside and was now wearing an Arsenal football shirt (this later caused some speculation that there was a further suspect), demanded that his victim, Geof Ho, lie down, before stabbing him in the throat, chin and abdomen.

After wiping the bloody knife on his beard, Butt and his two accomplices left.

By this time, reports of a terrorist attack had reached the police control room. Armed assets were dispatched to the location, with information that there were men armed with knives stabbing people. One of these assets was the City of London ARV, which had been stationed just north of London Bridge. The ARV quickly made its way over the bridge, bearing right towards the covered market.

True to form, the attackers spied an easier victim who was crossing the road in front of the pub listening to music on his phone, his headphones blocking any sound that could have alerted him. As he got to one of the concrete columns supporting the railway viaduct, they ran up behind him and set about stabbing him. He looked at the first one with some confusion and

The pubs and restaurants in Stoney Street, many with diners out on the pavement, which the attackers targeted. (*Stephen Smith*)

Above: The concrete pillar where the three set about their final victim just prior to the arrival of the ARV. (*Stephen Smith*)

Right: As the City of London ARV arrives on scene you can see the back of one of the terrorists as he stabs the man by the concrete pillar.

then the other two joined the first and there was no escape. They were later described as 'like a pack of hungry wolves'. Thankfully he was to be their last victim.

The final scene was played out as the City of London ARV arrived, and this undoubtedly saved the life of that young man (he later recovered from serious stab wounds). As the armed car pulled up in Stoney Street by the Wheatsheaf pub, the three murderers looked up and stepped backwards, leaving their victim in a pool of blood.

First out of the ARV was the officer in the front passenger seat, who began firing his G36 carbine at one of the attackers before giving chase as the murderer fled towards the market.

The driver and rear-seat passenger debussed simultaneously from the driver's side, stepping out then moving across the front of the ARV. In his haste to get out, the driver had failed to take the automatic vehicle out of gear and the BMW X5 began moving forward slowly. Both officers were now aware of the vehicle nudging against their legs and were forced to withdraw back to where they started. This may have saved their lives as one of the terrorists appeared out of the shadows, wielding his knives. Both officers fired at him while moving backwards. One of the officers, the driver, stumbled backwards onto the pavement. His colleague continued moving backwards and firing at the attacker. The driver ended up on his back on the ground and was firing directly upwards at the terrorist who was moving in for the kill. But having been shot multiple times by both officers, he collapsed almost on top of the officer. In the video taken from market security cameras you see the officer on the ground struggling to get up and kicking out at his attacker.

Above left: City ARV crew debus onto the pavement, moments before engaging in a life-and-death struggle with the three armed terrorists.

Above right: As the Met ARV arrives on scene, you can see the City car further up the road as officers fight a running battle with the remaining terrorists.

LONDON BRIDGE AND BOROUGH MARKET ATTACK

The empty ARV continued moving slowly up Stoney Street. As the officers fired at the remaining two attackers, people threw chairs and rubbish bins at the terrorists. A Met ARV, which had been assigned from SC&O19's south base at Lambeth, arrived moments later and deployed its officers in support of the City of London crew. These officers also engaged the terrorists, all of whom were fatally hit. Other armed police moved in. The three terrorists had all been shot dead within a small area – one lay on the pavement directly outside the Wheatsheaf, another in the road opposite and the third lay across the road, where he had charged at the driver of the police car.

In total, forty-eight, high-velocity .556 calibre rounds were fired from both the three City of London officers' Heckler & Koch G36 carbines and five of the Met's officers' SIG MCX carbines. Miraculously there was only one civilian casualty from police fire. He was a customer in the Wheatsheaf, who by his own admission had ignored advice to take cover under a table and had gone to the window to look out. A .556 round fired at the terrorist outside the pub had ricocheted through the pub window and hit the man in the head. The injured man, an American, went on to survive his wounds and make a full recovery.

It had taken just twenty seconds from the arrival of the officers to neutralize the three suspects. However, owing to the potential of explosive devices being on the suspects, officers

The Wheatsheaf pub in Stoney Street outside which one of the terrorists was shot dead. Note the replaced windows, which had been shattered by police gunfire. This wounded an American tourist who, against advice, was looking out of them when shot. (*Stephen Smith*)

The doorman looking over the body of one of the terrorists who is wearing a fake suicide vest. In the distance is the body of a second terrorist and the last wounded victim.

fired further shots at them after they perceived some were still moving and they could not afford the possibility of one of the fallen terrorists detonating themselves and injuring further victims.

As the dust settled and the screams died down, police, ambulance crews and helpful civilians went from victim to victim, offering help and first aid. Further armed officers were quickly on scene, including CTSFO officers who had been on standby at the north base at Leman Street. As in most situations of this nature, confusion reigned. Control needed information: how many victims? How many terrorists? Was this part of a larger attack? As more officers arrived, a thorough search of the streets and the locations they'd entered was carried out.

A control was set up in a pub where an ARV sergeant did his best coordinating the search for what was believed to be one further suspect. The information room received hundreds of calls, some claiming there were armed suspects in a nearby tube station, others claiming to have seen men with knives stabbing people after the three had been shot. They all needed to be checked out. At one point, a Special Forces helicopter put down on London Bridge containing a squad of SF operators who, on instructions from the Home Secretary, were held nearby in case this was indeed part of a larger attack.

A building-to-building search was instigated using every resource available. They could not afford to miss any outstanding members of the terrorist team. There were fears that one had gone to ground in the ancient Southwark Cathedral. As they could not gain entry, authorization was given to the SAS for one of the ancient doors of the cathedral to be blown in with EMOE as there could be life at risk (the Met later donated £10,000 to the cathedral and paid a specialist carpenter to fix the door). The coordinated search took many hours. Armed police from SC&O19, BTP and the City of London Police with search dogs and bomb disposal officers searched hundreds of premises within the 'warm zone' (area surrounding the incident). No other suspects were found.

At 1.45am, a controlled explosion rocked the market area as police bomb disposal experts made the three devices safe. All the surrounding buildings were evacuated and nearby tube and train stations shut down. London Bridge would not reopen until 14 June. The Victorian iron balustrade hit by the terrorists' van remained behind hoardings for well over a year. Following this attack, and the Westminster Bridge attack, new security measures were implemented using concrete barriers on eight central London bridges to reduce the likelihood of further vehicle assaults. The Met issued its famous 'run, hide and tell' notices advising anyone caught up in a situation like this to do those three things and remain calm and vigilant.

Eight people were murdered during the attack, three by the vehicle on the bridge and five in and around the market area. These were Frenchman Xavier Thomas, 45, who was thrown into the Thames; Spaniard Ignacio Echeverria, 39; Frenchman Sebastian Belanger, 36; Australian Sara Zelenak, 21; Frenchman Alexandra Pigeard, 26; Australian nurse Kirsty Boden, 28; Londoner James McMullan, 32; and Canadian Chrissy Archibald 30, who died in the arms of her fiancé. There were also forty-eight injured, ten of them seriously.

In 2018, twenty people involved in the attack received awards for bravery. These included, Ignacio Echeverria and Kirsty Boden who were both posthumously awarded the George Medal. BTP officer Wayne Marques and Met officer Charlie Guenigault also received the George Medal. BTP officer Leon McLeod received the Queen's Gallantry Medal for his actions in helping victims in the aftermath of the attack. Romanian baker Florin Morariu received the Queen's Commendation for Bravery. These were just a few of the people who displayed a special type of courage that night, fighting back or refusing to walk away and leave the injured behind. Sadly, some paid with their lives.

It had taken armed police just eight minutes to respond to the call, which although quick, must have seemed like a lifetime for those in mortal danger. Commenting on the police officers' actions, Metropolitan Police Federation chairman Ken Marsh said: 'There can be no doubt that the swift response of our colleagues, both armed and unarmed, saved further lives from being lost. There are barely words to describe the bravery of the officers who ran towards danger with no thought for their own safety.'

The bravery of the public was outstanding and displayed tenacity reminiscent of the 1909 Tottenham Outrage where they took on armed and dangerous men using anything that was to hand and never gave up.

Following the attack, twelve arrests were made in and around East London but after further investigation, all were released without charge.

The attack was condemned not only by all sides of the British Government but also by the Muslim Council Of Britain, along with over 130 imams who released a statement to say the attackers did not represent Islam. They were all refused Muslim burials.

There was a viable fear of a backlash from the far right following the attack and it would not be long coming.

Finsbury Park Mosque Attack

Vehicle-Ramming Assault on Muslims 19 June 2017

Nothing is more sickening than to hear of a cowardly, callous attack on innocent people going about their lawful business. But this happened, yet again, on the streets of London in Finsbury Park on 19 June 2017.

The incident unfolded fifteen minutes past midnight as a group of Muslims left the Muslim Welfare House just 100 metres from the Finsbury Park Mosque in North London. It was the month of Ramadan and they had been at night time prayers. They came across a Muslim man, Makram Ali, who had been taken ill and was being administered to on the pavement at Whadcoat Street on the junction of Seven Sisters Road.

None of them could have imagined that they would be targeted by a British man who had planned his attack against Muslims in revenge for the terrorist attack at London Bridge and Borough Market, which had occurred just over a fortnight earlier.

Darren Osborne, 47, from Cardiff was a father of four. He, like many others, was known to the security services prior to the attack and was described by his neighbours as 'aggressive and strange'. He had apparently suffered from depression and, according to his sister, had attempted to take his own life a few weeks earlier.

Osborne's family stated that he was not racist but had become agitated and had turned against Muslims following the screening of a documentary on TV about the Rochdale child abuse scandal.

He hired a van, which he had been sleeping in, and on the eve of the attack drove to London. That night, he was apparently heard boasting in a pub that he was going to attack the Muslims at the International Quds Day celebration, which was held on the last Friday of Ramadan to express support for Palestinians.

Osborne had been seen driving around the Finsbury Park area and had obviously been looking for a suitable target when he spotted a group of Muslim men congregating at the junction. They were administering first aid to Makram Ali.

Osborne sped up and drove his van at them. Many of the men were hit by his vehicle; eleven of them sustaining injuries of varying seriousness and eight requiring hospital treatment. Makram Ali, who had been helpless on the ground, was killed.

Osborne was dragged out and beaten by the survivors. However the imam of the mosque, Mohammed Mahmoud bravely managed to calm them down and stop the beating. Osborne was restrained until police arrived five minutes later. He was heard to shout: 'I want to kill Muslims!' and 'I did my bit.'

FINSBURY PARK MOSQUE ATTACK

The attack was declared a terrorist incident and Osborne was charged with terrorist-related murder and attempted murder. On 21 December 2017, he pleaded not guilty. He was tried the following January at Woolwich Crown Court and sentenced to life imprisonment with a minimum tariff of forty-three years.

Unfortunately, this attack on Muslims within the UK is not an isolated incident. Many Muslims live in fear of reprisal attacks and suffer abuse and assaults on a regular basis. In 2013, Ukrainian-born Pavlo Lapshyn stabbed and killed 82-year-old Mohammed Saleem as he was returning home from Green Lane Mosque in Birmingham. Lapshyn also attempted to bomb three mosques in the West Midlands. His motive was pure racism.

Although this has little to do with armed policing, it demonstrates how delicate the situation is here in Britain and how important it is to focus on terrorism in all societies. Each attack is as bad as another, irrespective of what race, nationality or religion the perpetrators are.

It is sadly inevitable that there will be similar attacks in the UK and we must all pull together against the common enemy that is terrorism.

Knifeman Arrested Outside Parliament

ARVs Prevent Knife Attack at Westminster 16 June 2017

At around 10am on Friday, 16 June 2017 an ARV was deployed to Parliament Square to detain a man suspected of planning a knife attack on Parliament.

The ARV was told the man was in his thirties and wearing a grey hoodie and black trousers. At 11.10am, as the ARV moved forward into the square, they identified him standing on the pavement in front of Westminster Hall. He had his fists clenched and a witness said 'he looked very angry'.

The ARV crew deployed on foot towards the man. Local officers ran at him and seeing he was holding a knife, one shouted, 'Knife! Knife! Knife!' The local officer grappled with the man, who was quickly engaged by the ARV officers who used their Taser. The man collapsed to the ground where he was handcuffed and detained. During the initial struggle the local police officer received cuts to his arm.

As this was only three months after the devastating attack on Parliament, they could not take the risk and a lockdown was called.

Eniola Mustafa Aminu, 27, was detained for assessments under the Mental Health Act.

At Southwark Crown Court he said he was carrying a knife because he wanted the police to shoot him and he felt unable to kill himself because of his religion. Prosecutors said it was unclear which religion Aminu followed.

Aminu was able to receive the medical care he needed.

PART 11

FIGHTING THE GOOD FIGHT

A Covert CTSFO 4X4 Gunship, lays in wait during a counter terrorism exercise at an airfield in Surrey. (*AH*)

Ongoing and Recent Incidents

These incidents are some that SCO19 have been involved with in recent years. While I cannot write about them in detail as they are part of ongoing investigations, I have included the briefest of information just to give an idea of what is happening on London's streets.

Thanks to the presence of the ARVs, we are able to safely deal with these instances of armed criminality. The UK has one of the lowest incidents of police-related shootings in the world.

Suspect Shot Outside Courthouse 11 December 2015

I can only give a brief summary of events leading up to and following the shooting of Jermaine Baker. All the material below is from open-source records.

Izzet Eren was on remand at Wormwood Scrubs Prison, awaiting trial following charges for firearms offences. While in his prison cell, he planned his own breakout. Using a smuggled mobile phone he contacted his accomplices on the outside and arranged how and when this would take place. The intention was for five accomplices to stop the prison delivery van as it travelled to Wood Green Crown Court and then by using firearms, including an imitation Uzi submachine gun, force the guards to free Eren.

Unbeknown to him, the police had become aware of his plans. So on Friday, 11 December 2015, an armed operation was authorized with the intention of disrupting the escape attempt and arresting the suspects, along with recovering any firearms which may be in their possession.

Having carried out what was later described in court as 'anti-surveillance moves', the vehicle containing 28-year-old Jermaine Baker from Tottenham, and two other men, was parked in Bracknell Close, near to the court, waiting for the delivery van.

SC&O19 CTSFOs were deployed to a location nearby and their primary role was to prevent the escape attempt and arrest the offenders. It was during the arrest phase of the operation that one officer, code name W80, opened fire, hitting Baker who was in the rear seat of the car and fatally wounding him. A non-police firearm was found in a holdall in the rear of the vehicle. Three other men were arrested in connection to the planned breakout.

The IPCC immediately launched an investigation and within days arrested W80 on suspicion of murder. He was interviewed and released on bail but remained suspended while the CPS decided on their next course of action.

In June 2016, both Eren Hasyer and Ozcan Eren (Izzet's cousin) were found guilty at Woolwich Crown Court of being involved in the escape plot. Nathan Mason and, Gokay

Sogucakli had already pleaded guilty to their part in the intended escape and each received sentences of between five-and-a-half and eight years' imprisonment.

Detective Chief Superintendent Tom Manson described the escape attempt as 'a bold, well planned and carefully thought out conspiracy that bears all the hallmarks of a professional crime.'

Eighteen months later, in June 2017, the CPS decided there was insufficient evidence to prosecute W80 for any offences. Jermaine Baker's family immediately made an application under the Victims' Right to Review scheme. This had been introduced to allow relatives or partners in homicide cases to request a review of the CPS's decision not to charge. In March 2018, the CPS upheld its decision that there was insufficient evidence for any charges.

However, in May 2018, the now rebranded IOPC directed that W80 should face gross misconduct proceedings for using excessive force when he shot Mr Baker. At the time of writing this is still ongoing. It has now been over two-and-a-half years since the incident and this will, no doubt, add to the officer's long and stressful ordeal.

Officers Open Fire in Hackney 19 March 2018

On Monday, 19 March 2018, at 10.50pm, police responded to reports of robbery in Mandeville Street, Hackney. In fact, it was an armed-vehicle hijacking. ARVs were assigned and, on arrival, two deployed and six armed officers began a search of the local area.

The officers attended an address on the road, identified the armed suspect and challenged him. He pointed what they believed to be a shotgun at them and officers reacted to the threat by firing thirteen times. The 21-year-old suspect was hit multiple times and was rushed to the Royal London Hospital.

It was later confirmed that a non-police firearm had been recovered from the scene.

The IOPC released a statement regarding the shooting: 'A young man is in hospital in a critical condition…we have been provided with a large amount of body worn video footage… we will be conducting a robust investigation.'

Once again, the body worn cameras were able to provide a wealth of evidence about the man's actions prior to being engaged by the officers. He went on to make a full recovery and was sectioned under the Mental Health Act. He was not charged with any criminal offences.

The officers who opened fire were returned to full operational duties following a brief investigation by the IOPC.

ARV Officers Open Fire in Petrol Station 1 April 2018

In the early hours of Sunday, 1 April 2018, SC&O19 ARV officers responded to a call about a man armed with a shotgun in a house in Collier Row, Romford in East London. When they arrived they were told the 40 year old had left the address with the firearm.

Just under an hour later, at 4.45am, ARV officers located the suspect at a petrol station near to his home address. As officers approached him, they responded to his actions and opened fire, wounding him fatally.

A statement released by the Met said: 'Police were called by a man making threats and claiming he was in possession of a firearm…. . Firearms officers attended the location and were informed that the man had left the location with a firearm… . At approximately 4.45am [the man] was shot by police…and pronounced dead at the scene.'

This incident is under investigation by the IOPC and therefore I cannot go into details at this stage.

Shootout in Leytonstone ARV Exchanges Shots with Gangsters in Car 26 July 2018

On Thursday, 26 July 2018, at around 10.45pm, a CO19 (as it reverted to being called between July and September 2018) ARV on patrol in the Leytonstone area noticed a black BMW containing four men. Checks identified that the vehicle was of interest to police and had been involved in an earlier firearms incident at premises in East London. They got behind the vehicle and flashed it to stop.

One can only assume the occupants of the BMW believed that they were being asked to pull over by a normal police patrol car and thought they could scare them off, because the passenger leant out of the window brandishing a sawn-off shotgun, which he fired at the ARV. Far from putting the police off, the ARV commenced a high-speed pursuit, which would take them over a mile before its conclusion in Bective Road, Forest Gate. A second ARV managed to get behind the first and witnessed the exchange of gunfire between the two vehicles.

During this pursuit, the front-seat passenger repeatedly reloaded and fired the shotgun at the police car. The front-seat passenger in the police car returned fire using his SIG MCX carbine, shooting through his own windscreen and hoping to neutralize the suspect.

Then, in an attempt to bring the pursuit to an end, the driver nudged the rear of the suspect's car. Nothing happened, so in a last-ditch attempt to stop it, the ARV driver made stronger contact in one corner, making the car lose control and forcing it to come to a halt. However, the manoeuvre did not go to plan and ended with the BMW sideways on to the police car, presenting the shooter, who again fired at the ARV. The officer in the front passenger seat had no other option but to return fire with his MCX carbine, which he did so firing several times.

Realizing they were seriously outgunned, the occupants gave up, apart from the driver who managed to get out of the vehicle and run (he would be arrested two days later.)

The ARV officers quickly deployed and, with weapons ready, approached the vehicle. They removed the remaining occupants and placed them on the ground where they were handcuffed and arrested.

All the suspects were in their early twenties and were all charged with three counts of attempted murder and possession of a firearm with intent to endanger life, and possession of offensive weapons. A sawn-off shotgun was recovered from the scene along with an axe, a 'zombie-killing knife' and facemasks.

Amazingly, apart from one of the ARV officers who received minor wounds, no one was seriously hurt. The BMW X5 ARV was peppered with hits from the shotgun and even had wadding from a shotgun cartridge embedded in the radiator grill. The suspects' black BMW also had several police bullet holes in the bodywork.

Chief Superintendent Richard Tucker said of the incident: 'This is just one example of the danger officers put themselves in day in, day out, to protect Londoners.'

Once again, these officers displayed the trademark courage that has become the signature of SCO19 – never giving up and always willing to take on dangerous assailants. Sadly, armed criminals who are willing to take on the police to avoid arrest are a growing danger to the public.

What's in a Name?

The Met's firearms unit has had many different names over its fifty-plus years and this has been confusing. For many specialist units, a name is something to be proud of and when that name achieves a global reputation, mess with it at your peril. Here I will try and explain why the name changes occurred and what they mean.

The firearms unit began its life in 1967 as D6, a small training unit attached to 'D' department. It soon became a department in its own right and that same year became known as D11. It maintained this title, achieving a reputation as a professional training and operational unit until 1987 when, in a major force restructuring, it became PT17, which stood for Personnel and Training.

Although this new title was not welcomed by the officers, the unit adopted its new name and achieved a reputation once again for professionalism and courage, taking on the IRA and carrying out thousands of successful armed operations in the capital as armed crime grew.

In the 1990s the changes came thick and fast. The first and most significant came in 1992 when PT17 left the training stable and came under the control of Specialist Operations for the first time. It was given yet another new initial and number, this time becoming SO19.

This change coincided with the formation of the ARV and SFO teams. It also recognized that the department was focused more on operational matters than training. This also came with a bigger budget, with more money being invested in training and equipment. SO19 soon became known and respected on the world stage alongside other specialist police and SWAT units.

The unit became known as 19 for short. The officers embraced this and soon had the Roman numerals XIX as an unofficial motif. This appeared to be recognized by the powers that be as when the force restructured in 2005, SO19 was allowed to keep the 19 and became CO19, which stood for Central Office. Central office was actually New Scotland Yard, which was now responsible for the unit who no longer came under the control of Specialist Operations and their big budgets. However, world events and the growing terrorist threat brought new challenges and extra funding and personnel to CO19.

CO19 would remain a solid name for the unit while it continued to grow and extend its reputation worldwide with the ATLAS Network. Then in 2012, another restructuring moved it back to Specialist Operations, this time naming it Specialist Crime and Operations 19 or SC&O19. The officers were not overly worried as they once again kept their lucky 19.

For a brief time between July and September 2018, they were known again as CO19, this time meaning Central Operations. Then for an even briefer time during September 2018 they were MO19, which stood for Met Operations. However, I am reliably informed their current title SCO19 (they've lost the &) is here to stay – until the next change. I hope for the sake of all of us they keep their lucky 19.

Above left: XIX shoulder patch, the adopted international trademark of SCO19. (*Stephen Smith*)

Above right: A current SCO19 shoulder patch. (*Stephen Smith*)

Ironic coincidence: XIX on the door to the 'Gladiator's Cell' at the Coliseum in Rome.

PART 12

REMEMBERING
THE PAST

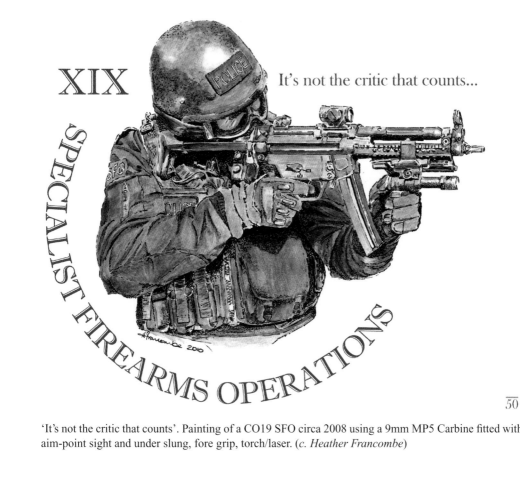

XIX

It's not the critic that counts...

SPECIALIST FIREARMS OPERATIONS

50

'It's not the critic that counts'. Painting of a CO19 SFO circa 2008 using a 9mm MP5 Carbine fitted with aim-point sight and under slung, fore grip, torch/laser. (*c. Heather Francombe*)

Museum of Armed Policing

Chatteris Police Station, Cambridgeshire Opened in 2018

In 2009, veteran SCO19 federation representative Mark Williams and a few others helped form an association for police firearms officers called, unsurprisingly, the Police Firearms Officers Association (PFOA). It wasn't an attempt to form a kind of union, it was aimed at filling a void that existed within the police force whereby some officers were given support and counselling while others were not. Mark wanted to guarantee that not just every officer, but also their families, would have access to counselling and receive any support they felt was necessary.

The PFOA soon exceeded all expectations, as firearms officers joined from all over the UK. Funded by subscriptions, donations and sponsorship, the PFOA soon received charitable status and was able to assist its members and their families by providing, among other things, a twenty-four-hour phone support line.

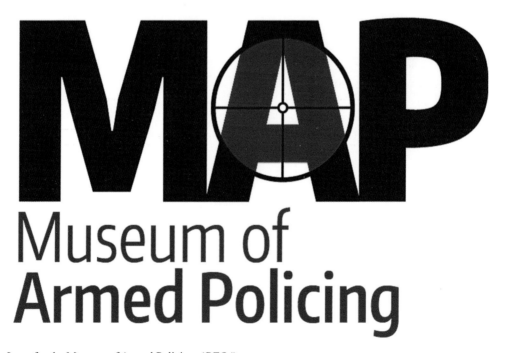

Logo for the Museum of Armed Policing. (*PFOA*)

In 2013 Mark Williams retired from the Met and became the PFOA's chief executive officer. At about this time he also started PFOA training, which won a contract with the College of Policing to deliver post-incident management training to all British forces. This training is vitally important to ensure firearms officers and all those involved in a police shooting are treated correctly. PFOA training also delivers post-incident courses to the Police Federation and to UNISON, which is one of the largest unions for the police.

The PFOA has also raised the profile of its members within the public arena and clarified some of the procedures, which are sometimes treated as suspicious, such as when officers can confer after a shooting incident.

In 2014 the PFOA secured a long lease on an empty police station in Chatteris, Cambridgeshire, which would become its new headquarters. Mark is a personal friend of mine and had helped me through some difficult post-incident investigations during my firearms career. I also had the pleasure of working closely with him during the 2012 London Olympic Games, covering the post-incident contingencies for any police shootings during the Games (thankfully we were not required). So, one afternoon while having coffee with Mark in a London coffee shop, he showed me the plans for the new PFOA headquarters. He knew my passion for police firearms history, and when I pointed to a large area at the back, which had been used as garages and jokingly said, 'And there's the National Firearms Officers Museum,' he said, 'What a great idea.'

Like all great ideas – even ones that start out as a joke – they take time to materialize, but Mark's passion for the project never slackened. He worked hard at getting private funding from sponsors and donations. He explained that the museum would be used as an educational tool for students and visitors and also as a showpiece to other armed officers from around the world. It would also welcome the media, and help educate and explain to journalists what it is like to be put in that exact moment of stress, that split second where you have to make a life or death decision to shoot or not shoot, and suffer the possible consequences.

The Museum of Armed Policing opened at the end of 2018, and both Mark and I expect it to become a great success. You can read more about it here: www.pfoa.co.uk.

Now, the book opened with an historic account of an incident in 1909 so it seems right to finish with a few accounts of some earlier operations covered in my first book *Stop! Armed Police!* Hopefully you will find them interesting, if not amusing.

Balcombe Street: Were the SAS There?

December 1975

Some questions remain regarding the siege of Balcombe Street, when the IRA held an elderly couple hostage, such as were the Special Air Service (SAS) ever deployed and, if so, what was their involvement?

We all remember the 'big one' – the Iranian Embassy siege in 1980 – but while I was researching this book I came across some photos of what was, unmistakably, SAS troopers practising an entry to a building. I assumed they were standard training photos dated around the same time as the Iranian Embassy siege, but on closer inspection a friend and I identified that the balcony they had mocked up was the balcony at Balcombe Street, even down to the fire buckets they had placed in position to represent the flowerpots.

D11 officers take the surrender of the Balcombe Street gang following a four-day siege.

266

BALCOMBE STREET: WERE THE SAS THERE?

Above left: Three SAS troopers rehearse a hostage rescue on a mock up of the balcony at Balcombe Street.

Above right: The same three SAS troopers practise deploying a gas or stun grenade through the balcony window while others cover with Ingram submachine guns.

The three SAS troopers in the photos were armed with Ingram submachine guns and practising for an opposed entry off the balcony using stun grenades. These photos are rare and unique and deserve to be seen in the context of this book.

They date from December 1975, predating the Iranian Embassy siege, which made the SAS a household name. They provide a snapshot into UK Special Forces who were there in support of D11 (the forerunner of SCO19), who were containing the stronghold at Balcombe Street where the IRA terror cell were holed up with two hostages.

The siege ended peacefully with a negotiated surrender and no shots fired. The four-handed team of terrorists, known thereafter as the Balcombe Street Gang, were imprisoned for their crimes.

It was pleasing to observe that as far back as forty-four years ago, D11 had been working in collaboration with UK Special Forces and have maintained a good working relationship ever since.

What we don't know is this: was the terror cell aware of the presence of the feared SAS? If so, was that one of the reasons they surrendered so hastily when they appeared?

Stansted Hijacking: The Talking Bush

February 2000

During the Stansted hijacking between 6 and 10 February 2000, rifle officers from Essex and those sent up to support them from the Met firearms unit, not only had to deal with containing a hijacked aircraft, but also freezing temperatures. The strong winds added to the chill factor, making it very uncomfortable for those doing long stints on the containment.

Add to that the army of press camped just outside the perimeter fence, vying to get better photos of the stricken Ariana aircraft with its cargo of miserable and frightened passengers from Afghanistan, and the job was not the most pleasant.

Rifle officers in position in a wooded area, carrying out containment duties similar to those at the hijacking of an Ariana aircraft at Stansted in 2000.

STANSTED HIJACKING: THE TALKING BUSH

After many days, and not a lot of information to report on, some resourceful reporters decided to make their own news. Somehow they managed to crawl under the perimeter fence and work their way into a wooded area, from where they hoped to get closer shots of the aircraft and some of the police activity, which was screened off from them outside the fence.

As they crawled through the undergrowth their advance was brought to an abrupt stop when a mysterious voice said: 'I suggest you stop there. I cannot guarantee your safety if you go any further, and if they don't shoot you I might do it myself!'

The reporter and his cameraman couldn't see where this mysterious voice was coming from until they realized it was from a pile of foliage 4 feet away.

After a brief conversation around the laws of trespass, they promised to leave the way they had come in, and not enter 'Sniper Wood' again.

True to their word they returned to the city of tents and managed to piece together a story to put out on the evening news. The firearms officers watching the news in the control room found it amusing when the reporter gave an account of his adventure, commenting that 'after a conversation with a very polite bush I was advised to leave.'

The siege ended peacefully on the fourth day when the terrorists on board gave up. The freezing-cold riflemen were kept busy throughout the period, especially when the pilots and cabin crew descended down a rope ladder from an escape hatch in the cockpit. One of the pilots also wandered into Sniper Wood and was detained by the polite-talking bush.

The Hackney Siege: Pet Recovery

December 2002

In my previous book's account of the Hackney siege that began on 26 December 2002 and concluded twenty-three days later, with Eli Hall's suicide and a huge fire that he ignited, I mentioned the mechanics of the siege, including the negotiation, the containment and the disruption it caused to the community.

However, I hadn't considered the effect it might have had on some of the residents' extended families – their pets.

It wasn't until I was reminiscing with an old colleague, who played a big part in all aspects of this siege – which saw Hall hold 22-year-old student Paul Okere hostage – that he explained an unusual duty to which he had been detailed.

On about day four of the siege, when it dawned on senior management that the standoff might not be over any time soon, they called my friend – whom I shall refer to as 'Dave' – over to the control room where he was introduced to a local council animal welfare officer.

Apparently, many of the residents that had been evacuated from local houses close to where Hall had barricaded himself and Okere inside, were complaining that their pets had been abandoned and needed feeding.

The officer in charge decided Dave would be the ideal person to be an armed guide for the welfare officer. They were given the task of visiting all the premises that fell within the police cordon where people had said their pets might be. Yet of all the skills he had, pet rescue was one he had not been trained for. He was instructed that those he could not bring back, he should leave food for.

Dave was not amused, but as an animal lover he knew it would be a good thing to do. So, armed with thick gloves, dog-catcher poles, cages and a selection of pet food for any animals they could not coax out, they set off on their mission of mercy.

As they passed through the first cordon and hugged the building line, the council officer said, 'I don't like the look of this. I'm not paid enough to take these kinds of risks.' Dave was now on his own.

He told the petrified welfare officer to wait outside the cordon and he continued with his equipment and bunches of keys.

After opening the door of the first premises, he was greeted with the unpleasant smell of animal faeces. 'Here kitty, kitty,' he called out and saw movement in his peripheral vision. He went into the lounge and, finding the four-legged culprit, put his gloves on and opened the cage ready to take his first rescued hostage. But like any carefully prepared firearms operation it did not go to plan.

A view along the Hackney street outside the flat where Eli Hall was under siege for twenty-three days.

As Dave attempted to corner the big black cat, it jumped at him and tried to escape. He said it was like trying to land a huge fish but he managed to grab a rear leg. The cat struggled to break free, scratching and biting to get away from this stranger dressed in black.

He finally got the cat in the cage. He cast a look back at the carnage in the room with his dirty footprints adding to the cat mess on the lovely beige carpet.

Dave only managed to get to one premises on his first attempt. He returned to the control room to get reinforcements and was greeted with strange looks and comments of, 'What the hell is that smell?' He didn't feel inclined to tell them he was attacked by a cat he was trying to save. It just shows how dangerous some firearms operations can be.

Like any dedicated firearms officer Dave returned, along with other team members, and managed to recover and feed all the animals.

Chandler's Ford: The Robbers Return

September 2007

In September 2007, a prolific gang of armed robbers were active in the Home Counties, committing eighteen armed robberies and netting over £500,000.

Their reign of terror was brought to a sudden end when the gang were ambushed by SFOs from CO19 and detectives from the Met's Flying Squad in the quiet Hampshire town of Chandler's Ford.

The gang had planned to rob a cash-in-transit delivery to an HSBC bank but, unbeknown to the robbers, armed police lay in wait. Due to the serious threat to the custodian guard in the delivery van, they had also placed two riflemen in a commercial premises opposite the bank.

Leroy Hall (left) received six-and-a-half years while Leon McKenzie (right) got six years for their part in a second string of robberies. This included an almost identical raid at the same HSBC Bank in Chandler's Ford where two of their gang were shot dead by police five years earlier.

CHANDLER'S FORD: THE ROBBERS RETURN

As one of the robbers, Mark Nunes, approached the guard, he lifted a pistol to his head but a shot rang out and he dropped to the ground. A second robber, Andrew Markland, picked up the handgun and brought it up to threaten the guard again, but a second shot rang out and he too dropped to the ground. Both were dead.

In total, seven other gang members were arrested and charged with serious offences, including conspiracy to commit armed robbery. The surviving members of the gang were sent to prison for between five and seventeen years.

It would be reasonable to assume that an operation like this, which had been foiled, left two robbers dead and the others with lengthy prison sentences, should have acted as a deterrent to others, especially to those who served time for it.

This was not the case. Two of the gang, Leroy Hall and Leon McKenzie, who had been jailed in November 2008 for seven years apiece were released on license in 2011, and returned almost immediately to their life of crime.

They embarked on a series of robberies across the Home Counties once again. One of the robberies committed on 24 November 2011 was at the same HSBC Bank in Chandler's Ford where their fellow gang members, Nunes and Markland, had been shot dead five years earlier. This time the gang successfully held up the G4 security van making off with £25,000.

When investigating the string of robberies, the Serious Organised Crime Agency noticed they had the same blueprint as the previous ones and quickly arrested four gang members, including Hall and McKenzie, just before they set off to commit another. Hall received six-and-a-half years while McKenzie got six years' imprisonment.

Postscript

The role of today's firearms officers has changed dramatically in the past decade as we've seen an increase in home-grown terrorist activity. Officers still have a responsibility to maintain the peace, fulfil a support role to their unarmed colleagues across London and act as a deterrent to armed criminals and would-be terrorists, while being prepared at any moment for a major terrorist attack.

In 1983, excluding the non-Home Office forces, such as the CNC and MOD Police, I was one of 13,200 officers in England and Wales authorized to carry firearms. In 2016 there were just 5,639.

It is fair to say these 5,639 officers are trained to a far higher standard than their predecessors and, unlike former colleagues, they are, on the whole, armed permanently.

While we, as a nation, have resisted the temptation of falling in line with the rest of Europe and arming all our police officers, is it inevitable that we will do eventually? Yes, I suppose it is, but not in the near future. Although having said that, we are always only one incident away from change.

I have heard fellow officers say, 'How can we be expected to protect the public when we cannot even protect ourselves?' It's a fair comment and I believe the Met may eventually vote with their feet, as the BTP did following the attack on London Bridge and Borough Market when they voted in favour of being armed.

On the flipside, we must consider events in Liege, Belgium in May 2018 when a terrorist attacked two patrolling officers with bladed weapons, then relieved one of their issue sidearms, which he used to shoot members of the public and other officers.

Whichever way you look at it I believe that, in London, arming the police in general will not prevent acts of terrorism. However, it would give the officers and the public a greater feeling of security and protection. Maybe there is an acceptable balance in the number of officers who are armed that would satisfy everyone. We shall see how this debate plays out over the next decade until a decision is made.

One thing I know for sure – we must support our officers both armed and unarmed. They need the public and the press behind them in this war on armed crime and terrorism as they cannot do the job without that public backing. We still have the best police service in the world and the lowest numbers of police-related shootings.

I hope this book gives you a better understanding of how we police with firearms in London and the UK. Thank you for reading *London's Armed Police Up Close and Personal*.

Stephen Smith

CTSFO team sergeant uses his favoured SIG 516, rifle. He has a set of night vision goggles fitted to his ballistic helmet. (*AH*)

The author on set for Channel 5's documentary *Armed and Deadly: Police UK*. (*Hassan Ghazi*)

Appendix

Timeline of Events in the Evolution of The Force Firearms Unit SCO19

Below is a chronology of events detailing the evolution of SCO19 since the ruthless murders of three unarmed officers at Shepherd's Bush in 1966. The earlier incidents feature in my first book, *Stop! Armed Police!* I have not included changes in legislation affecting firearms or the department, and this list is by no means a comprehensive one. I hope you find it a useful guide to events that shaped armed policing in London and the UK.

1966

August The three-man crew of unmarked police Q-car, Foxtrot One One, are shot dead at Shepherd's Bush causing a public outcry.

December Formation of D6, the firearms training wing. A core of serving ex-Army constables are recruited as instructors and sent for Army small arms training at Hythe Ranges.

1967

April D6 given responsibility for developing tactics to deploy CS irritant against armed besieged criminals.

May Ten instructors are confirmed in post and the first four-day defensive firearms courses are run within the Met.

July Following the force restructure, D6 becomes D11 firearms training unit. Training commences at Lippitts Hill in Epping Forest.

1968

December Sergeant Bob Wells passes his firearms instructors' course on the top floor of Old Street Police Station. He would later become chief superintendent and lead the force firearms unit 1984-89.

1969

May A total of 115 traffic division officers are added to the list of authorized firearms officers.

December The Home Office approves a dual operational and training role for D11. Officers are on call to give tactical advice at sieges as well as to deploy CS irritant. D11 is also authorized to provide rifle support to Heathrow Airport on twenty-four-hour call for hijackings.

APPENDIX

1970

April D11 instructors sent on SAS pistol courses at Hereford. Instructors also sent to military sniper courses and the FBI Academy in Virginia US to bring back new skill sets.

1971

January 900 officers apply for thirty places as force riflemen.

July The first deployment of CS irritant occurs during a domestic siege in Greenwich. The Browning Hi-Power pistol is adopted by D11 as a standard sidearm.

1972

March Savage and Viking shotguns are introduced for delivery of CS irritant.

October Lee Enfield L42A1 sniper rifle is adopted by D11.

December PC Peter Slimon shoots two bank robbers in Kensington, one fatally.

1973

February Armed Special Patrol Group officers shoot dead two terrorists at the Indian High Commission on Aldwych.

December D11 take delivery of the Enfield Enforcer sniper rifle.

1974

March Attempted kidnapping of Princess Anne in the Mall.

June IRA bomb Parliament.

July IRA bomb the Tower of London.

October Met Police adopt the Smith & Wesson Model 10 revolver as the standard police sidearm. Formation of the Diplomatic Protection Group. IRA bomb two pubs in Guildford killing five and wounding sixty-five.

November IRA bomb Birmingham pub killing nineteen.

1975

February The murder of PC Stephen Tibble by the IRA.

September Spaghetti House siege in Knightsbridge lasts six days.

November Home Office authorize D11 to provide firearms teams to combat armed crime and terrorism. The Met becomes a national centre for firearms training.

December Six day Balcombe Street siege ends when four Provisional IRA terrorists surrender to D11.

1976

January Home Secretary authorizes two Sterling submachine guns to be purchased by D11 to counter the terrorist threat from the IRA.

1977

June D11 introduce the new lightweight (still heavy by today's standards) Kevlar body armour to replace the heavy steel-plate system.

October The Heckler & Koch MP5 carbine is adopted by D11. Following a nine-day siege against a man with a knife, D11 deploy a purpose-built cage into the room, disarm and arrest the subject.

1978

December All Met dog handlers have their firearms authorizations taken away when a handler is photographed pointing his Model 10 revolver at his dog's head. It was the camera angle but the complaint stood.

1979

March/August IRA kill Airey Neave and Lord Mountbatten with bombs.
September D11 officer fractures both legs in first abseil training course.
December D11 carry out a rapid entry in Holland Park Road arresting three IRA suspects planning an audacious prison break of fellow members. D11 take delivery of first purpose-built armoured Land Rover.

1980

D11 given responsibility for high-risk convoys, including movement of dangerous prisoners between prison and court.
April D11 teams help contain the Iranian Embassy during the six-day siege, which ends when the SAS storm the building. The new 50-metre range complex is completed at Lippitts Hill training centre.

1983

January Armed detectives shoot Stephen Waldorf, mistaking him for fugitive David Martin. The two officers are later acquitted of his attempted murder. New guidelines for police use of firearms are published. The police basic firearms course is extended to two weeks and the term AFO (authorized firearms officer) adopted.
August IRA plant bombs in Regents Park and Hyde Park killing eleven soldiers and wounding many more.
December IRA bomb Harrods killing six.

1984

April D11 are actively involved in the ten-day siege at the Libyan People's Bureau, which followed the shooting of eight people and the murder of WPC Yvonne Fletcher.
August The Firearms Working Committee meets to try and reduce the number of AFOs in the Met from 4,851 (that number is now under 2,500).

1985

January The hunt for armed robber Anthony Baldessare comes to an end with his suicide following a three-day siege in Streatham.
March A two-day siege of a van in Earls Court ends with murderer James Baigre's suicide.
September Cherry Groce is mistakenly shot by local police during a search of her home in Brixton, sparking the Brixton riots. Her shooting leads to changes in firearms training and tactics.

December A two-day siege in Northolt ends with the premises being stormed, a 4-year old hostage rescued and murderer Errol Walker shot and wounded by D11.

1986
February Home Office gives permission for overt carriage of the MP5 carbine at Heathrow Airport.

1987
January Force restructures with D11 renamed PT17 (Personnel & Training).
June Formation of PT17 level 2 teams brought in following recommendations after the Cherry Groce shooting.
July Following a robbery at an abattoir in Greenwich, PT17 level 1 officer shoots three suspects, two fatally.
August Hungerford Massacre, Berkshire. Michael Ryan shoots thirty-one people, sixteen fatally. PT17 called to assist with the search before Ryan kills himself.
November PT17 level 2 officers ambush robbers in Woolwich. During the shootout, one robber is killed and one officer wounded.

1988
December Central London Diplomatic Protection Group riflemen shoot and wound hostage-taker Michael Rose aka 'Mental Mickey' in the first ever directed rifle fire by a senior officer.

1989
April PT17 level 1 officer shoots three robbers, two fatally, in Harrow following an attempted armed robbery. IRA bombing campaign kills ten Royal Marines at Deal in Kent.

1990
April PT17 level 2 officers ambush two robbers, shooting one dead in Brentford.
July PT17 successfully end the siege at Tokyo Joe's nightclub, Mayfair, after releasing all the hostages and arresting the suspect. IRA bomb the Stock Exchange in the City of London.
November Following an attempted armed robbery and kidnapping of security van custodians at Woodhatch in Reigate, Surrey, PT17 level 1 and 2 officers shoot two robbers, one fatally.

1991
July PT17 armed response vehicles (ARVs) begin patrolling London and first ARV base is established at Old Street Police Station.
September PT17 host first ever female officers' open day in hope of attracting more women firearms officers.
October PT17 sends six level 1 officers to Turks and Caicos Islands to prevent prisoner being rescued by Colombian drugs cartel.
November Female ARV officer wounded in Acton following a shootout with man armed with shotgun. He is shot by ARVs.

1992

January PT17 restructure level 1 and 2 teams forming five specialist firearms officer (SFO) teams. Six unmarked semi-armoured Range Rovers are obtained for use by SFOs on covert operation.

February Following yet another restructure, PT17 is renamed SO19 (Specialist Operations).

June The first recorded 'suicide by cop' occurs in London when hostage-taker Peter Swann points a firearm at SO19 officers forcing them to shoot him.

September An SO19 SFO officer is wounded while chasing robbers in Bow when his pistol accidentally discharges into his own leg.

November SO19 help recover £160 million worth of drugs following a joint operation on fishing boat *Fox Trot Five*.

December IRA bomb Manchester.

1993

February Robber Steven Charalambous is shot and wounded by SFO officers while threatening a security van custodian with a gun.

March SFO officers are shot at as they raid an IRA bomb factory in Stoke Newington. Two terrorists are arrested.

July SFO officers arrest IRA bomber in Cricklewood.

October ARV officer shoots a robber dead after an exchange of shots in a woodyard in North London.

1994

July ARV officer shoots John O'Brien following a siege at his house in Holloway in another suicide by cop.

August ARV officer is shot and wounded after a robbery and foot chase in Putney. The robber shoots himself dead after being wounded by police. The Model 10 revolver is phased out as the Met's standard AFO firearm and replaced with the Glock 17 self-loading pistol. IRA declare ceasefire.

October SO19 officers sent to Saint Kitts to protect detectives working on a gang-related murder case on the island. Number of ARV officers increases from seventy-five to 120 following the murder of PC Derek Robertson.

December Female ARV officer wounded in shootout following domestic dispute. Suspect Alan McMinn shot and wounded by ARV officers.

1995

Body armour is issued to front-line officers in answer to a marked increase in gun and knife crime.

February ARV officer shoots dead unarmed robber David Ewin in West London. The officer is later acquitted of his murder following three retrials.

September SFOs ambush and wound hitman Michael Boyle after he shoots and wounds his intended victim David Brindle. A second ARV base is opened south of the river at Lambeth.

APPENDIX

1996
SO19 begin Chemical, Biological, Radiological and Nuclear (CBRN) training.

February IRA blow up Canary Wharf killing two members of the public and ending their ceasefire.

June IRA bomb a shopping centre in Manchester.

July SO19 raid addresses in South London and arrest six IRA suspects.

September SO19 arrest three IRA suspects and shoot a fourth dead in a hotel room in Hammersmith, preventing them from detonating a massive bomb in the City of London.

1997
November ARV officers wound female robbery suspect Jane Lee after she drove her van at police.

1998
December SO19 carry out huge drugs raid in Charing Cross arresting over 100 suspects and recovering substantial amounts of drugs.

1999
February SO19 officers help end a three-day siege at the Greek Embassy in Holland Park after it was taken over by seventy Kurdish protesters.

April George Knight arrested by SO19 following a short siege in Feltham after going on a shooting rampage.

September Harry Stanley shot dead by ARV officers when he points what they believe to be a sawn-off shotgun at them wrapped in a plastic bag. It turns out to be a table leg.

2000
February SO19 help end the four-day hijacking at Stansted Airport.

August ARV officer wounds a man with an axe in a supermarket in New Cross.

October SFO sniper shoots dead hostage-taker Kieran O'Donnell as he attempts to kill hostage.

November SO19 play major part in thwarting a diamond heist at the Millennium Dome in Greenwich.

2001
SO19 relocate bases from Old Street to Leman Street, East London. SO19 join European counterparts in finding solutions to counter gun crime and terrorism and the ATLAS Network is formed.

July ARV officers shoot dead hostage-taker Derek Bennett who is suffering from mental illness and armed with an imitation firearm. Heckler & Koch baton launcher adopted by SO19.

September Islamist terrorists attack the Twin Towers in New York killing over 2000.

November ARV officers shoot dead Michael Malsbury in another suicide-by-cop incident.

2002
ARV south base temporarily relocated to Clapham Police Station. The baton launcher is routinely carried on ARVs as a less-than-lethal option.

September SO19 carry out its first armed maritime patrol on the River Thames.

December SO19 participate in the fifteen-day Hackney siege. It ends when fugitive Eli Hall sets fires to the flat and shoots himself.

2003

Firearms training is moved from Lippitts Hill to the new Firearms and Public Order Centre at Milton in Gravesend.

January Following operational trials, the M26 Taser is issued to SFO teams before being issued to ARVs later that year.

2004

May SFOs shoot dead Nicholas Palmer in Thornton Heath. He is armed and wanted for firearms offences.

November Tactical Support Teams (TST) are formed to support SFO operations. Independent Police Complaints Commission created to investigate complaints against police.

2005

April After yet more restructuring, SO19 changes its name to CO19 (Central Office 19). SFO shoots Azelle Rodney dead following a vehicle stop in Edgware. Officer later acquitted of his murder. ARV permanent south base is reopened at Lambeth.

July Islamic suicide terrorists attack the London transport system killing fifty-two. CO19 involved in a massive manhunt to arrest four failed suicide bombers following a second almost identical attack the following week. SFOs shoot dead Jean Charles de Menezes, who is mistaken for one of the attempted bombers on a tube carriage at Stockwell.

2006

CO19 send officers on courses to teach and use explosive method of entry (EMOE) to aid entry to premises in special circumstances.

June During a CO19 raid on a suspected bomb factory in Forest Gate, a suspect is accidentally shot in the arm. X26 Taser introduced to replace M26 used by CO19.

October SFOs shoot dead robber Robert Haines in New Romney, Kent after he fires a shotgun at police.

2007

May SFOs shoot dead Terry Nicholas after he opens fire at them using a pistol concealed inside a sock. A dedicated sniper team is formed to provide sniper cover in support of armed operations.

September Two armed robbers are shot dead by CO19 snipers during an armed robbery at Chandler's Ford in Hampshire.

2008

Operation Makepeace is set up by CO19 to educate young people against knife and gun crime and reach out to schools and the community.

APPENDIX

May CO19 officers shoot dead Mark Saunders after he points a shotgun at police from his flat in Chelsea.

October ARV officers shoot dead Andrew Hammond, who is armed with an assault rifle (possible suicide by cop).

2009
April ARV PC Gary Toms dies during an arrest of suspects in a vehicle after sustaining serious head injuries.

October ARV officers shoot dead Richard Hiorns in a suicide-by-cop scenario. Heckler & Koch G36 assault rifle adopted by CO19 SFO and later ARVs.

2010
CO19 begin training officers for working in smoke-filled environments.

July CO19 sends TST officers to Northumbria to assist in the manhunt for murderer Raoul Moat who commits suicide when cornered.

2011
August Gang member Mark Duggan shot dead by TST officers following a vehicle stop in Tottenham. It sparks rioting and violence across the UK.

2012
January Another name change as CO19 becomes SC&O19 (Specialist Crime and Operations directive 19).

February ARVs shoot and wound man attacking them with machete.

April SIG 516 adopted by SFOs.

May Combined Response Firearms Teams formed for the 2012 London Olympic Games. These are later rebranded Counter Terrorist Specialist Firearms Officers (CTSFOs).

July-September SC&O19 take an active role policing the London Olympic Games.

2013
May Fusilier Lee Rigby murdered by two Islamic terrorists. ARV officers shoot and wound both murderers.

2014
May First non-Home Office armed officer arrests gang member following a shootout in Tottenham, earning himself the George Medal for bravery.

September ARV officer shoots hostage-taker Dean Joseph dead in his flat in Haringey saving his hostage.

2015
Body Worn Video (BWV) cameras taken out operationally by SC&O19 officers to help with post-incident investigations.

January *Charlie Hebdo* attack in Paris causes British Government to plan for possible attacks in the UK.

February ARV officers shoot and wound Mark Bryan after he discharges a shotgun at them.

April Operation Temperer devised to counter the event of the national threat level reaching 'critical'.

June Biggest ever anti-terrorist exercise staged in London by SC&O19 to test emergency services' response to Mumbai-type attack in the capital.

August ARV officers shoot and wound Nathaniel Brophy outside a flat in Lambeth after he threatened police and housing officials with a pistol. ARV officers shoot James Fox following an armed confrontation at his flat in Enfield.

October Operation Trident detective wounded during arrest of armed suspect in Tottenham.

November Terror attacks in Paris shock Europe and London braces itself.

December Islamic terrorist attacks and injures passengers with a knife at Leytonstone tube. Taser deployed and suspect arrested. CTSFOs shoot dead Jermaine Baker in a car outside court.

2016

SC&O19 adopt the SIG MCX weapons systems. DPG get the Heckler & Koch G36.

April The Met contract out basic firearms training to outside forces.

2017

Two further ARV bases are opened, one in Lillie Road in Fulham and the other at Limehouse Police Station in the East End. SC&O19 start to use drones as a means of gaining aerial footage of firearms scenes and incidents. Conflict Management Dogs introduced as another less-lethal option when combatting violent armed criminals and terrorists.

March Lone Islamic terrorist carries out vehicle attack on Westminster Bridge killing four and injuring twenty-nine then stabs PC Keith Palmer to death in New Palace Yard. Terrorist shot dead by police.

April Female terrorist suspect shot during raid on house in Willesden by CTSFOs. Three other female suspects arrested. Khalid Omar arrested outside Parliament by ARV foiling a terrorist knife attack.

May Manchester Arena bomb exploded by Islamic suicide killer. Twenty-three killed and 500 injured. First deployment under Operation Temperer as threat level rises to 'critical'.

June Three Islamic terrorists carry out vehicle attack on London Bridge followed by knife attack in Borough Market. All three are shot dead by ARV officers. Finsbury Park Mosque attack. Right-wing activist drives van into worshippers outside mosque, killing one and injuring others.

September Islamic terrorist partially detonates a bomb on the tube at Parsons Green injuring passengers. Operation Temperer initiated across the country for the second time in a year.

2018

The two-shot model X2 Taser adopted by the Met replacing the X-26.

March Six ARV officers open fire wounding an armed man in Hackney.

April Two ARV officers shoot dead a man armed with a shotgun on a petrol forecourt, in a possible suicide-by-cop incident.

June In a department restructuring SC&O19 becomes CO19 (Central Operation) once again.

July ARV officers exchange shots with armed suspects in a car following a chase in Leytonstone. Four suspects arrested.

September Following a brief return to the title CO19 and even MO19 (M for Met), the unit is renamed SCO19.

November Museum of Armed Policing opened at old Chatteris Police Station in Cambridgeshire.

December SFOs shoot a suspect wanted for conspiracy to rob, during a raid on his home in Wimbledon.

2019

January ARVs shoot a suspected kidnapper in Blackheath, after stopping a car he was travelling in. No offences were disclosed.

Glossary

AFO – Authorized Firearms Officer
Title given to an officer who has passed a basic firearms course.

Al-Qaeda – Extremist Islamic terrorist organization
One of the first Islamic extremist groups led by Osama bin Laden. Responsible, among other things for the 9/11 terrorist attacks on the Twin Towers.

ARV – Armed Response Vehicle
An overt police vehicle containing three uniformed armed officers.

APP – Approved Professional Practice
Procedures set out by the College of Policing which all forces should adhere to.

BTP – British Transport Police
Responsible for policing the UK transport systems, above and below ground.

BWV – Body Worn Video
A personal body worn camera system developed specifically for firearms officers to record incidents in which they become involved.

CARV – Covert Armed Response Vehicle
An unmarked police vehicle containing up to three plain clothed armed police officers. (See also Gunship.)

CBRN – Chemical, Biological, Radiological and Nuclear
Name given for incident where any of the above are detected.

CNC – Civil Nuclear Police
Non-Home Office police force responsible for protecting UK nuclear assets.

COBRA – Cabinet Office Briefing Room A
Meetings convened as part of the civil contingencies committee, which plans government responses in times of emergency.

GLOSSARY

CO19 – 2005-12 Central Office 19. Between July and September 2018 it changed to Central Operations 19
Department name given to the firearms unit of the Metropolitan Police – previously known as D11, PT17, SO19, SC&O19 and finally, SCO19.

CRFT – Combined Response Firearms Teams
Set up to provide a specialist firearms response during the 2012 London Olympic Games.

CTSFO – Counter Terrorist Specialist Firearms Officer
Title given to all UK SFOs who are specially trained in counter-terrorist tactics. In use since 2012.

DHS – The Department of Homeland Security
Title given to the US federal states' government cabinet department responsible for public security, anti-terrorism, border security, immigration and customs.

DIG OUT – To 'dig out' an armed suspect from an address
SCO19 term used to denote the tactic of arresting an armed suspect at their home address.

DPS – Directorate of Professional Standards
Police body set up to investigate misconduct within the Metropolitan Police.

EMD – Emotionally or Mentally Distressed
Refers to anyone who is emotionally or mentally unstable, or vulnerable, and can include those under the influence of drink or drugs.

ENFORCER – Hand-held kinetic battering ram
Mechanical breaching tool used to swing at a door forcing it open using kinetic energy. The action causes 3.5 tonnes to be delivered to a small area the size of the faceplate.

FPOTC – Firearms and Public Order Training Centre
The Metropolitan Police firearms training site opened in 2003.

FRIS – Fire Retardant Immersion Suit
Protective clothing used when working on the River Thames.

GUNSHIP – SCO19 or Flying Squad Covert Armed Response Vehicle
Police term to describe the vehicle in which they are deployed. (See also CARV.)

HASAW – Health and Safety at Work
Employment legislation to protect workers.

HATTON GUN – Shortened shotgun
Dedicated to firing the patented 'Hatton round', developed to deliver a one-ounce lead/wax round into a tyre or door hinge/lock and designed to have no ricochet.

HOOLI BAR – SCO19 name for the stainless steel wrecking bar
One of the tools used in conjunction with the enforcer to breach doors, used in the main on outward opening doors and grills. Real name, Halligan bar, named after its inventor, New York Fire Department Deputy Chief Hugh Halligan, it has a duck bill and spike.

KRATOS – Tactic of firing critical shots to neutralize suicide killers
Developed by London's Metropolitan Police Service for dealing with suspected suicide bombers, most notably firing shots to the brain stem without warning.

IED – Improvised Explosive Device
Bombs and incendiary devices used by terrorists to kill and maim.

INLA - Irish National Liberation Army
Irish republican socialist paramilitary terrorist group formed in December 1974.

IOPC – Independent Office for Police Conduct (see IPCC)
Government body set up to investigate serious complaints against the police. Replaced the IPCC on 8 Jan 2018.

IPCC – Independent Police Complaints Commission (see IOPC)
Replaced the PCA (Police Complaints Authority) in 2005.

IRA – Irish Republican Army
Irish republican paramilitary terrorist organization formed in 1919.

ISIS/IS – Islamic State (radical Muslim fundamentalist terrorists)
Set up following the war in Syria intent on forming a Muslim caliphate.

JANKEL – Police Armoured Support Vehicle
Named after its British designer Robert Jankel. Used since 1995 for sieges and retrieving wounded casualties.

LFBS/LFB – London Fire Brigade Service
All London firefighters come under this title.

MASTS – Mobile Armed Support to Surveillance
Configuration and tactic used by SCO19 when supporting surveillance operations.

MODP – Ministry of Defence Police
Armed Police Force responsible for policing MOD facilities.

MOE – Method of Entry
The mechanical equipment used for breaching a door for entry by the team.

GLOSSARY

MONEY BOX – Flying Squad speak for 'cash-in-transit' security vehicle
One of the many alternative terms used in radio transmissions in the early days to confuse anyone listening in.

MPD – Metropolitan Police District
Refers to the area of the UK policed by London's Metropolitan Police.

MPS – Metropolitan Police Service
Generic term used for the Metropolitan Police as a whole.

NCA – National Crime Agency (see SOCA)
A non-ministerial government department set up in October 2013 to take over from SOCA. Includes child exploitation and online protection.

NDMM – National Decision-Making Model
All policing decisions should be made using the NDMM.

OFC – Operational Firearms Commander
Commands a group of officers carrying out functional or territorial responsibilities related to a tactical plan.

OPERATION TEMPERER
Name given to the government's plan to deploy armed troops on the streets in response to a terrorist threat, thus releasing armed officers to patrol vulnerable areas.

OPERATION TRIDENT (also known as SCD8)
Set up in 1998 to combat the growing number of black-on-black shootings in London.

PFEW – Police Federation for England and Wales
Member organization representing officers from England and Wales.

PFOA – Police Firearms Officers Association
Registered charity set up in 2010 in support of all UK firearms officers and their families.

PIM – Post Incident Manager
Specially trained senior officer responsible for the integrity of an investigation following a police-related shooting.

PIP – Post Incident Procedure
Process officers go through following a police-related shooting or any event resulting in an IOPC investigation.

PIRA – Provisional Irish Republican Army
Irish republican terrorist organization.

PSNI – Police Service of Northern Ireland
Polices Northern Ireland. It replaced the Royal Ulster Constabulary (RUC) in 2001.

Q-CAR – Police slang for unmarked police crime car
Referring back to the First World War when the British Navy disguised warships as cargo ships, known as Q-boats to trick the enemy. The police Q-car has a crew of three: a police class 1 driver and two detectives.

SAS – Special Air Service (see UKSF)
The British Army's elite fighting force, whose responsibilities include counter-terrorist work.

SBS – Special Boat Squadron (see UKSF)
The elite Special Forces unit of the Royal Navy who work independently and alongside the SAS.

SCD7 (2) – Projects Team, part of Specialist Crime Directorate 7
Responsible for proactive investigations into contract killings, serious crime groups, major drug importation, trafficking and distribution.

SCD7 (5) – Flying Squad, part of Specialist Crime Directorate 7
Set up to investigate commercial armed robberies and other serious armed crime.

SCD8 – See Operation Trident

SCD11 – Dedicated Surveillance, part of Specialist Crime Directorate 11
Police surveillance teams used by police departments to track movements of criminals to gather evidence prior to arrest.

SC&O19/SCO19 – Specialist Crime and Operations 19
The Force Firearms Unit was named SC&O19 from 2012 to July 2018, however, between July and September 2018, it reverted to Central Operations 19 (and even MO19 for a month – M stands for Met). It is now SCO19, having dropped the &.

SERT – Specialist Entry Recovery Team
ARV officers trained by the fire brigade in the use of firefighting equipment and breathing apparatus to perform search and rescue in smoke-filled environments using firearms.

SFC – Strategic Firearms Commander
Retains strategic oversight and overall command and responsibility.

SFE – Smoke Filled Environment (trained)
CTSFOs who have received extra training to carry out an assault on a building on fire to rescue hostages or neutralize an armed suspect.

GLOSSARY

SFO – Specialist Firearms Officer
Title given to all SFOs between 1992 and 2012 who had completed the specialist training required for that role.

SLP – Self-loading pistol
A pistol which harnesses the energy of a discharged round to cycle the slide back then forward, thus chambering a fresh round into the breech from the magazine. Known as a semi-automatic or just plain automatic pistol in the US.

SO18 – Specialist Operation 18
Aviation Security Operational Command Unit, responsible for policing the airports within the MPD.

SO19 – Specialist Operation 19
Force Firearms Unit 1992-05. See also D6, D11, PT17, CO19, SC&O19 and now SCO19.

SOCA – Serious and Organised Crime Agency (see NCA)
Set up in April 2006 as a national law enforcement agency sponsored by the Home Office. Replaced by the NCA in October 2013.

SPG – Special Patrol Group (see TSG)
Reserve of patrolling officers, many trained in firearms and surveillance. Replaced by the TSG in 1987.

STICK – Order of march for armed officers approaching a premises
Term used to denote officers moving up to an address or outside a front door.

STRONGHOLD –The location or seat of hostile activity during a siege
Used in armed police situations to identify the location of hostages or armed besieged criminals or terrorists.

TA – Tactical Advisor
Advises on tactical options, limitations and capabilities.

TASER –-Thomas A. Swift's Electric Rifle
Trademark name of the company, which produces and supplies the M-26, X-26 & X2 Tasers. The name is an acronym of Thomas A Swift's Electric Rifle, inspired by a book in the *Tom Swift* novel series from 1911. It is now made by Axon.

TFC – Tactical Firearms Commander
Develops, commands and coordinates the overall tactical response in accordance with strategic objectives.

TMD – Tottenham Man Dem
Criminal street gang involved in violence and drug dealing.

TSG – Territorial Support Group

The Met's commissioner's reserve. Replaced the SPG in 1987.

TST – Tactical Support Team

SC&O19 officers with tactical skill set between SFO and ARV formed into firearms teams to provide support to the SFO teams from 2004 until 2012.

UKSF – United Kingdom Special Forces

Combined reference to SAS and SBS assets.

Select Bibliography

Barton, G. (2017). *The Tottenham Outrage And Walthamstow Tram Chase*. Waterside Press.

Block, L. (2007). *Europe's Emerging Counter-Terrorism Elite: The ATLAS Network* – The Jamestown Foundation, Jamestown.org.

Eur-Lex. (2008). *On The Improvement Of Cooperation Between The Special Intervention Units Of The Member States Of The European Union In Crisis Situations*. Eur-Lex.europa.eu.

Flashbang Magazine (2012). DA Limited Editions.

Garden Court Chambers. (2015). *Jury Finds Metropolitan Police Firearms Operation Which Resulted In Dean Joseph's Death To Have Been 'Inadequate'*. Gardencourtchambers.co.uk.

Gould, R.W., Waldren, M.J. (1986). *London's Armed Police*. London: Arms and Armour Press.

Gov.UK. (2017). *Keeping The Nation Safe: Ministry Of Defence Police Rise To The Challenge*.

Imperial War Museum. (2018). *A Brief History Of Drones*. Iwm.org.uk.

Long, T. (2016). *Lethal Force: My Life As The Met's Most Controversial Marksman*. Ebury Press.

Metropolitan Police. (2017). *MPS - Body Worn Video*. met.police.uk.

Metropolitan Police. (2018). *Statement following judgment [sic] - Joseph, Coburn and Sammy v Commissioner*. met.police.uk. National Archives. (2015). *Azelle Rodney Inquiry*.

National Archives. (2015). *Inquest Into The Death Of Mark Duggan*.

New York Police Department. (2011). *Active Shooter Report*. nyc.gov.uk.

Police Firearms Officers Association. (2017). *IPCC Under Fire Over Firearms Officers*. pfoa.co.uk.

Police Foundation. (2009). *The Briefing: Tasers*. series 1/edition 3. police-foundation.org.uk.

Rennie, J. (2011). *River Pirates On The Thames*. eastlondonhistory.com.

Rifkind, M. (2014). Report On The Intelligence Relating To The Murder Of Fusilier Lee Rigby. Williams Lea Group.

Rumbelow, D. (2009). *The Houndsditch Murders And The Siege Of Sidney Street*. The History Press.

Russell-Pavier, N. (2017). *The Shepherd's Bush Murders*. Penguin Books.

Smith, S. (2013). *Stop! Armed Police!* Robert Hale.

Waldren, M. J. (2007). *Armed Police: The Police Use Of Firearms Since 1945*. The History Press.

Worksafetexas.com. (2018). *3 Steps To Surviving An Active Shooter*.

Index

INDEX

INDEX

INDEX

INDEX

INDEX

INDEX

309